Welfare, Law and Citizenship

Hartley Dean

University of Luton

PRENTICE HALL
HARVESTER WHEATSHEAF

LONDON   NEW YORK   TORONTO   SYDNEY   TOKYO   SINGAPORE
MADRID   MEXICO CITY   MUNICH

First published 1996 by
Prentice Hall/Harvester Wheatsheaf
Campus 400, Maylands Avenue
Hemel Hempstead
Hertfordshire, HP2 7EZ
A division of
Simon & Schuster International Group

Typeset in 10/12pt Times
by Hands Fotoset, Leicester

Printed and bound in Great Britain by
Biddles Ltd, Guildford and King's Lynn

Library of Congress Cataloging-in-Publication Data

Dean, Hartley, 1949–
    Welfare, law and citizenship / Hartley Dean.
      p.   cm.
    Includes bibliographical references (p.) and index.
    ISBN 0-13-355264-0 (pbk.)
    1. Public welfare–Great Britain.   2. Welfare rights movement–
Great Britain.   3. Welfare recipients–Legal status, laws, etc.–
Great Britain.   4. Public welfare administration–Great Britain.
5. Welfare state.   6. Social justice.   7. Civil rights.   8. Welfare
rights movement.   9. Great Britain–Social policy–1979–   I. Title.
HV248.D35   1996
361.941–dc20   95–21621
                                               CIP

British Library Cataloguing in Publication Data

A catalogue record for this book is available from
the British Library

ISBN 0-13-355264-0

---

1 2 3 4 5   00 99 98 97 96

CONTENTS

TABLES AND FIGURES

INTRODUCTION

This is a book for believers and sceptics alike; for those who regard welfare rights as a realisable project and for those who regard them as an ideological fiction. Both will find enough here with which to quarrel. More importantly, perhaps, it is also a book for those who wish to sample the debates about the nature of welfare rights and to learn about the social legislation which gives rise to them. They, I hope, will find enough that is useful to enable them to make sense of the daily workings of what is still usually called the 'welfare state'.

Social policy textbooks have a tendency to address the issue of welfare rights with reference to abstract debates about the nature of citizenship and the welfare state and to describe social legislation only in terms of principles and generalities. Welfare rights guides and handbooks, on the other hand, have a tendency to focus narrowly on the exercise of individual rights and to describe social legislation in technical detail without regard to wider theoretical and philosophical debates. This book is neither a textbook of the genre described, nor a handbook. It seeks to bridge the gap between these two approaches and to present an account which will provoke new insights into the role and meaning of welfare rights, while being practically relevant to those who are concerned with the daily implementation and impact of social legislation. The book will explore the concept of welfare rights in a comparative, historical and critical context. From within that framework it will specifically discuss the development of British social legislation, the rights and duties this has imposed on the citizen, and the citizen's rights of enforcement and redress.

Part I focuses on the philosophical debates associated with social rights and the development of welfare citizenship. The intention is to draw together key insights from politics, sociology and jurisprudence, as well as from the social policy literature, and to situate these insights in relation to the emergence in advanced capitalist societies of various forms of welfare state. Chapter 1, therefore, sets the scene with a discussion of the concept of social rights and the antagonism between class and citizenship; between the market and the state. Chapter 2 moves on to consider the concepts of needs and poverty, the way that needs may be translated into rights and how welfare rights may succeed or fail in addressing the problem of poverty. Chapter 3 takes a comparative perspective and examines different kinds of welfare state and different ways in which rights to welfare may be understood. Finally, Chapter 4 discusses various critiques of the welfare state and arguments that the rights it confers are conditional, having more to do with controlling behaviour than meeting need.

Part II deals substantively with the rights and duties of welfare citizenship in Britain. Specifically, it focuses on three areas of welfare rights: income maintenance, employment and housing. In outlining the rights and duties of citizens under existing policy, no attempt is made to present an exhaustive account. Rather, the object is to link specific description to the theoretical underpinnings broached in Part I. None the less, sufficient detail is provided to enable readers to refer to the current editions of welfare rights handbooks and to put flesh on the bones of my account (or perhaps, to reverse the metaphor, to discover the underlying structures and principles which the outer body of the welfare system so often obscures). In these chapters I have refrained as far as possible from the use of jargon and shorthand notations. I even avoid citing current levels of cash benefits since my aim is as far as is practicable to allow for the ineluctable process of change (or 'reform') to which the legislative provisions described will be subject. Inevitably, however, some elements of the account will be out of date before this book even appears in print. In the welfare rights arena more than any other, readers need to be aware that nothing stands still. Chapter 5, therefore, outlines the British social security system and considers specific provision for children, older people and disabled people; Chapter 6 considers the various rights of people in employment; while Chapter 7 addresses the role of rights in relation to housing.

Part III focuses on rights of redress in relation to the administration of welfare. The emphasis is on the principles and mechanisms for redress, but with a discussion of the functioning and effectiveness of such mechanisms. Thus, Chapter 8 critically examines the part which the courts have played in relation to welfare provision and Chapter 9 discusses the role of administrative tribunals, ombudspersons and complaints procedures.

Finally, Part IV consists of a single concluding chapter which draws together the common threads from the first three parts, while focusing on current debates about social justice and the future of welfare rights.

At the end of each chapter, I provide some recommendations for additional reading and some questions for reflection. It is hoped that these will be helpful to all readers, although they may prove especially so to students and teachers. The recommendations for additional reading are not intended in any way to be comprehensive, merely to signal some of the more readily available key sources to which a reader may wish to turn for a better understanding of the chapter s/he has just read: a full bibliography is provided by way of references at the end of the book. The questions for reflection are not meant to be susceptible to clear or unequivocal answers, but are intended to provoke thought or discussion.

Finally, I should like to express my considerable appreciation to Vic George for suggesting the idea for a book along these lines and who additionally read and helpfully commented on early drafts of some chapters. Thanks are also due to Martin Hewitt for reading and commenting on the whole manuscript. I am grateful too to the University of Luton for allowing me some time for the writing of this book. It should be made clear, however, that responsibility for the inadequacies of what is included in the following pages – and for what has been left out – is mine alone. I do not pretend that this book provides a definitive account of its chosen subject, not only because it would be arrogant to do so, but because time and space necessitate a degree of selectivity, and because the purposes of the book require that it should be reasonably succinct and accessible. None the less, the book is offered to a wide readership as a considered contribution to further debate and exploration.

To Pam

PART I

CHAPTER 1

CLASS, CITIZENSHIP AND COMMODIFICATION

Each of the terms 'welfare rights' and 'social legislation' can mean different things at different times. On the one hand, we often use the term welfare rights very specifically to refer to social security or cash benefit entitlements, and the term social legislation to refer to certain specialised kinds of Acts of Parliament. On the other hand, we may also speak of welfare rights in a much broader sense as the entitlements of citizenship in a welfare state, and of social legislation in terms of all those policies and actions of government which reflect broad societal objectives. This apparent ambiguity arises partly from the looseness with which language is so often used, but partly too because, for those of us who live in welfare state societies, our entitlements to welfare benefits and services are both specifically defined *and* generally situated; they result both from particular legislative rules and regulations *and* from wider policies and principles. This book will use the terms in both senses: not because there is any intention of fudging the difference between different meanings, but because it is important to think about these questions in both a practical and a theoretical way.

The intention is to begin at the level of the general and to work towards more particular applications of welfare rights and social legislation. This chapter therefore starts with a discussion which fuses the terms welfare rights and social legislation into a single expression: 'social rights'.

The amelioration of class

Social rights according to the sociologist, T. H. Marshall (1950), are the unique achievement of the twentieth century. In Britain the struggle to achieve civil rights (i.e. property and legal rights) had by and large succeeded by the eighteenth century and the struggle to achieve political rights (i.e. voting and democratic rights) took major strides in the nineteenth century. The establishment of social rights – that is, entitlement to basic standards of education, health and social care, housing and income maintenance – was completed with the formation of the 'modern' welfare state after the end of the Second World War. Marshall may be accused of overgeneralisation, particularly in his broad-brush characterisation of different historical periods, but this ought not to obscure the importance of his argument. His contentions were, first, that social inequalities based on class divisions have been ameliorated through the development of citizenship and, second, that full citizenship requires three components – not just civil and political rights, but social rights as well.

The first of these points finds favour in the writings of many commentators and supporters of the welfare state, especially those on the Fabian Left (see George and Wilding 1985). However, Marshall's use of the term 'amelioration' had in fact been drawn directly from the works of the nineteenth-century economist, Alfred Marshall. It was in a series of lectures in memory of Alfred Marshall that T. H. Marshall advanced the proposition that the welfare state founded by the post-war Labour government represented the 'latest phase in an evolution of citizenship which has been in continuous progress for some 250 years' (1950: 7). In so doing, he claimed he was addressing a question raised by his erstwhile namesake some seventy years before, namely:

> whether . . . the amelioration of the working classes has limits beyond
> which it cannot pass . . . [or] whether progress may not go on steadily,
> if slowly, till by occupation at least, every man is a gentleman.
> (Alfred Marshall 1873; cited in T. H. Marshall 1950: 4–5).

Marshall the nineteenth-century economist was no egalitarian, least of all so far as women were concerned. The equality he foresaw was an equality of opportunities and lifestyle rather than a material equality of incomes or wealth. Technological advances, he believed, would ameliorate the arduous nature of manual labour, while compulsory elementary education would civilise the manners of the working classes. Marshall the twentieth-century sociologist similarly believed that 'equality of status is more important than equality of income' (1950: 33). The development of a range of social services and cash benefits financed by taxation clearly did involve an equalisation of incomes, but this was not its only, or even its primary, achievement:

> What matters is that there is a general enrichment of the concrete substance of civilised life, a general reduction of risk and insecurity, an equalisation between the more and the less fortunate at all levels – between the healthy and the sick, the employed and the unemployed, the old and the active, the bachelor and the father of a large family. Equalisation is not so much between classes as between individuals within a population which is now treated for this purpose as though it were one class. (*ibid.*)

The argument, then, is that social rights abolish class differences; gender differences were not considered. Academic commentators in the Fabian tradition, such as Titmuss (1958; 1968), argued that the development and maintenance of state welfare provision constituted a moral imperative in so far as it represented the peaceful means of mitigating the unacceptable consequences of class inequality; social rights were a civilising force which compensated for the diswelfares of the capitalist system. Other Fabians, like the Labour politician Tony Crosland (1956), went so far as to argue that the development of social legislation and the rise of labour and trade union power had together shifted the balance so far against the capitalist class system as to promise the imminent realisation of a democratic form of socialism.

It is important, however, to grasp the extent to which Marshall's concept of citizenship was not necessarily consistent with socialist pretensions. Marshall saw citizenship, particularly through the effects of a truly meritocratic state education system, as an alternative instrument of social stratification (1950: 39). Certainly, he believed the emergence of social rights signalled the extent to which *laissez-faire* capitalism had been superseded. But the result would be a society based on status and desert, rather than contract and mere good fortune: 'Social rights in their modern form imply an invasion of contract by status, the subordination of market price to social justice, the replacement of the free bargain by the declaration of rights' (*ibid.*: 40). Ironically, shorn of any commitment to economic equality, this view of social rights can be rendered consistent with a form of one-nation Toryism and the kind of call for a 'classless society' which the British Prime Minister, John Major, made following his 1992 election victory (*Guardian*, 10.4.1992).

The instability of citizenship

We do not, of course, live in a classless society. None the less, the class structure of Britain has changed since the creation of the 'modern' welfare state, although this has been driven by changes in the nature of capitalism, rather than by any influence of the welfare state (see Bottomore 1992; also Sarre 1989). The faultline in Britain's occupational structure now lies not so much between a manual working class and a non-manual middle class, as between secure, highly trained, well-paid 'core' workers and vulnerable, low-skilled, poorly paid 'peripheral' workers. What is more, since the late 1970s the growth of the welfare state has been curtailed and the extent of social and economic inequality in Britain has worsened (see Hills 1990; also Oppenheim 1993). Some commentators suggest that Britain and similar precariously placed Western economies could now face a 'Brazilianisation scenario' in which up to a third of the population will be more or less permanently excluded from economic activity (Therborn 1989). I shall examine the implications of such issues – not least for social stability – in Chapter 2.

For the moment, however, I shall return to the second limb of Marshall's argument, which was that civil, political and social rights are all necessary to full citizenship. Marshall recognised the sense in which citizenship based on a broad equality of rights was potentially in conflict with the workings of a capitalist market economy. In later writings, however, Marshall (1981) stressed that full citizenship need not inhibit a market economy, provided a state of equilibrium can be sustained between political, social and civil rights in what he characterised as the 'hyphenated' society, *democratic-welfare-capitalism*. The hyphens in this formulation symbolise the interconnectedness of a democratic polity, a welfare state and a mixed economy, all functioning in harmony. The maintenance of a flourishing 'hyphenated' society is, therefore, a matter of achieving the right balance between the constituent components of citizenship.

On this premiss, if too much emphasis is being placed in Britain, for example, on our rights as producers and consumers and not enough on our rights to a guaranteed living standard and social provision, then in as much as this creates an imbalance between the civil and social aspects of citizenship, it poses a potential threat to social stability. Similarly, social upheavals in the former Soviet Union and Eastern Europe might be regarded as a consequence of violent shifts in the equilibrium of citizenship. Under former Stalinist regimes, social rights had been guaranteed, while civil and political rights were either suppressed or neglected, but now political rights have been promoted at the expense of social rights and without an adequate framework of civil rights (see, for example, Bottomore 1992).

Marshall's sociological model of citizenship clearly has its applications and attractions. It may be criticised, however, first for 'state-market essentialism' and second for its inherent functionalism.

The charge of state-market essentialism is levelled by Barry Hindess (1987), who complains that Marshall's sophisticated model assumes an over-simplistic conception of the antagonism between the state and the market. Hindess points out that there are aspects of capitalist market relations which are in tune with equal citizenship and aspects of state welfare systems which are not. As we shall see later, not all the changes to welfare systems which have been occurring since the 1970s in countries like Britain have diminished the social rights of citizenship. Although there are obvious limitations, it is possible for the market as well as the state to contribute to the realisation of social rights.

Marshall's functionalism is evident in his treatment of social class. Although he examines the effects of social citizenship on social class, as Bottomore (1992) points out, Marshall fails to account for the impact which social classes have had on the development of citizenship. The development of civil rights and the beginnings of political rights resulted from the struggles of an emerging capitalist class to wrest power from the feudal aristocracy. The more recent development of political rights and aspects of the beginnings of social rights owed much to the struggles of working-class organisations – the Chartists, the trade unions, socialist and social democratic parties. Marshall expresses the conflicts from which citizenship has emerged in terms of clashes between opposing principles rather than between opposing classes. The development and maintenance of welfare states have been analysed by other commentators (e.g. Korpi 1983; Offe 1984; Esping-Andersen 1990) with reference to the influence of corporatism – the effect of which is more relevant in some European countries than in others. Corporatism, in this context, is a process of tripartite negotiation between the representatives of capital, labour and the state. What is often involved in the development of social rights is not an impersonally established equilibrium between formal principles, but a directly negotiated compromise between substantive class interests.

There are, as we shall see, two very different ways of looking at rights: they may be regarded as being founded on abstract or constitutional doctrines or as arising from claims or demands established in the process of political struggle.

The origins of rights

Where then do rights come from?

To the extent that welfare rights founded in social legislation are inevitably embodied in legal form, it can be difficult in practice to sustain a distinction between welfare rights and legal rights. The form of rights in 'hyphenated' democratic-welfare-capitalist societies is inescapably bound up with attempts in the seventeenth and eighteenth centuries to establish both the inalienability (or 'freedom') of property and second, the formal separation of civil society (the economy) from the state (politics).

In feudal society there were no rights other than the right to govern, which had supposedly been bestowed by God on the sovereign and the nobility. To the extent that there were paternalistic duties attaching to such rights, then privileges and gratuities might be conferred from time to time on the common people (Kamenka and Tay 1975), but they enjoyed no rights in the modern legal sense. The doctrines of 'natural' law on which feudal beliefs and practices were founded afforded absolute power to a potentially capricious crown and aristocracy, while imposing constraints on property ownership. Natural law, therefore, frustrated the market freedoms necessary to the economic foundation of capitalist society. Belief in natural law had therefore to be replaced over time by liberal beliefs in 'man-made' laws. (Women, it should be noted, had no legal status at that time and, as we shall see in Chapter 4, can still be systematically disadvantaged before the law.)

Bob Fine has argued that the doctrines of classical jurisprudence which laid the foundations for these man-made laws were inseparable from the doctrines of political economy. The ultimate objective of classical jurisprudence was 'that of creating a synthesis between individual freedom and collective authority' (Fine 1984: 65). This could be achieved by making believe that the authority of the state *is* the will of every rational individual. Hobbes and Rousseau, for example, albeit in rather different ways, advanced the idea of a 'social contract' by which each egotistic individual subject could empower a national legislature to act as guarantor of rational governance on his behalf.

A more pragmatic approach was taken by Adam Smith. Smith is best known for his notion that human affairs can be governed through the 'invisible hand' of free market forces and his insistence that government should not encroach on the liberties of the property-owning subject. He was none the less quite clear about government's role in relation to the four 'great objects' of law, namely police, justice, revenue and arms. Most interesting here is Smith's use of the word 'police' in its archaic sense, referring not to a body of officers responsible for the maintenance of law and order (a comparatively recent invention), but to the general regulation of good order and mannerly or 'polite' conduct (see M. Dean 1991: 55–6). Most particularly, Smith asserted, 'some attention of government is necessary in order to prevent the almost entire corruption and degeneracy of the great body of the people' (1776: 613). To this end he expressly advocated elementary state education.

Hegel's jurisprudential theory went further in advocating that 'police' within a liberal state required the provision of welfare for the poor and public health care, as well as education and public works (see Fine 1984: 59). Hegel's contribution to classical jurisprudence is significant, not only because it provided the starting point for Marxist critiques (to which I shall return in Chapter 4) but because it provided the clearest expression of the form of law and of 'rights' under liberal governance. Rights, he argued, are not bestowed and they do not inhere 'naturally' to the individual subject: 'Right is . . . the immediate embodiment which freedom gives itself as an immediate way, i.e. possession which is property ownership' (Hegel, *Philosophy of Right* [1821], cited in Fine 1984: 57). In other words, the origin of rights is ownership. Rights and equality before the law are universal only in the formal and abstract sense that in an ordered (capitalist) society everybody has to relate to and respect everybody else as *proprietors*. Even people without land or goods at their disposal may 'own' (and therefore sell) their labour-power. More recent theorists have suggested that welfare rights are, or ought to be, directly analogous to property rights, and that 'government largesse' (such as welfare benefits, subsidies, grants, education, etc.) constitutes a kind of property which may be subject to the same legal rules and categories as other property forms (Reich 1964).

This is one way of looking at welfare rights: as an expression in legal form of the logic of individual ownership. In the case of many recipients of state welfare, this logically driven formulation may seem bizarre. Many 'clients' of the welfare state are ostensibly propertyless and their 'rights', to means-tested social security benefits for example, are governed specifically by legislation (see Chapter 5). None the less, such benefits – provided all the conditions of eligibility are met – are available as an entitlement rather than as a gift, and the principles which give rise to that entitlement are supposed to operate with indifference to the personality and status of the recipient. They are rights within the liberal definition of the rule of law.

A radically different view of the character of the rights which are conferred by social legislation has been provided by Paul Hirst (1980). Like the classical jurists, Hirst rejects the notion that rights can have any natural or ontological attributes, but argues that welfare rights serve socially determined policy objectives. The rights which social legislation bestow do no more than assign or regulate the responsibilities and conduct of persons appointed to fulfil particular tasks. Rights are no more and no less than specific capacities, conferred by law. The rights created by social security legislation for example do not relate to any inherent or unconditional claim by the citizen, but to the precise duties of state departments and officials. These rights merely define the limited circumstances in which social policy will permit assistance to be given.

In contrast, the traditional rhetoric of welfare rights campaigners and activists is often cast in terms of doctrinal or ontological rights. This is a tradition which can be traced back to the Owenites and Chartists whose opposition to the Poor Law Amendment Act of 1834 was founded on the romantically conceived 'birth rights' of free Englishmen, that is to say:

> the right to have a living out of the land of our birth in exchange for labour duly and honestly performed; the right in case we fell into distress, to have our wants sufficiently relieved out of the produce of the land, whether that distress arose from sickness, from decrepitude, from old age, or from inability to find employment. (William Cobbett, cited in Thompson 1968: 836)

The modern equivalent of such demands are the right to work, the right to a living wage, the right to an adequate income in the event of incapacity, unemployment or retirement, and the right to education, health care and affordable housing. Claims to such benefits are founded on conviction: they may well be politically realisable, but they are not necessarily substantive rights. Such conviction explains, for example, the outrage expressed in a satirical cartoon which appeared in Child Poverty Action Group's *Welfare Rights Bulletin* (Issue 60) in July 1984. The cartoon (see Figure 1.1) sought to ridicule the remarks of a Social Security Commissioner who had said:

> At the end of the day, the supplementary benefit scheme [the then prevailing basic means-tested benefit in the UK] is not something to which there is a divine right: it is nothing more than an arbitrary compromise, sanctioned by Parliament, between the demand for benefits on the one hand and the availability of public funds to finance it. (R(SB)55/83)

In one sense, the Commissioner had a point: the welfare rights which we enjoy are not founded on doctrine, but come out of struggle and often arbitrary compromises between competing interests. Welfare rights are the outcome of campaigns (by organisations such as Child Poverty Action Group) for enhanced benefits and *better* compromises.

Figure 1.1 'You do not have a divine right
to your benefit . . .' (*Source:* from *Welfare
Rights Bulletin*, Issue No. 60 (July 1984),
p.8. Reproduced by kind permission of
Child Poverty Action Group.)

The privatisation of rights

The language or 'discourse' of rights is shot through with
ambiguities. Not only is there a distinction to be drawn between the
kinds of rights which are prescribed by doctrine and the kinds of
rights which people establish for themselves through struggle, there
is also a distinction between 'negative' rights which protect the
individual from external interference and 'positive' rights which
guarantee state intervention. The distinction between negative and

positive 'liberties' was drawn by Isaiah Berlin to mark the difference between a 'right' to forbearance by others, as opposed to 'the freedom which consists in being one's own master' (Berlin 1967: 149). Strictly speaking, of course, the words 'liberty' and 'right' are not synonymous and it should also be noted that there is a narrow legal positivist tradition which refers to any right which is legally defined as a 'positive' right as distinct from a mere 'moral' right which is unspecified and unenforceable. This book is concerned with rights in a broad sense. Hohfeld (1923, cited in Weale 1983) identified four kinds of rights: liberties, claims, immunities and powers. I shall argue that liberties and immunities are what might be called negative rights because they signal a *freedom from* something, whereas claims and powers are positive rights because they signal an *entitlement to* something.

In general, negative rights ('freedoms from') are supported from the political Right, while positive rights ('entitlements to') are more usually championed on the political Left. This, however, is a crude generalisation. The entitlements created by positive rights are often subject to conditions. As we shall see in Chapter 4, welfare rights in particular may also be the means of enforcing certain duties of citizenship. The authoritarian (neo-conservative) rather than the libertarian (neo-liberal) Right may therefore be supportive of positive welfare rights where these are closely tied to the performance of obligations, particularly such private obligations as the duty to work and/or to support dependants (see Roche 1993). Conversely, there are those on the libertarian Left who are mis-trustful of the conditional nature of positive welfare rights and seek also to emphasise the negative rights of citizens against the welfare state such as the right to 'privacy, dignity and confidentiality' (Esam, Good and Middleton 1985: 38).

The rights defined *doctrinally* by classical jurisprudence in the seventeenth and eighteenth centuries were realised and consolidated *politically* by the early nineteenth century through the ascendancy of the industrial bourgeoisie. This new middle class was concerned both with the negative rights required for individual autonomy in a free market and the positive rights required for the collective authority of an effective state. The architects of such nineteenth-century social legislation as the Poor Law Amendment Act 1834, against which the Owenites and Chartists so vigorously protested, were the middle-class utilitarians, represented by

Jeremy Bentham and Edwin Chadwick. E. P. Thompson described these utilitarians as 'the main protagonists of the State, in its political and administrative authority . . . on the other side of whose statist banner were inscribed the doctrines of economic *laissez faire*' (1968: 90). The 'rights' of the poor were made strictly conditional and subject to the universal regimentation of the workhouse; the 'rights' of entrepreneurs to engage in free trade without state interference were to be unconditional.

The development of the modern welfare state has been achieved through a body of social legislation which has extended the 'positive' rights of citizenship, by expanding public services and reforming the conditions attaching to the availability of those services. Neo-liberal critics of the welfare state – sometimes characterised as anti-collectivists (George and Wilding 1985) – complain that the degree of state intervention involved and the scale of public services have been at the expense of all-important 'negative' rights. The freedoms which citizens must enjoy if a market economy is to prosper have been eroded by an interfering state which stifles initiative (Hayek 1960) and public spending which crowds out productive investment (Bacon and Eltis 1978). This kind of thinking informed a political project whose manifestation in the UK was 'Thatcherism' (Gamble 1988). Like the middle-class utilitarians of the nineteenth century, the Thatcher governments of the 1980s were concerned to promote both a free market *and* a strong state. This involved strengthening the 'negative' rights of businesses (through tax cuts and deregulation), while using the power of the state to control the rights of trade unions, unemployed people and welfare dependants. In practice, the degree of retrenchment suffered by the welfare state was relatively modest (see, for example, Hills 1990). Of far greater significance was a restructuring of welfare spending and a transition to what is widely termed the 'mixed economy of welfare' or 'welfare pluralism' (see, for example, Johnson 1987).

In the process of the shift to welfare pluralism welfare rights have also been restructured, or at least a different dimension has been introduced to the social rights of citizenship. There is a sense in which many rights have been 'privatised', although such a term runs the risk of obscuring the complexity of the processes involved.

The concept of welfare pluralism rests on the idea that, instead of the public sector (the state) being the principal provider of welfare goods and services, a significant level of provision should also come from the 'informal' sector (families and communities), the 'voluntary' sector (independent self-help or non-profit-making organisations) and the 'commercial' sector (private enterprise). The suggestion is not that the state should no longer guarantee the welfare rights of the citizen, but that that guarantee should not necessarily be honoured through the direct provision of services by public sector organisations. The state might instead fund the provision of services by other agencies, or it might do no more than regulate the standards of provision made by such agencies.

The promotion of the *informal* sector lies at the heart of the development of policies of community care. In practice the greater part of everyday health and social care takes place within households (Rose 1988) and, for everyday needs, most people do tend, in the first instance, to look for help from members of their family (Beresford and Croft 1986). At the same time, for some thirty years there has been widespread agreement throughout the Western world that the institutional forms of care – for physically disabled people, people with severe learning difficulties, people with mental health problems and frail elderly people – should be replaced by alternative forms of community-based care. In seeking to give expression to this objective, the British government has emphasised that care *in* the community should increasingly mean care *by* the community, and that the contribution to care by family, relatives, friends and neighbours should be maximised (see, for example, Walker 1990). The government has justified this in terms of giving people the right to choose where and how they should be looked after (DHSS 1989). In practice, choice may be limited and the right which the legislation (NHS and Community Care Act 1990) has given people is an inferred right to a needs assessment conducted by their local authority Social Services Department. The intention is that, as far as possible, care in public institutions should be avoided and that people should be enabled, through domiciliary care packages, to live independently in their own home. The character of the citizen's right has been altered to the extent that the provision of a substantive service (rather than a formal needs assessment) may in some circumstances become contingent on the imposition of an obligation on a close relative to act as an informal carer.

The government's promotion of the *voluntary* sector has been accompanied by attempts to advance the concept of Active Citizenship. Towards the end of the 1980s two British government ministers, Douglas Hurd and John Patten, in particular sought to ameliorate the essentially amoral premisses of Thatcherism by encouraging voluntary action, especially on the part of successful citizens. Active Citizenship was described as 'a necessary complement to that of the enterprise culture' (Hurd 1989) and entailed charitable giving and voluntary service. As a concept of citizenship it was one that emphasised, not the rights of disadvantaged citizens, but the duties of those with time and money to spare:

> we have to recognise that it is no longer acceptable to buy your way out of your obligations to society. Tax cannot remain the only way in which citizens discharge their obligations: time and commitment have to be added to money. (*Guardian*, 16.9.1988)

Ruth Lister (1990) has suggested that this amounted to an attempt to 'privatise' citizenship and negate welfare rights. The implication of a shift of social obligations from the sphere of tax-financed benefits to the sphere of charitable and voluntary service is a return to the feudal notion of *noblesse oblige* (that the divine rights bestowed on the nobility obliged them to be charitable to their subjects). Appeals to the ideal of Active Citizenship have been less in evidence in the 1990s, although continued support has been given by government to the use of voluntary organisations and volunteers in the provision of social services, both through requirements directly imposed on Social Services Departments relating to the contracting out of work to independent providers (including the voluntary sector) and through the direct financing of projects like the 'Make a Difference' scheme (see *Guardian* 2.3.1994) intended to encourage people to take part in voluntary community service.

The government's promotion of the *commercial* welfare sector (see Papadakis and Taylor-Gooby 1987) has affected citizenship rights in a number of ways. The encouragement given during the 1980s to insurance-based private health care and pensions was given on the basis that such arrangements would afford citizens independence from the state: the intention was that people should substitute civil rights, based on a contract of insurance, for social rights, based on citizenship status. The promotion of home-ownership through the Right to Buy scheme for public sector tenants similarly sought directly to substitute property rights for social rights. In other areas of social policy, however, the partial privatisation of public welfare was intended to create competition between public and private sector providers and so alter the ethos of public service provision. Where citizens had a right to a service, they should have a choice between providers: even if no payment were required at the point of service delivery, the rights of a service user should be more akin to the civil rights of a paying customer than the social rights of a citizen. What is more, this could be achieved without transferring services to the private sector. In the 1980s and 1990s three other methods were employed towards this general goal.

The first of these devices found expression in the doctrine of New Public Management (Hood 1991; see also Gray and Jenkins 1993). The idea was that, if public services were not to be relocated in the commercial sector, the business practices of the commercial sector could none the less be imported into public services. To this end, for example, the principles of general management were introduced into the National Health Service (Butler 1993); the administration of social security benefits was hived off to an 'arm's length' executive agency governed by performance targets (H. Dean 1993). The essence of the New Public Management doctrine is a change in the culture of public service delivery and a deliberate attempt at the level of discourse to reconstitute the client, the patient or the claimant as a 'customer'.

Second, in a number of social policy areas the emphasis in the late 1980s and early 1990s shifted in favour of the introduction of 'quasi-markets' (Le Grand 1990a). This found its most explicit expression in the NHS 'internal market', in which District Health Authorities and fund-holding general practitioners became the 'purchasers' of health care on behalf of their patients, while hospitals and community health care units became 'providers' competing for the custom of the purchasers. The community care reforms described above have had a similar effect for local authority Social Services Departments, which must now operate separate commissioning and provider operations with contracts for residential care, day care and domiciliary services being placed both internally and externally (Lawson 1993). In education the introduction of open enrolment and formula funding has effectively put state schools in competition with each other for pupils and funding (Taylor-Gooby 1993).

Third, in 1991 John Major introduced the *Citizen's Charter* (Prime Minister's Office 1991). At first sight the *Citizen's Charter*, aimed at improving the standards of public services, represented a retreat from Thatcherism and a return to a more social democratic concern with the positive rights of the citizen (Miller and Peroni 1992). The stated aim of the *Charter* was to make services more open and accountable, but as Miller and Peroni put it: 'it creates few new rights. The drafting skilfully blurs the distinction between what is new and what merely confirms past practices and promises' (1992: 256). The *Charter* claimed to provide a 'tool kit' of initiatives and ideas, among which were:

> more privatisation; wider competition; further contracting out; more performance related pay; published performance targets – local and national; comprehensive publication of information on standards achieved; more effective complaints procedures; tougher and more independent inspectorates; better redress for the citizen when things go badly wrong. (Prime Minister's Office 1991: 5)

Central to the idea of the *Citizen's Charter* is the link between payment for services (whether directly or through taxes) and the quality of those services. The competent citizen is therefore the successful consumer, able to get the best out of services. The users and providers of services are cast as opponents of each other's interests. What is more, the 'business' of service provision is uncoupled from the 'politics' of welfare: policy-makers may evade responsibility for policy failures (because customers are encouraged to blame the providers of services) and the collectivist ethos of the welfare state is diluted (because service provision is driven by individualised incentives rather than policy, or vocational or professional commitment). In Marshall's terms the *Citizen's Charter* strengthened civil rights (the kind of rights 'customers' enjoy in the marketplace) *at the expense of* both political rights and social rights.

Commodification and decommodification

An alternative way to address the changing nature of welfare rights and social legislation is provided through a discussion of 'commodification' and 'decommodification'. Although interest in these concepts has resurfaced only recently, their roots may be traced to the Marxist critique of classical political economy and to a reinterpretation of that analysis by Polanyi (1944).

Marx contended that it was the commodity form which was constitutive of capitalism. He argued that when the products of labour are traded as commodities they assume values related not to their actual utility, but to the amount of human labour which they embody. At the same time, because labour-power itself is reduced to a commodity which is bought and sold (supposedly) like any other, the labourer becomes alienated from the products of his/her labour. So it is that 'a definite social relation between men . . . assumes . . . the fantastic form of a relation between things' (1887: 72). The development of capitalism entailed the socialisation of commodities and the commodification of social life.

It was Karl Polanyi, however, who pointed out that labour-power is in reality only a fictitious commodity. Unlike ordinary commodities, labour-power cannot be separated from its owners and, what is more, is uniquely dependent for its existence on the health and well-being of those owners. While it is possible for the owners of ordinary commodities to withhold them from sale until the price is right, the owners of labour-power cannot do so unless they can secure an alternative means of subsistence. If labour-power is to be traded as if it were a commodity on a labour market, certain conditions must be met, including certain decommodified support systems. In a sense, welfare rights are a precondition of the commodification of labour-power, and Offe suggests that Polanyi's theory therefore contradicts that of Marshall. The development of social rights did not take place *after* the development of the legal and economic infrastructure of capitalism; on the contrary, 'a supportive network of non-commodified institutions is necessary for an economic system that utilizes labour power as if it were a commodity' (Offe 1984: 263).

The development of welfare rights undoubtedly has been messier and more complex than Marshall suggested, and Esping-Andersen has developed the concept of decommodification as a means to explain the development of different kinds of welfare state in different countries. He makes clear that

de-commodification should not be confused with the complete eradication of labor as a commodity; it is not an issue of all or nothing. Rather the concept refers to the degree to which individuals, or families, can uphold a socially acceptable standard of living independently of market participation. (Esping-Andersen 1990: 37)

I shall return to Esping-Andersen's work in Chapter 3, which examines how welfare rights can differ between countries, but this chapter now considers a particular element of his argument about the development of welfare rights and social legislation. Esping-Andersen suggests that, historically, there were three kinds of response to the commodification process, reflecting in effect three different ways of thinking about social rights. He defines these in terms of the classical paradigms of conservatism, liberalism and socialism.

The conservative approach resists commodification because it undermines traditional authority. Characteristically, therefore, this approach favours 'rights' in a paternalistic sense: the kind of rights which come from imposing obligations on employers to look after their workers; from encouraging corporatist guilds and mutual self-help societies; or from state intervention in a paternal-authoritarian mode (e.g. compulsory national insurance schemes).

The liberal approach does not resist commodification and seeks to intervene only to the extent that intervention will assist the commodification process or correct 'market failures'. Characteristically, this approach favours 'rights' of a highly conditional nature (such as strictly means-tested social assistance schemes).

The socialist/social democratic approach resists commodification because it is the basis of social alienation and class exploitation. Characteristically, this approach favours 'rights' which are emancipatory, which minimise stigmatising conditions and maximise equality. What Esping-Andersen's analysis seeks to demonstrate is that all welfare state regimes are in fact compromises between these competing notions of what welfare rights should achieve.

A similar analysis, but with more of a structuralist emphasis, is offered by Claus Offe. Offe claims that advanced capitalist societies face a paralysis of the commodity form, precisely because of the competing tendencies towards commodification and decommodification. In the face of this, neither inaction and a return to economic *laissez-faire*, nor the further development of an extensive and fiscally unviable welfare state is tenable. The alternative which Offe identifies as the underlying basis of policy in welfare state societies is 'administrative recommodification' (1984: 125). What Offe anticipates is the use of the administrative power of government to sustain the commodity form. This may be achieved by regulating the self-destructive tendencies of market competition; by investing in the 'supply-side' of the economy (in education, training, research and development, transport and communications systems, etc.); by introducing new forms of joint decision-making and financing (which Offe calls neo-corporatism). Some elements of such approaches are evident in British government policies, others conspicuously less so.

None the less, the notion of administrative recommodification provides the basis for a valuable insight into the changing nature of welfare rights and social legislation. Certainly, it is a term which captures the sense in which the shift to welfare pluralism and the introduction of devices such as the *Citizen's Charter* are transforming the social rights of citizenship. It is not that welfare rights are being extinguished, rather that they are being made less emancipatory and more akin to the property rights of classical jurisprudence. Welfare rights are now less concerned with enabling people to exist independently of the market, and rather more with requiring them to participate in markets, including 'quasi-markets' for welfare services. Ironically, however, welfare rights are no less administrative in nature; it is simply that administrative power has been made more technical than political in character.

Conclusion/summary

All our rights are ideological constructions. When we speak of welfare rights we are dealing with an abstract idea rather than with concrete realities. None the less, it is welfare rights which give expression to the effects (if not always the intentions) of social legislation and the substantive exercise of state power. This chapter has examined a range of theoretical explanations concerning the basis of welfare rights and the social legislation which gives rise to them.

We have been concerned, first, with the extent to which welfare rights are founded in a form of mature citizenship which has displaced class as a basis for social organisation. If this view were accepted, in place of a society founded on class antagonisms and inequalities we would now have a society based on a broad equality of citizenship. It is difficult, however, to reconcile this view with the realities of contemporary welfare state societies, although there is a sense in which the idea of welfare (or social) rights represents only a part of a wider project in which property (or civil) rights and democratic (or political) rights must also play a part if capitalism is to work.

We have also considered the extent to which the concept of rights under capitalism is problematic. Essentially, the basis of individual 'rights' stems from the definition of private property. Welfare rights, however, are bestowed by the collective authority of the state. While it is possible to speak of welfare rights as if they were property rights, in practice they are defined with reference to obligations imposed on both those who administer and those who benefit from such rights. To this extent, welfare rights are also political in character, because they may represent negotiable claims made by or on behalf of groups in society.

Clearly, therefore, welfare rights are not static attributes of citizenship. They change over time, and we have considered how recent welfare reforms have resulted in sometimes subtle transformations to the nature of welfare rights and social legislation. In particular, we have examined how the privatisation of certain aspects of welfare and changes to the way in which public services are administered have been reflected in a more consumer-oriented form of rights. Following from this, we have discussed commodification, decommodification and recommodification; concepts which provide a particular perspective on the development of welfare rights in capitalist societies and an explanation of the contradictory potential of welfare rights (as rights to an existence independent of the market) and their ambiguous status (when deflected into the form of consumer rights).

The next chapter will move on from broad definitions of social rights as a component of citizenship to a discussion of poverty and need and, specifically, the extent to which welfare rights address poverty and need.

Recommended additional reading

Esping-Andersen, G. (1990) *The Three Worlds of Welfare Capitalism*, Polity Press, Cambridge, Chapter 2.
Lister, R. (1990) *The Exclusive Society: Citizenship and the poor*; a pamphlet published by Child Poverty Action Group, London, Part I.
Marshall, T. H. (1950) 'Citizenship and social class', an essay reproduced in Marshall, T. H. (1963) *Sociology at the Crossroads and Other Essays*, Heinemann, London; and in Marshall, T. H. and Bottomore, T. (1992) *Citizenship and Social Class*, Pluto Press.

Questions for reflection

In a 'hyphenated' democratic-welfare-capitalist society is the right to social security the same sort of right as the right to enforce a contract, the right to religious freedom or the right to vote? If not, in what way does it differ?

The development of the social rights of citizenship has been associated with processes of 'class amelioration' on the one hand and 'decommodification' on the other. Will a trend towards 'recommodification' (the introduction of private or marketised forms of welfare provision) necessarily entail a loss of rights and a restoration of class inequality?

CHAPTER 2

POVERTY, NEED AND RIGHTS

Chapter 1 discussed social rights as a component of citizenship within a democratic-welfare-capitalist state. Just as rights to political participation and legal protection are supposedly guaranteed, so citizens are also entitled to have certain basic human needs satisfied. But which needs?

The Beveridge Report (1942), which provided the blueprint for Britain's post-war welfare state, identified five metaphorical 'giants' to be banished: Disease, Idleness, Ignorance, Squalor and Want. The social ills which these giants represented reflected the needs which the welfare state promised to underwrite; the need for health, employment, education, housing and the means of subsistence. Of the five giants, it is Want – what we might now call poverty – which has proved the most difficult to defeat, not least because this giant tends to shield itself behind its companions. The right to an adequate means of subsistence is difficult to guarantee, not least because overall adequacy of living standards can be dependent on a complex array of life chances, including good health, employment prospects, educational opportunity and decent housing. An issue to which I shall return is that of whether Want, in the sense that Beveridge spoke of it, implies a universal concept of human need and therefore a set of rights to welfare which are both specifiable and general. First, however, this chapter will discuss the concept of poverty.

Under the Poor Laws which preceded the 'modern' British welfare state people who received state assistance were defined as 'paupers'. Paupers were not citizens. They were disqualified, for

24

example, from voting in elections. By repealing the Poor Laws the modern welfare state sought not only to banish poverty, but to abolish pauperism. Welfare rights for all implied a formal equality of citizenship. Poverty represents 'a strategically important *limit* for the concept of social citizenship' (Roche 1993: 55). If poverty persists in capitalist welfare states this implies a failure by citizens to secure their rights and a failure by the welfare state to honour those rights. Poverty is the 'limit case', the 'litmus test' or 'yardstick' against which the effectiveness of welfare rights and social legislation is to be defined and judged.

Defining poverty

The trouble with 'poverty' is that politically and technically it is a highly contested concept (see Alcock 1993 for an excellent introductory text on poverty) and at the level of popular discourse it is an especially elusive and ambiguous term (see H. Dean 1992).

Absolute or relative?

The traditional battlelines in the debate about poverty have been drawn between those who subscribe to an absolute definition of poverty and those who subscribe to a relative definition. The absolute definition, broadly speaking, is that favoured by Victorian poverty investigators (Booth 1889; Rowntree 1901) and by contemporary politicians of the New Right (Joseph and Sumption 1979; Moore 1989). It is a definition which restricts the term poverty to people with insufficient resources for physical survival. The relative definition is that favoured characteristically by Fabian academics (Townsend 1979; Donnison 1982) and the so-called 'poverty lobby' (see, for example, Oppenheim 1993). It is a definition that expands the term poverty to include people with insufficient resources for normal social participation. From this classic debate stems a number of related controversies of a technical, explanatory and political nature.

First, there is no agreed way of measuring poverty. Rowntree, for example, sought to apply an absolute or primary poverty line based on the cost of providing 'the minimum necessaries for the maintenance of merely physical efficiency' for a household of any given size or composition. Rowntree's approach was to be a direct methodological influence on the setting of social assistance benefit levels in the 1940s. This is now called the 'budget standard' approach to poverty measurement. It has been extended in recent years by the University of York's Family Budget Unit, which has developed not only a 'low cost' budget standard but a 'modest but adequate' budget standard, reflecting as it were a relative as well as an absolute definition (Bradshaw 1993a). It should be noted that the Family Budget Unit calculated that, at 1993 prices, families with young children in the UK needed incomes around one third higher than the prevailing levels of social assistance benefit in order to achieve even a 'low cost' budget standard. Alternatively, it is common practice in some Western countries, officially or unofficially, to define a 'poverty line' with reference to the level of income at which people qualify for means-tested social assistance benefits or a level of income equivalent to some arbitrary proportion (generally 50 per cent) of average household incomes, although neither of these indices strictly speaking is a measure of poverty (see Veit-Wilson 1994). Other commentators prefer statistical or 'income proxy' measures which seek to identify the level of income below which need demonstrably replaces choice as the principal determinant of household expenditure (Orshansky 1969) or below which prevailing public opinion believes it impossible to make ends meet (Van Praag *et al.* 1982). Rather than measure incomes only, some sociologists have sought to measure 'deprivation'. This may be achieved by applying either a range of expertly determined indicators relating to diet, consumption patterns, housing, working conditions, family and community activity levels (Townsend 1979) or a consensually determined range of 'socially perceived necessities' identified through public opinion surveys (Mack and Lansley 1985).

Second, there are explanatory controversies. The conflict here is between explanations of poverty based on pathology and explanations based on structural causes (Holman 1978). Pathological explanations blame poverty on the failures of the poor. Poverty is seen to arise from the inadequacies of the individuals, families or communities affected. As a result of their genetic make-up or their personalities or through sheer bad luck individuals may be inept, lazy or incapacitated. Deficient parenting or a deprived family background may result in the transmission of poverty and inappropriate behaviour patterns from generation to generation (Joseph 1972). In certain localities or communities a ghetto sub-culture may develop which reinforces and perpetuates economic dependency and poverty (Murray 1984). The alternative structural explanations focus on the part played by society. These blame poverty on the inevitable 'diswelfares' of the competitive market economy (Titmuss 1968), the nature of class relations (Townsend 1979), or on the consequences of patriarchy and racism (see, for example, Williams 1989).

Third, there are political controversies concerning what role (if any) the state should play in relation to poverty and whether the objective of social policy is to prevent poverty, or merely relieve it if it occurs. There are those on the far Right who are critical of the welfare state, not only for eroding individual freedoms (see the discussion of 'negative rights' in Chapter 1), but also for perpetuating poverty (Boyson 1971; Murray 1984). They suggest that the kindest thing the state can do for 'the poor' is to stand out of their way. Most right-wing opinion, however, acknowledges that the state should have a minimalist role in relieving poverty (Hayek 1944; Anderson 1991), as indeed the British state had done for three and a half centuries under the Poor Laws. To the centre and left of the political spectrum it is widely believed that the state should provide more than an 'ambulance' service to relieve the casualties of poverty, and that it should attempt to cure the causes of poverty and so prevent poverty from happening in the first place. The social legislation to which such an approach gives rise ranges from social insurance to the provision of universal benefits. These will be discussed in Chapter 5.

For the moment, I should like to go behind the old debate about absolute and relative poverty since this has been in some respects eclipsed – first, by new debates about how poverty relates to citizenship; and second, by new approaches to the definition of human need. To the second of these issues this chapter will turn shortly, but first it will be useful to open up some rather different arguments bearing on the idea advanced by 'relativists' that poverty represents an exclusion from citizenship, or at the very least a form of 'second-class' citizenship (see, for example, Lister 1990).

The discourses of poverty and citizenship

The figure who can claim the greatest credit both for Britain's 'rediscovery' of poverty in the 1960s and for major advances in the theory and analysis of poverty in the 1970s is Professor Peter Townsend. Townsend pioneered a structural analysis of poverty and devised an index of relative deprivation based on living patterns. From the findings of a major survey he sought to demonstrate that people with incomes of up to one and a half times the prevailing level of social assistance benefits were likely to suffer relative deprivation; that is, to a greater or lesser extent to be excluded from socially acceptable living patterns. Townsend's (1979) contention was that there is an income band or threshold below which the risk of relative deprivation increases disproportionately. In 1981, in the columns of *New Society*, a celebrated exchange took place between Townsend and David Piachaud. Piachaud criticised Townsend's index of relative deprivation because it did not allow for the diversity of people's lifestyles and behaviour; it assumed uniformity and so denied individual choice and freedom. At first glance, Piachaud's attack appears conventionally right-wing and 'absolutist', but the main thrust of his argument lies in his contention that 'There is a continuum from great wealth to chronic poverty and along that continuum a wide diversity of patterns of living. The poor in Britain are worse off than others; but for the most part, they are members of society, not outcasts' (1981: 118). Piachaud readily concedes that 'The term "poverty" carries with it an implication and a moral imperative that something should be done about it' (*ibid.*: 119), but it is precisely because this requires the making of political or value-judgements that there can be no objective measurement of relative deprivation. Piachaud compares Townsend's quest for a poverty threshold with that for the Holy Grail.

The issue therefore is whether it is more helpful to think in terms of poverty as a discursive or social construct, rather than as an objective phenomenon. Tawney once wrote that 'What thoughtful rich people call the problem of poverty, thoughtful poor people call with equal justice a problem of riches' (1913, cited in Alcock 1993: xi). John Scott (1993) has sought to move the debate beyond Townsend's definition of *poverty* as 'relative deprivation', in order to define *wealth* as 'relative privilege'. Like Piachaud, Scott posits the idea of a continuum between the extremes of wealth and poverty. Exclusion, he argues, occurs at both extremes of the continuum, though it is an exclusion which relates not merely to living standards, but to *citizenship* (cf. Lister 1990): 'Citizenship describes the institutionalised conception of what it is to have "full membership" in the public world of society. It thus refers to the norms and practices which define who possesses the rights (and the corresponding obligations) which allow full participation in public life' (Scott 1993: 21). The deprived poor and the privileged rich have in common an exclusion from that which is 'public'. Scott reminds us that 'The words "privilege" and "deprivation" have a common root in the Latin "*privatus*", which was also the origin of the modern word "private" . . . "private" means withdrawn from public life, kept or closed from the public, or belonging to a particular individual' (*ibid.*: 24). I understand the exclusion of which Scott speaks as being primarily symbolic in nature. The 'poor' are dispossessed from the rights of citizenship as the 'rich' are immune from the duties of citizenship. The thread which links them is the public sphere of citizenship beyond whose opposing boundaries they stand. They may or they may not be literal outcasts, but the threat of poverty and the possibility of wealth are symbols of fear and awe respectively to the whole community of citizens.

Chapter 1 has described how Adam Smith, the classical political economist and advocate of the free market, identified a role for the state in the 'policing' of social order. Smith is also credited with the prescience to have advanced an oft-quoted 'relative' definition of poverty. While arguing against the taxation of 'necessary' commodities, he wrote: 'By necessaries, I understand not only commodities which are indispensably necessary for the support of life but whatever the *custom* of the country renders it indecent for *creditable people*, even of the lowest order, to be without' [emphasis added] (1776: 691). Although a linen shirt is not a necessity of life, an eighteenth-century English labourer would have been 'ashamed', according to Smith, to appear in public without one. It might be argued that the advent of twentieth-century social citizenship has turned 'customs' into 'rights' and 'creditable people' into 'citizens'. However, as Seabrook points out, twentieth-century capitalism has also brought with it a reformulation of our understanding of poverty: 'For within capitalism that which it seemed to promise,

. . . sufficiency, is inadmissible. Enough is anathema to a system devoted to its accumulation' (1985: 12). The promise of the democratic-welfare-capitalist state was of more than sufficiency, but of social security. As Michael Ignatieff says, 'What we need in order to survive and what we need in order to flourish are two different things' (Ignatieff 1984: 11). Therefore, if citizenship involves a social as well as a political and civil element, then the expectations it engenders are not only those of what it would be shameful to go without, but also those of what it is to flourish. The welfare state fulfils a function not foreseen by Adam Smith: in ways which mere custom could not, it helps 'police' both the fear of poverty and the desire for wealth; the fear or the desire of being beyond the security or the discipline of citizenship.

It is precisely because 'the poor' are for the most part, as Piachaud contends, 'members of society, not outcasts' that they remain subject to the fears and desires of all citizens. Though they are excluded from a range of life chances, they are not formally excluded from citizenship, nor from the cultural values, prejudices and aspirations of society at large (for an empirical defence of this assertion, see Dean and Taylor-Gooby 1992).

Chapter 4 will examine critiques of the welfare state which suggest that it functions not as a means of relieving poverty, but as a means to define and regulate it. Among those critiques is a work by this author which, drawing on the work of Foucault, outlines an alternative theory of poverty (H. Dean 1991). I have argued that, just as for example 'criminality' is a social construct generated through the discourses of the criminal justice and penal systems, so 'poverty' is a parallel social construct generated through the discourses of social policy and the social security system. This is not to say that either crime or material deprivation are mere phantoms: on the contrary, they are very tangible. It is the discursively constructed phenomena of 'criminality' and 'poverty' which are so elusive and contentious. Poverty in this sense represents a process of subjection; subjection through the distinctions drawn between 'the poor' and 'the not poor'; but subjection too because the social rights of citizenship make the risk or potentiality towards poverty inherent to the identity of all citizens, wherever they stand on the wealth–poverty continuum.

Defining need

Closely related to the concept of 'poverty' is that of 'human need'. Need is a no less problematic concept, albeit for rather different reasons. The controversies tend to stem more from philosophical than from political concerns. At root, however, human need like poverty is beset by a dichotomy between absolute and relative definitions.

Absolute or 'basic' human needs might be supposed to arise from the requirements of biological survival and protection from physical harm. Relative needs or mere 'wants' might be supposed to arise from culturally or socially determined expectations. The distinction, however, is one which melts away as soon as one tries to specify what is 'basically' necessary to human survival. What constitutes adequacy of diet or shelter, for example, is fundamentally related not only to sociocultural considerations, but also to physiological, physical, geographical and climatic factors. Exact scientific or clinical criteria even for 'starvation' and 'hunger' are not easy to find (Townsend 1993: 132) and strict medically or biologically derived definitions are likely to be at best arbitrary and at worst meaningless, unless they can be situated in a substantive human context.

Theoretical approaches to human need have tended to be polarised not simplistically between the absolute and the relative, but between notions of needs which are inherent to the human individual and needs which are creatures of policy. An instance of the former is provided by Maslow (1943), who argued that humans' basic drives are (in descending order of potency) physiological; for physical safety; for love and belonging; for self-esteem; and for 'self-actualisation'. An instance of a policy analyst's approach is provided by Bradshaw (1972), who proposed a very different taxonomy of need, distinguishing the 'normative' needs defined on our behalf by professionals and experts; the 'felt' needs which we might identify when asked what we need; the 'expressed' needs articulated through political demands for the delivery of services; and the 'comparative' needs which may be said to exist when there is a shortfall or deficiency in the services received by one person or group relative to those received by another similarly placed person or group. Maslow's approach cannot account for the potency of socially constituted needs and the fact that, for example, in affluent societies people on low incomes may opt to go hungry in order to maintain forms of consumption by which to 'keep up appearances'. Bradshaw's approach fails to prioritise different kinds of need or to say which needs should inform social legislation. Should people be allowed to determine their own needs and interests? Given that people are not always best placed to identify or to safeguard their own interests, who should be the arbiter and guarantor of their needs?

Probably the most systematic attempt to wrestle with such questions has been provided by Doyal and Gough (1984; 1991). They have argued that a conception of human need is implicit in almost every ideological stance, even those that rail against the possibility of defining basic human needs. They argue that:

- Orthodox economists believe that the market is the ideal medium through which needs or 'preferences' may be formulated and expressed. They must none the less concede that 'demand' in the marketplace may be artificially created or suppressed, that 'consumers' may act irrationally or from ignorance and that markets often fail to function in the wider public interest.
- The political New Right goes further than orthodox economists in that they see the free market not merely as efficient but as a morally superior way of articulating and satisfying human need, since intervention by the state is an affront to liberty. In practice, however, most strands of New Right or neo-liberal opinion recognise a role for the state in guaranteeing the functioning of a free market and, to this end, will concede a minimalist welfare 'safety net'.
- Marxists, for rather different reasons, also eschew the notion of predetermined or 'basic' needs since, they would argue, human needs are historically fashioned through economic processes. Implicit none the less to the Marxists' call for struggle against social injustice and the privations of oppressed classes is that there must be basic needs or rights which capitalism violates.
- Critics of cultural imperialism, anti-racists, feminists and ecologists respectively condemn the false needs defined on behalf of oppressed peoples or groups by colonialists, by patriarchal white society and by Western 'scientism'. Yet even the most radical of cultural relativists appear to subscribe to principles – such as an opposition to human misery or ill health – which plainly transcend cultural specificity.

- Radical democrats who embrace the idea that needs are discursively constructed tend to over-romanticise the prospects of group morality and should concede that a fully democratised civil society would still require forms of public regulation predicated on a theory of human need.
- The extreme relativism of phenomenologists is criticised because there plainly are objective social realities (such as war) which are demonstrably capable of occasioning harm to human beings.
- Finally, Doyal and Gough criticise Townsend, whose concept of relative poverty we have discussed above. They accuse Townsend's account of deprivation of 'vacillating' between relativism and absolutism (1991: 33).

Doyal and Gough go on to advance and defend a theory of human need as a 'universal' rather than a relative concept. Ironically, there is a sense in which Doyal and Gough might be accused like Townsend of a search for some Holy Grail. Just as Townsend sought an elusive threshold absolutely to determine the extent of relative poverty, so Doyal and Gough seek an absolute definition of need capable of application in a relative context across different cultures and societies. Doyal and Gough specify the universal preconditions for human action and interaction in terms of physical health and personal autonomy. The need for physical health requires the protection of all people from harm as well as the provision of the means of subsistence, shelter and health care. The need for personal autonomy requires that all people should have knowledge, capabilities and opportunities, which would seem to imply education/training and the prospect of productive and satisfying work. Personal autonomy, however, has societal preconditions, and the historical process of human liberation may be construed as the struggle to optimise the satisfaction of human need. Like Rousseau and Durkheim before them, Doyal and Gough argue passionately that to be a social being is to be the bearer of responsibilities. The moral reciprocity that is the universal foundation for all human societies is such as to sustain a belief that the needs of all people should be satisfied not only to a minimal, but to an optimal extent:

> For if humans do possess the power to alter history, the task is to keep trying to bring about those alterations which are necessary

conditions for human liberation – the satisfaction of the health and autonomy needs of as many humans as possible to the highest sustainable levels. (1991: 110)

This is a powerful defence for a positive conception of welfare rights. It is a conception very much in the Enlightenment tradition. That is to say, it is a normative conception of how progress in history is to be made and of the relationship between abstract ideals and individual conduct.

The needs which Doyal and Gough define are universal in an *a priori* sense. It may be argued that such 'needs' are no more than abstract formulations and that what is objective and concrete is not 'need' so much as 'dependency' (see Dean and Taylor-Gooby 1992: 174). What defines our social being is not our individual moral responsibility, but our mutual interdependence as human subjects. Rights, duties and morality flow from the manner in which people are dependent on each other. What matters is 'our loyalty to other human beings clinging together against the dark' (Rorty 1980, cited in Doyal and Gough 1991: 19). The seminal concerns of sociology, especially in the Durkheimian tradition, had been the growing complexity of the social order in the Western world. The greater the social division of *labour* within a society, the greater the extent of human interdependence. It was within this tradition that theorists of the 'modern' welfare state, such as Titmuss (1958), began to analyse social divisions of *welfare* and the basis on which to posit collective (i.e. state) responsibility for 'dependent people' (*ibid.*: 42).

Spicker (1993) has suggested that the problem of defining or conceptualising 'need' is resolved when one regards needs as claims. Chapter 1 has already considered the argument that 'rights' are not propensities which vest naturally in every individual but represent specific demands or claims for resources and/or services. Certainly, a 'need' becomes a 'right' when it is formulated as a 'claim'; but there is a sense in which needs, rights and claims are all expressions of human dependence. They are neither absolute (capable of *a priori* prescription) nor relative (mere cultural artefacts), but relational. They are created neither by rational precept nor chance of circumstance, but through the way people interact in time and space. Needs, rights and claims may be defined or satisfied by family members, kin, lovers, friends, community members, voluntary associations, within a market or by a welfare state, but their common moral nexus is the dependency of all upon all.

Rights and equality

Social legislation within a democratic-welfare-capitalist state gives expression to certain needs, rights or claims. A fundamental question for this book is the effect such legislation has. Has the formal equality of citizenship promised by the welfare state succeeded in banishing Want? During the 1970s and 1980s it was widely argued that the welfare state had failed. (For an accessible review of such arguments, see Taylor-Gooby 1991.) The more theoretical or ideologically-based critiques of state welfare will be visited in Chapter 4, but here I should like briefly to mention debates concerning the empirical effects which state welfare has had on social equality.

Inequality and poverty are not the same thing. The basis of the post-war welfare consensus (see, for example, Mishra 1984: ch. 1) was a general acceptance that the state should play some role in ameliorating Want, through the provision of a 'national minimum'. Implicitly, the formal equality of citizenship was to be accompanied by a greater degree of substantive equality, albeit at such a level as to provide a modest floor below which none should fall, rather than a generous ceiling above which none might climb (Beveridge 1942). Kincaid, however, suggested that by 'extraordinary ingenuity' the welfare state managed to avoid any considerable influence in levelling post-tax incomes (1975: 219). Worse, in a highly influential book entitled *The Strategy of Equality*, Julian Le Grand (1982) found that public expenditure in such areas as health, education, housing and transport exacerbated inequality by benefiting higher and middle income groups more than lower income groups. In a later review of the welfare state in Britain between 1974 and 1987, Le Grand more reassuringly concluded that, in spite of the economic difficulties faced by Labour governments of the 1970s and the ideological hostility to welfare exhibited by Conservative governments of the 1980s, the welfare state had continued successfully to 'smooth income over the life-cycle of each individual' and progressively to reduce 'the gap between "original" (i.e. market) incomes and "gross" incomes (original incomes plus cash benefits)' (1990a: 340). He was obliged none the less to concede that the welfare state had been less successful in ameliorating a widening gap since 1979 between the richest and the poorest in terms of original incomes.

Between 1979 and 1991 the poorest sixth of the UK population experienced a fall in real income after housing costs, while that of the richest tenth doubled (Jenkins 1994). Looked at over a longer period of time, the income *share* of the poorest tenth of the population fell from 4.2 per cent of national income in 1961 to 3.0 per cent in 1991, while that of the richest tenth rose from 22 per cent to 25 per cent (with most of this fluctuation occurring in the 1980s) (Goodman and Webb 1994: 66). In spite of the welfare state, Britain is a more unequal society than it was thirty years ago. Whether this means the welfare state has failed depends, as Taylor-Gooby puts it, 'on how redistributive you expected it to be in the first place' (1991: 40). Hindess (1987), for example, has taken issue with the supposition that the welfare state ever embodied a grand 'strategy of equality' and has suggested that the process of social legislation has been informed by far more limited and pragmatic objectives.

It is difficult therefore to establish in any overall sense how effective welfare rights have been, although it is possible to establish who has benefited least from such protection as welfare rights do afford. While accepting that poverty is a contested concept, it is possible to observe the extent to which the composition of the poorest section of the population changes over time. Such changes, both in Britain and in other developed countries (see for example Room *et al.* 1989), have led to the emergence of what are sometimes called the 'new poor'. The 'old poor' of the Beveridge era were principally pensioners and 'large' working families, for whom the risk of financial hardship arose from the vicissitudes of the life-cycle. The 'new poor' tend to be unemployed people, people on low pay, lone parents and their families (regardless of size) for whom the risk of financial hardship arises because of the consequences of economic restructuring and social change.

Table 2.1 shows the changing proportions of different family types and economic groups both within the general UK population and within the bottom income decile. To the extent that the poorest

Table 2.1 The changing risk of 'poverty' in the UK: 1979–1990/91[1]

	As a proportion of total population			As a proportion of poorest 10%[2]			Change of risk factor[3]
	1979 %	1990/91 %	Change	1979 % (under/over-representation)	1990/91 % (under/over-representation)	Change	
By family type							
Pensioner couple	9	9	0	20 (+11)	5 (−4)	−15	−15
Single pensioner	8	8	0	11 (+3)	6 (−2)	−5	−5
Childless couple	18	22	+4	9 (−9)	12 (−10)	+3	−1
Couple with children	47	38	−9	41 (−6)	49 (+11)	+8	+17
Single without children	14	16	+2	10 (−4)	18 (+2)	+8	+6
Single with children	4	6	+2	9 (+5)	11 (+5)	+2	0
By economic status							
Self-employed	6	10	+4	10 (+4)	18 (+8)	+8	+4
Single/couple all in FTW[4]	24	23	−1	2 (−22)	2 (−21)	0	+1
1 FTW[4] & 1 PTW[5]	20	15	−5	2 (−18)	2 (−13)	0	+5
1 FTW[4] & 1 not working	21	15	−6	9 (−12)	9 (−6)	0	+6
Single/couple all in W[5]	6	6	0	10 (+4)	7 (+1)	−3	−3
Head/spouse aged 60+	15	17	+2	33 (+18)	14 (−3)	−19	−21
Head/spouse unemployed	3	5	+2	16 (+13)	28 (+23)	+12	+10
Other	5	8	+3	18 (+13)	21 (+13)	+3	0

Notes:
1. Based on Department of Social Security (1993) *Households below Average Income: A statistical analysis 1979–1990/91*, HMSO, London.
2. i.e. as a proportion of bottom income decile group *after* housing costs.
3. i.e. overall change in under/over-representation in poorest decile.
4. FTW = full-time work (> 30 hours per week).
5. PTW = part-time work (< 30 hours per week).

tenth of the population are in fact worse off than they were in 1979 (Jenkins 1994), we are not dealing here with a consistent, still less an objective measure of poverty (see Veit-Wilson 1994). However, changes in the number of percentage points by which groups are under- or over-represented within the poorest tenth may be taken as a crude index or 'change of risk' factor. It may be seen clearly that:

• Pensioners are less at risk of poverty, though single pensioners (among whom women are disproportionately represented) remain much more at risk than pensioner couples; and it should also be noted that a greater number of pensioners are living on or below half average household incomes than was the case even in the 1960s (see Goodman and Webb 1994).

• Couples with children are demonstrably at greater risk than in the 1970s. This relates partly to the increased risk of unemployment, but also to the extremely high risk of poverty faced by unemployed households. While households containing a full-time worker are consistently under-represented in the poorest tenth, it is significant that their risk of poverty has been increasing.

• Lone-parent households remain consistently over-represented in the poorest tenth. It should be borne in mind that the proportion of households with children headed by a lone parent has more than doubled since the 1970s, from 8 per cent in 1971 to 19 per cent in 1991 (Burghes 1993) and that, although the risk of poverty did not appear to change in the 1980s, it is proportionately very high and, in one sense, could not have got much worse.

One conclusion is that rights to welfare have not been consistently secured over time or for all social groups. This was a concern expressed in Titmuss's (1958) seminal analysis of the social division of welfare. Titmuss had identified a threefold division between the fiscal, occupational and state welfare systems, and he pointed to the relative advantages and disadvantages which these systems created for different social classes. Those who are most marginal to the labour process must place greatest reliance on rights to (inferior) state welfare, rather than more highly prized fiscal or occupational alternatives. More recent theorists have additionally pointed to a sexual division of welfare (Rose 1981) and, indeed, a case can be made 'for identifying a racial division of welfare, an age division and other specific divisions based on the failure of welfare to cater for the needs of the various and disparate groups which constitute the poor' (Mann 1992: 26).

'Rights', as socially and politically constructed phenomena, are with few exceptions unmindful of such dimensions as gender, 'race', age and disability and welfare rights may be seen in many respects to have failed women, 'black' people (that is people from ethnic communities), older people and people with disabilities. The implicit assumptions on which the 'modern' welfare state was founded have been outlined by Hermione Parker as including:

> that all poverty is due either to 'interruption or loss of earnings' or to 'failure to relate income during earning to the size of family'; that society consists of happily married couples (no divorce), widows (no widowers) and heterosexual celibates living either alone or with their parents; . . . that all married women are financially dependent on their husbands; . . . that it is within the power of governments to maintain full employment; . . . that full employment means regular full-time work for men, aged 15 to 65, with minimal job changes . . . (1989: 23–9)

The legacy of these assumptions, in spite of more recent piecemeal reform, is that women (see Glendinning and Millar 1992), black people (see Amin and Oppenheim 1992), older people (see Townsend 1991) and people with disabilities (see Oliver 1990) have been systematically marginalised from welfare citizenship's mainstream. In Part II we shall explore some of the ways in which the explicit rights accorded to such groups may in practice have been compromised, but here I simply underline the point that welfare rights are not equal rights.

Citizenship and welfare

Ruth Lister is one of many commentators who fear that the social rights of citizenship in the UK have been eroded as a result of legislative changes made during the 1980s. She argues:

> it is not possible to divorce the rights and responsibilities which are supposed to unite citizens from the inequalities of power and resources that divide them. These inequalities – particularly class,

race and gender – run like fault lines through our society and shape
the contours of citizenship in the civil, political and social spheres.
Poverty spells exclusion from the full rights of citizenship in each of
these spheres and undermines people's ability to fulfil the private and
public obligations of citizenship. For people with disabilities, this
exclusion is often compounded . . . [T]he resurrection of the
citizenship ideal, expressed in the language of social justice (and
located firmly in the sphere of public morality), could potentially
provide the basis for building a more united society. If this is to
happen, it first must be transformed from the monolithic concept of
the post-war citizenship theorists to one which embodies, in
particular, the dimensions of race and gender. (1990: 68–9)

Lister's concept of citizenship certainly reaches beyond that implied
in the *Citizen's Charter* (see Chapter 1), but also beyond that
articulated by T. H. Marshall. This is an ideal of social citizenship
closely articulated with a concept of poverty as exclusion and of
rights based on needs. For all its rhetorical power, therefore, it is
inescapably prone to certain underlying ambiguities. Where and
how are the 'full rights of citizenship' determined?

Bryan Turner (1990; 1991) has identified different historical
kinds and various dimensions of citizenship. One of the key
distinctions he draws is between passive citizenship derived from a
'descending' view and active citizenship derived from an 'ascending'
view: 'In the descending view, the king is all powerful and the
subject is the recipient of privileges. In the ascending view a free
man was a citizen, an active bearer of rights' (1990: 207). The first
is typified by the English constitutional settlement of 1688 by which
the rule of the sovereign-in-parliament was established over
subjects-as-citizens. The latter is typified by the aspirations of the
French Revolution of 1789. The essential critique of 'bourgeois'
citizenship within modern parliamentary democracies by Marxists
such as Michael Mann (1987) is that it is passive: that it represents
a ruling class strategy for the regulation of citizens – an argument
to which I shall return in Chapter 4. In contrast, Turner argues:

> active and radical forms of citizenship will be grabbed from below
> by struggle in societies which emphasise the moral importance of the
> public domain. . . . Radical citizenship should produce norms which
> would challenge the marginalization of the elderly, the alienation of
> unemployed youth or the isolation of the chronically sick. Active
> traditions of citizenship should produce an inclusive and extensive

social policy of reform. In short, active citizenship should be the basis of an extensive social welfare programme. (1991: 36)

Harking back to Habermas (1976), however, Turner expresses the fear that this form of active citizenship runs the risk of generating expectations which cannot be fulfilled, of creating a 'legitimation deficit' and therefore social instability. Lister's 'resurrected' citizenship, though inclusive by intent, is essentially a passive citizenship; it would seem to lie within a beneficent Fabian tradition which involves a 'top down' prescription of social rights and moral obligations. Though Lister is mindful of 'inequalities of power' and is concerned not to invoke a 'monolithic concept of citizenship', what seems to be implied could easily exemplify the kind of approach characterised by Alan Hunt as an 'oppositional project conceived of as if it were constructed "elsewhere", fully finished and then drawn into place, like some Trojan horse of the mind, to do battle with the prevailing dominant hegemony' (1990: 313). Turner's vision in contrast is of a more revolutionary active citizenship in which the determination of rights and obligations would be 'bottom up', but which he suspects may not be sustainable.

Intersecting with this dilemma about the nature of citizenship and welfare is another dichotomy; between what may be called the 'politics of discourse' and the 'politics of agency'. To the former, citizenship itself is the key, while to the latter it is class, party or interest which takes precedence. The politics of discourse is embraced by a group of commentators whom Doyal and Gough (1991) have characterised as 'radical democrats'. Among them they include Laclau and Mouffe (1985) and Keane (1988). Laclau and Mouffe are 'post-Marxists' who have abandoned the classical Marxist stress on class struggle as the driving force of history and have instead embraced the postmodernist notion of the 'discursive position': political struggles over citizenship and welfare in a postmodern age will be conducted, they believe, not between classes but at the level of discourse. Keane similarly rejects the idea of an historical agent of emancipation and argues for a democratisation of civil society: our diverse and different welfare needs should be determined and met through processes of voluntary co-operation in which the state should have only a minimal role as mediator and guarantor. Critiques of Laclau and Mouffe have been provided by Wood (1986) and of 'postmodernism' generally by

Callinicos (1989), both of whom seek to hold on to a theory of structure and agency; the belief that human welfare can result from reasoned human action; 'the idea that there is no cure for the wounds of Enlightenment other than the radicalized Enlightenment itself' (Habermas 1986, cited in Callinicos 1989: 95). Doyal and Gough's theory of human need which I have outlined above is very much an attempt to recapture the Enlightenment tradition. They argue for a hard-headed compromise or 'dual strategy' which combines a mixed economy of welfare with elements of central planning. The 'tragedy' of relativism, they say, is that 'through proclaiming the incoherence of debates about how [the optimisation of needs satisfaction] should be achieved, its supporters – whatever their intentions might be – lend support to those who wish to prevent such change' (1991: 110–1).

Finally, another intriguing if controversial rejection of relativism – relating specifically to conceptions of poverty – has been espoused by Amartya Sen (1984; 1985), who argues that the social exclusion by which relativists identify poverty is not subjective, but an objective curtailment of people's capabilities. What is required for physical and social functioning may vary between societies, but the fundamental capabilities which all people require are the same. In a social context in which daily journeys are unnecessary, the absence of a bicycle, a car or the inaccessibility of public transport will not be a problem, but in a context in which one must travel to obtain the means of subsistence such things are not luxuries but commodities or services possessing essential characteristics. Thus, as Sen rather obscurely puts it, 'poverty is an absolute notion in the space of capabilities but very often will take a relative form in the space of commodities or characteristics' (1984: 335).

On the one hand, this rather subtle account articulates with the 'relational' view of needs, rights and claims which I outlined earlier in this chapter, and with the idea that needs, rights and claims are materially grounded in social practice. On the other hand, Sen's account also chimes with Paul Hirst's definition of 'rights' as 'capacities' conferred by law (see Chapter 1 above). Hirst's argument is that rights 'serve socially determined policy objectives and interests' (1980: 104), that they represent codified objectives by which a democratic society must secure its own regulation, whether that be a utopian socialist society or a democratic-welfare-capitalist society.

The dilemma remains. Do we address poverty by imposing citizenship from above and regulating people's capabilities or capacities; or is such an objective to be achieved by seizing citizenship from below and democratically reconstituting the discourses through which needs are identified, formulated and legitimised as claims? Unfortunately, the resolution of this dilemma remains beyond the scope of this book, but it remains an issue for anyone concerned with the theory and practice of welfare rights.

Conclusion/summary

The modern welfare state was ostensibly created to remedy poverty and meet needs through the creation of social rights of citizenship.

This chapter has tried to tease apart some of the complex arguments about how to define poverty and human need. A central theme in both sets of arguments is the conflict between absolutism and relativism. At one level absolutism is associated with individualist explanations of poverty and restrictive approaches to state welfare, while relativism is associated with structural explanations of poverty and expansive approaches to state welfare. At another level, however, relativism can also be associated with forms and notions of citizenship which are disciplinary in effect, and with a failure to specify and therefore to guarantee that which may be fundamental to human emancipation.

Second, this chapter has sought to demonstrate that social rights of citizenship have not made Britain a more equal society. Indeed, some groups in society (women, black people, older people and people with disabilities) remain more unequal than others. This has led to a discussion about what it is that social citizenship should achieve. Remedying poverty and meeting need requires a society that is inclusive not exclusive, but this need not imply any single model of citizenship. There is a tension between an essentially relativist vision of a democratic, discursively constructed citizenship of postmodernity, and what is in one sense an absolutist vision of a democratically regulated citizenship in the Enlightenment tradition.

It may be seen that controversies about the fundamental nature of welfare rights do not always fit neatly with the left/right political conventions with which readers may be familiar. It should also be emphasised that such issues are certainly not unique to any one country, nor will they necessarily be resolved in the same way in all parts of the world. Accordingly, the next chapter will extend the analysis to consider welfare rights and social legislation in a global context.

Recommended additional reading

Alcock, P. (1993) *Understanding Poverty*, Macmillan, Basingstoke, Chapters 1, 2 and 4.
Doyal, L. and Gough, I. (1991) *A Theory of Human Need*, Macmillan, Basingstoke, Chapters 1, 2 and 3.
Lister, R. (1990) *The Exclusive Society: Citizenship and the poor*, a pamphlet published by Child Poverty Action Group, London, Part II.

Questions for reflection

Is it possible to establish rights which both prevent poverty and guarantee that basic human needs are satisfied? Why might these objectives be different?

Does the existence of poverty signal a failure of citizenship? If so, how is citizenship to be reformed?

CHAPTER 3

SOCIAL RIGHTS IN GLOBAL PERSPECTIVE

This book is primarily concerned with welfare rights and social legislation in a particular democratic-welfare-capitalist state, namely Britain. There are however dangers in concentrating on the British case. First, the classic view of social citizenship expounded by T. H. Marshall (see Chapter 1), because it related so specifically to the British case, is profoundly ethnocentric and provides only a limited understanding of the scope and limits of social citizenship. Second, the future of the welfare state in Britain and elsewhere is increasingly dependent on global influences. This chapter aims to widen the discussion and consider the role which social rights might play in alleviating poverty in different parts of the world. It will also discuss alternative models of social citizenship and the different kinds of welfare state which exist around the globe.

Different explanations are offered for the existence of poverty in a national context and these were discussed in Chapter 2. Broadly speaking, these divide between individualist explanations based on notions of pathology and structuralist explanations based on the idea that poverty has social causes. Vic George has observed that explanations of wealth and poverty at the international level – or of what is often called 'development' and 'underdevelopment' – can be divided along similar lines. There are commentators who attribute the failure of some countries to 'modernise' to techno- logical, cultural or political deficiencies which are internal to those countries. Other commentators attribute the continued disadvan- tage of the so-called Third World to external factors and, in particular, the structured economic dependence of poor and weak nations on rich and powerful ones (George 1988: ch. 1).

That the world is divided between rich and poor is beyond dispute. In 1988, according to data assembled by the United Nations Development Programme, the per capita GDP (adjusted for purchasing power parity) of the world's richest nation, the United States, at $19,850, was twenty-seven times greater than that of the poorest country for which data were available, namely Bangladesh at $720 (see Townsend 1993: Table 1.1). Whether we blame the losers for their own incompetence or the winners for unfair competition, the assumption it seems is that poverty at the international level reflects the outcome of a global race for economic development. Social ecologists like Penny Kemp have argued that 'Capitalism needs poverty in order to survive' (1990: 3) and 'Greens' in general argue that there are finite global limits to economic growth (Meadows *et al.* 1972). Certainly, the ascendancy of international capitalism and the universal quest for economic growth must at least raise questions about how feasible it is for poor nations ever to 'modernise' and to develop their economies in the manner of their richer competitors. If the hope is that economic development will overcome poverty, there appears to be, not an environmental, but an empirically demonstrable limit to this process.

According once again to the United Nations Development Programme some 1.4 billion of the world's 5.3 billion people live 'in poverty'. Of that 1.4 billion, 1.2 billion live in 'developing countries' (the Third World). However, around 100 million live in the former USSR and Eastern Europe (the Second World) and 100 million live in Western industrialised countries (the First World), including 30 million in the USA, the richest country of all (cited in Townsend 1993: 13). Economic growth does not guarantee the elimination of poverty. So what is the role of social rights in protecting against poverty and what is the relationship between social rights and economic prosperity?

There is a view propounded by Wilensky that the development of social rights is a direct result of economic prosperity. Wilensky (1975) has sought to demonstrate a positive correlation between social security spending as a proportion of GNP and economic development as measured by per capita GNP and he infers a causal relationship between the two. Opponents of this view (for example

Castles 1982; Alber 1983) argue that it takes insufficient account of the part which political processes play in determining the level of spending on social security provision (for a fuller discussion see Taylor-Gooby 1991: 60–1; Ginsburg 1992: 19–20). Social rights, in other words, are political achievements and not the automatic outcome of capitalist development. The significance of social rights is therefore different in the different sectors of the world economy.

Social rights in the Third World

The first point to be made about the development of social rights in the Third World is that Third World countries do not represent an original or primeval stage of development. On the contrary, we should accept that the circumstances of these countries are to a greater or lesser extent a product or artefact of the prevailing condition of the world economy. Social policy in the sense that Westerners understand it may not be evident in many of these countries, but to the extent that entitlements approximating to social rights may have been adopted, some relate to practices 'inherited' from the West as a legacy of past colonial domination or directly 'borrowed' from the example of capitalist welfare states; other countries have formulated welfare provisions on quite different cultural or ideological premisses. For example, Islamic countries operate more or less organised systems of *Zakat* and the *Bait-Ul-Mal*, providing forms of poor relief or social security which accord with religious not state laws.

The second point which should be underlined is that the peoples of the Third World are not uniformly poor. There can be huge differences in wealth and income *within* these countries, some of which have wealthy, even profligate, elites as well as impoverished masses. There can also be huge inequalities *between* the countries of the Third World, a term which in fact encompasses affluent oil-exporting nations of the Middle East, rapidly industrialising nations on the Pacific Rim and in Latin America, large nations with huge populations like India and China, and the starving and famine-torn nations of sub-Saharan Africa. A full discussion lies beyond the scope of this book (see, however, McPherson and Midgley 1987). The focus here is necessarily a narrow one and I propose to do no more than cite some illustrative examples which suggest the contrasting forms in which welfare provision (with or without 'rights') can be embodied. The first of these will be drawn from among the newly industrialising countries. My purpose is to illustrate two very different strategies: 'Confucian' capitalism on the one hand, and Third World *laissez-faire* capitalism on the other.

Catherine Jones (1993) has coined the term 'Confucian welfare states' to characterise not only the far from underdeveloped Japan, but the emerging 'little tigers' of Hong Kong, Singapore, South Korea and Taiwan. These nations all spend proportionately less on welfare than Western-style welfare states and they certainly do not conform to the liberal ideal: 'there is far too much social direction and too little sense of individual rights' (Jones 1993: 214). These are welfare states without social rights in the sense defined by T. H. Marshall and run not so much democratically as by top down consensus, 'in the style of a would be traditional, Confucian, extended family' (*ibid.*). The approach to social provision is pragmatic rather than doctrinaire, sometimes borrowing and sometimes avoiding Western examples to make up their 'own brand' welfare states. Characteristically, these states offer education, limited housing and health care provision, a deliberately constrained social security system and no personal social services. Where services are provided, there is heavy reliance on voluntary action. The economic 'miracles' contrived by these countries rested on self-conscious policies of hierarchical community-building. Within the tradition of popular Confucianism, government represents a hierarchy with responsibility for national housekeeping. It is not the voice or the moral conscience of the people and it is not responsible for those duties which fall to families and communities.

In contrast, the *laissez-faire* capitalist countries of the Third World, of which Brazil is the biggest and best-known example, offer no systematic welfare, have poor human rights records and make no attempt to underwrite social rights or social stability. Brazil has none the less achieved relatively high rates of economic growth, but in so doing has created a society that is notoriously polarised and in which poverty on a deep and massive scale exists side by side with conspicuous affluence. In São Paulo, for example, more than half the population is undernourished in a city also noted for luxury and extravagance (Doyal and Gough 1991: 279–80). Economic growth generated by unregulated inward investment can be accompanied by high inflation (250 per cent plus per annum), which far outstrips desultory increases in minimum wages (Allen 1985, cited in George 1988: 151). This is the sub-minimalist welfare state. Unregulated poverty, in the form of high unemployment and low wages, represents the virtually explicit policy by which Brazil competes for inward investment.

The other contrasting examples on which I should like to draw are those of India and China. India is a country with an incipient welfare state owing much to its British colonial history. A substantial government bureaucracy produces impressive five year plans, which have included rural employment creation programmes, water supply schemes, health centres, education facilities and housing. The plans also purport to give special attention to the needs of women and vulnerable minorities. In practice, the bureaucracy and local oligarchies reputedly misappropriate much of the resources and benefits of anti-poverty programmes. Western-inspired egalitarianism fails to penetrate the dharma ethic which informs the Indian caste system. Imported Western health care and education practices are often ill suited to local needs and aspirations. At the same time India has, since Independence, allowed most land and industry to remain concentrated in private hands and it has relied heavily on overseas aid and expertise for its industrialisation strategy. As a result, India, like many Third World countries, produces cash crops and cheap consumer goods for the industrialised world, rather than subsistence crops and staple goods for its own population, and it remains locked into the world banking and finance system (see Townsend 1993: ch. 8).

A very different course has been pursued by communist China, which in the early 1950s nationalised most land and industry and gave it over to local collectives and co-operatives. China accepted very little external aid and emphasised a self-reliant path to industrialisation and endogenous styles of education and health provision. China's centrally planned approach has even extended to the curtailment of population movements and other freedoms, but the result has been much higher economic growth than India has managed to achieve (George 1988: 77–8). The People's Republic of China has been able substantially to honour the 'five guarantees' it makes its citizens – enough food, enough clothes, enough fuel, an honourable funeral and education for the children.

Critics of communism commonly complain that, notwithstanding the great strides China has made in realising the social rights of its citizens, it has also suppressed (sometimes brutally) the civil and especially the political rights of those citizens. This is true so far as it goes, but it misses the point that China does not provide *any* rights in the bourgeois liberal sense. There are no rights vesting in the individual Chinese citizen. Harold Pepinsky (1975) has drawn attention to the contrast between China, where there is no (or very little) formally promulgated legislation or written law, and a country like the USA, where rights and prohibitions are minutely prescribed by substantive written rules contained in public legislation. Western citizens have their freedoms guaranteed in writing and are enabled to calculate in advance whether any particular action may be liable to coercive restraint by agents of the state. By contrast, the Chinese citizen appears to the Western observer to enjoy no assurances against the prospects of social disorder and to be subject potentially to unlimited social control. Pepinsky argues, however, that very different kinds of freedom are involved. He contrasts the 'freedom of social mobility' enjoyed by citizens of Western countries, with the 'freedom of collective accomplishment'. Westerners are characteristically entitled to a high degree of geographical and occupational mobility, they are free (subject to the rules of marriage and divorce) to enter or to leave relationships with other human beings, and, increasingly, they rely on state authorities to resolve the disputes they may have with other human beings. Chinese citizens live and work where they are assigned and within a culture that emphasises reconciliation between disputants, the reintegration of the excluded and open criticism and 're-education' of the delinquent. Yet for all that, Chinese citizens are not subject so directly to the prescriptions of written law and substantive intrusion by the state. Official pronouncements in the People's Republic of China do not have the status of legislation: they may prescribe what collectives and communes should achieve but they do not prescribe the conduct required of individuals. Within the confines and strictures of their communities, Chinese citizens have freedoms to debate and participate, to adapt and innovate, to work and co-operate in ways which formal written law might even inhibit. This is not to romanticise what is in many respects a semi-feudal form of society. Indeed, policies of market liberalisation in the 1980s have resulted in a weakening of the collective social protection which had been in force when Pepinsky was writing and an increase in social inequalities (see Leung 1994). The purpose here has been to underline the culturally circumscribed way in which rights to welfare are guaranteed in 'developed' Western countries. It is possible to have welfare without rights (see Rose 1993).

Returning to the theories of development and underdevelopment which I briefly outlined earlier, the so-called 'modernisation' theorists assumed that there is a set path with predetermined stages which all nations must traverse in order to become mature civilisations. Closely associated with this view was the idea that, in a free world market, wealth would eventually 'trickle down' from rich to poor nations, just as it should 'trickle down' from rich to poor people within each nation. What mattered, in their view, was that the engine of economic growth and development should be kept running. So-called 'dependency' theorists and structuralists have resisted this view. Economic growth does not invariably lead to social development and the enhancement of welfare. In fact, there is tentative evidence that, in the case of developing rather than developed countries, the opposite applies.

Research by Newman and Thompson (1989) suggests that provision for basic needs (measured by indices of basic literacy, perinatal mortality and life expectancy) *precede* rather than result from economic development. This research involved correlations over a twenty-year period (from 1960 to 1980) of data from some forty-six developing countries. Given the diversity of the forms of social provision which are developing in the Third World, these findings support the case, not only for saying that the achievement of social rights is not dependent on economic growth, but that Western forms of welfare rights and social legislation are not the only way to secure social development.

Social rights in the Second World

Prior to 1989 the political, economic and social regimes which characterised the Soviet Union and its satellite states in Eastern Europe were sufficiently distinctive to justify their classification as a sphere of influence quite separate from that of either Western-style capitalism or the non-industrialised portions of the globe. The collapse of Soviet-style communism has dissolved the basis for that distinction. However, uncertainty over the future direction of the countries now emerging from the collapse still justifies their separate treatment for the purposes of this chapter.

To grasp the magnitude of the transition now occurring in the former Soviet Union and the ex-communist Eastern European states, it is first necessary to recall the nature of the ideological vision which originally set the Second World apart. Beatrice and Sidney Webb, whose influence on the Fabian wing of the British Labour Party played some part in informing social democratic perceptions of social policy, proposed that Soviet communism might amount to nothing less than 'A New Form of Civilisation' (1935). This expression (presciently qualified by the addition of a question mark) was incorporated as the sub-title of the book in which the Webbs made their case. The chapter devoted to the welfare provisions of the Soviet state was entitled 'The Remaking of Man'. Here the Webbs proclaimed that:

> Monarchs and parliaments, humane oligarchies and enlightened democracies have often desired the welfare of their subjects, and have even sometimes sought to shape their policy towards this end. But at best this has been more of a hope than a purpose. The Soviet Government from the first made it a fundamental purpose of its policy not merely to benefit the people whom it served but actually to transform them. . . . The following slogan of the Moscow Sports Clubs is significant: 'We are not only rebuilding human society on an economic basis: we are mending the human race on scientific principles'. (Webb and Webb 1935: 805)

The systems which were swept away during the tumultuous events following 1989 were but a pale reflection of these utopian objectives; nor had they ever been effective in banishing poverty (George 1993). None the less, the original intention had been clear. Social rights were to transform as well as serve the Soviet citizen.

The demands that led to the fall of Soviet-style communism were for the political and civil rights which the system withheld. In the months preceding the Soviet Union's final collapse in 1991, President Gorbachev's attempts at perestroika were not only too late, they also entailed a top down reconstruction of the system rather than reform from below. The people of the Second World continued to covet the political freedoms and economic rewards of the First World and they were in practice little enamoured of the social rights at their disposal.

The welfare systems of the Soviet Union and Eastern Europe had guaranteed a right to work; minimum wages at levels representing a high proportion of average wages; a free health service; free day care for children, three-year child care grants for women and the right to return to work; highly subsidised housing; and social insurance provision for retirement and sickness. Set against these benefits, however, there were drawbacks: the jobs which the state guaranteed to provide were often unproductive in nature or in reality non-existent; minimum wages fell consistently below poverty levels, while party and state bureaucrats enjoyed many valuable perks and undeserved privileges; health services were underdeveloped and bribes were often required to secure access to more advanced treatments; although women had the opportunity (if not indeed an obligation) to work, they were still expected to shoulder the burden of domestic and care work; state housing was often of poor quality and strictly rationed, with the best housing often going to state or party bureaucrats; social insurance benefits were not index-linked and, because the existence of unemployment and poverty was denied, there had been no unemployment benefit and grossly inadequate social assistance (for fuller accounts see Deacon *et al.* 1992; Deacon 1993; George 1993).

As the command economies of the Second World make their precipitous transition to market capitalism, the prospects of remedying these defects are bleak. Bob Deacon (1993) identifies four reasons for this. First, while the old system in many respects failed, it did create popular expectations of what housing, health care and pensions should be like. To compound this, domestic politicians and Western free-market ideologues also generated expectations that free markets would be more efficient and could deliver what central planning had not. Second, the standards of public health and housing and the extent of poverty are such that the scale of the investment and expenditure required to meet such expectations is considerable. Third, unemployment which had in any event been rising can be expected with the deregulation of the economy to reach crisis levels. Fourth, the collapse of the Soviet and Eastern European economies means that, pending a market-led recovery, there will be an insufficient and dwindling tax base from which to raise the revenue to address these issues.

What is sought is a shift from an egalitarianism of economic underdevelopment to a social justice founded on capitalist development. What this will entail is a widening of social inequalities and the privatisation of state services. There can be no doubt that, initially and for the immediately foreseeable future, there will be a radical curtailment of social rights. Writing specifically about the Hungarian experience since the 1989 'revolution', Zsuzsa Ferge (1993a; 1993b) observes that the shift has been from welfare statism and universal provision to welfare pluralism and selectivity. At the bidding of newly democratically elected conservative or neo-liberal politicians and on the strength of recommendations from the World Bank, Hungary has been seeking to curtail social spending; to target benefits selectively on the poorest; to replace free health services with a health insurance scheme; to reform or reduce state pensions and child allowances; to cut day care for children and force women back into full-time motherhood. According to Ferge, 'the transition has thoroughly undermined the security and living standards of the majority' (1993a: 84), and she admits that 'a glorious promise for everybody has to date profited citizens unequally' (*ibid.*: 90). Similarly, in Russia, the magnitude of impoverishment in the years following 1991 has been said to defy statistical quantification, though some estimates suggest that, in 1992, 75 per cent of the population of Moscow were living below subsistence levels (George 1993: 243–4). As in Hungary, women and vulnerable ethnic minorities have been among the worst affected. In spite of this, Ferge (1993a) insists that the old systems *had* to disappear and that the task is to find a less painful form of transition to a democratic system.

Having abandoned its utopian vision, the new aspiration of the Second World is to join the First World club. The danger, if not the likelihood, is that it will join the Third World.

Social rights in the First World

It is in the First World that welfare has become a matter of rights and that social development is regulated by social legislation. This does not however mean that there is any one example of the way in which social rights of citizenship have typically emerged. Nor does it mean that there is any dominant form of democratic-welfare-capitalist state.

Different roads to welfare citizenship

As has already been said, Marshall's theory of citizenship was based entirely on the British case, yet it is often presented as an evolutionary schema to account for all welfare states. That this is unsatisfactory has been pointed out by many writers, including Michael Mann (1987) and Bryan Turner (1990).

For Mann, the strength of Marshall's thesis was that it showed how the development of modern citizenship served to render class struggle innocuous. Its weakness was that it failed to demonstrate the full variety of the strategies by which the *anciens régimes* of the West have sought to institutionalise their conflict with class movements, both of the bourgeoisie and the proletariat. Mann suggests that, prior to the main phase of industrialisation, the West was divided into three kinds of regime:

1. constitutional regimes (Britain and the USA), in which civil citizenship and a limited form of political franchise had already developed,
2. absolutist regimes (such as Prussia, Austria and Russia), in which the monarch's despotic power was exercised partly by selective tactical repression, but also through 'divide and rule' negotiations with powerful corporate groups in society;
3. contested' or 'merged' regimes, in which conflict between absolutism and constitutionalists was either highly turbulent (as in France) or relatively peaceful (as in the Scandinavian countries).

From the nineteenth century onwards:

1. The constitutional regimes took different paths – the USA, liberalism; Britain, reformism. The early extension of a universal franchise (i.e. full political rights) in the USA meant that class struggles were diverted and fragmented into interest group politics. The consequent absence of a developed labour and trade union movement accounts for the late and relatively limited development of social rights in the USA. In comparison,

the much later development of political rights in Britain permitted the emergence of a strong labour and trade union movement requiring the accommodation of reformist strategies, more extensive social rights and the scenario depicted by Marshall.

2. The absolutist regimes turned to 'authoritarian monarchy'. They had no intention of granting universal citizenship rights, but found ways to incorporate both bourgeoisie and proletariat through 'modernisation'. The civil legal code required for the successful development of capitalist production, distribution and exchange was conceded and limited forms of social citizenship were offered to stem the threat of organised labour. The classic example is that of late nineteenth-century Germany, where the Chancellor, Otto von Bismarck, pioneered the introduction of social insurance. However, to the extent that political citizenship was allowed to develop, prior to the First World War, this was little more than a sham. Subsequent geopolitical upheavals were to play some part in the (temporary) emergence of fascism in Germany and authoritarian socialism in Russia.

3. The 'contested' regimes, such as France and Italy, endured protracted political upheavals until broad alliances between bourgeoisie, labour and small farmers could attain a lasting compromise between an absolutist inheritance and the emerging constitionalist tradition. The 'merged' regimes of Scandinavia in fact pursued what may be described as a corporatist style of reformism which, as Mann (1987: 344) points out, is probably closer to Marshall's vision than the British case!

This analysis, though incomplete, provides a very necessary historical perspective. It has none the less been criticised on three counts by Turner (1990). The first ground for criticism is that Mann's focus on class relationships ignores the significance for citizenship of other social divisions (an issue to which this book returns in Chapter 4). Second, Turner complains, it is necessary to consider the part which cultural and religious influences played in the development of the modern concept of citizenship and, in particular, the emergence of the idea of a distinction between the private sphere of the individual and the public spheres of civil society and the state. Third, says Turner, Mann 'cannot adequately appreciate the revolutionary implications of the oppositional character of rights' (1990: 199): citizenship is not necessarily always handed down from above, it can also be seized from below (this element of Turner's argument I have already touched on in Chapter 2). Turner alerts us to the complexity of citizenship and the dangers of overgeneralised analysis. He also incidentally reminds us of the possibility that social rights – rights to publicly guaranteed welfare – are not a necessary component of citizenship.

Different kinds of welfare state

This returns us to the point made earlier in this chapter, that social rights represent the outcome of political processes. It also returns us to the work of Esping-Andersen and the idea that there are different political responses to the process of 'commodification' which characterises capitalism (see Chapter 1). Esping-Andersen (1990) has suggested that there can be liberal, conservative or socialist responses which will modify the consequences of market relations by allowing, respectively, a relatively low, medium or high degree of 'decommodification'. He has constructed a quantitative index by which to measure the extent to which the social security systems of different OECD countries will allow aged, sick and unemployed workers to exist on a 'decommodified' basis, that is to say outside the labour market. He has complemented this analysis by the construction of 'stratification indices', which produce a quantitative measure for the extent to which the social security systems of different countries are based on selective social assistance principles (a liberal approach), class or status reinforcing social insurance principles (a conservative approach), or on egalitarian universal benefit principles (a socialist/social democratic approach). Using contemporary empirical data, rather than an historical analysis, Esping-Andersen has been able to demonstrate the existence of three 'clusters' of countries, exhibiting the characteristics of three different kinds of welfare state regime.

The first cluster contains liberal regimes. These are countries with minimalist welfare states such as the USA, Canada and Australia. State welfare in these countries is founded in the poor relief tradition, with emphasis on selectivity and the means testing of benefits and only modest levels of provision through social insurance or universal transfer schemes. Entitlement rules tend to be strict and benefit levels low, with encouragement being given to occupational fringe benefits and private or market-led forms of welfare provision.

The second cluster contains conservative or 'corporatist' regimes. These are countries such as Austria, France, Germany and Italy. State welfare provision in these countries is founded in a corporatist tradition: that is to say, there is an emphasis on policy negotiation between major corporate interest groups (especially tripartite negotiation between capital, labour and the state) rather than on democratic/parliamentary processes. It is a tradition preoccupied less with free markets than with the preservation of status differentials and, for example, a privileged and influential civil service. The emphasis is on social insurance-type benefits and universal family allowances. Levels of provision are usually high, and occupational and private market welfare provision is marginal. The character of these welfare states is strongly influenced by Catholicism and so, for example, services such as day care are underdeveloped, since motherhood and the traditional family are encouraged. Benefits for those excluded from the labour market or traditional family support may be selective and poor.

The third cluster contains socialist or, more precisely, social democratic regimes, most notably the Scandinavian countries – Sweden, Norway and Denmark. In these countries, state welfare provision is founded in a universalist tradition concerned to promote an equality of high standards. The emphasis is on universal transfers, supplemented by earnings-related social insurance. Levels of provision are or have been high (for some even luxurious) and occupational and private market provision is or has been effectively excluded. Full employment is an integral objective of policy, as are benefits and services for children and for parents wishing to work.

It is important to emphasise that what Esping-Andersen is describing are 'ideal-types' embodying features, tendencies or propensities which may be present in any given instance only to a greater or lesser extent and the balance of which will never be static. Changes in the political complexion of national governments can bring about shifts in the relative emphasis of policy, as has occurred, for example, in Sweden, where recently there has been a significant dilution of social democratic principles (see Gould 1993). Also, not all countries fit into the typology and may in fact represent hybrids, combining features of different regime types. Examples include Britain – which combines apparently contradictory liberal and reformist social democratic traditions – and Japan – which ostensibly combines liberal and corporatist tendencies but, at another level, might be regarded as lying outside Western European and Anglo-Saxon traditions (see the discussion above regarding Confucian welfare states).

Figure 3.1 maps Esping-Andersen's typology onto Mann's historical typology of citizenship strategies. This illustrates the development of strategies adopted or negotiated to accommodate the class conflicts and economic restructuring associated with the rise of industrial capitalism. From the old European absolutism have emerged corporatist welfare regimes, reflecting Catholic influences and providing developed social rights for workers, rather than citizens. From the early constitutionalist resistance to absolutism have emerged two very different kinds of welfare state: the Anglo-Saxon (predominantly Protestant) states have given rise to restrictive welfare regimes providing minimalist welfare rights primarily only for poor citizens; the Scandinavian (predominantly secular) states have given rise to extensive welfare regimes, albeit with a strongly corporatist tinge, providing universal social rights for all citizens. Britain, far from providing a model by which to understand the nature of modern welfare states, is an atypical and ambiguous case.

Towards a global form of social rights?

It is no part of the thesis presented here to suggest that there is any single tendency or movement towards convergence between the various forms which welfare states and social rights can take. On the contrary, the intention is to emphasise the fluidity of rights, both in form and in substance. Within the context of that fluidity, however, there are certain trends to be observed at an international level. Although the magnitude of the consequences varies from case to case, welfare states in the developed world have been subject during the last three decades of the twentieth century to similar pressures:

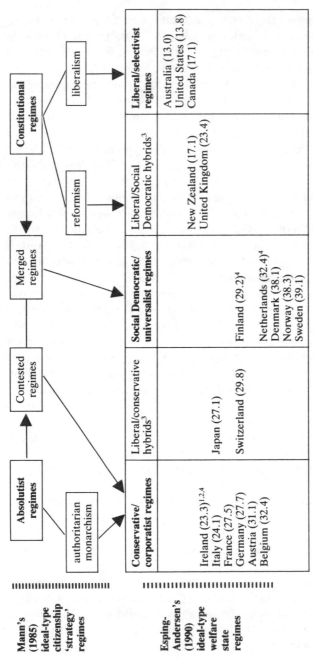

Figure 3.1 Citizenship 'strategy' and welfare state regimes.

Notes:
1. Countries listed are the eighteen OECD countries.
2. Figures in brackets are Esping-Andersen's 'decommodification index' scores calculated on 1980 statistics. The countries are arranged in descending rank order (i.e. the least decommodified countries are at the top, the most decommodified at the bottom).
3. Signifies author's assessment of hybrid status, based on Esping-Andersen's 'stratification index' scores (not shown).
4. Signifies ambiguous or borderline cases (allocations made by author).

- economic pressures, especially during the oil price and exchange rate crises of the 1970s and the impetus to labour market restructuring of the 1980s;
- political pressures resulting from the ascendancy in the 1980s in many parts of the capitalist world of New Right thinking, which was explicitly hostile to state welfare;
- social-demographic pressures arising because of commonly experienced trends to population ageing, accelerating rates of household formation and the growth of lone parenting (for a lucid summary of all these pressures, see Taylor-Gooby 1991).

The resilience of welfare state forms, in spite of such developments, has given rise to a number of explanations or theses, which Mishra (1990) succinctly summarises as the irreversibility, maturity and pluralist theses. Irreversibility theses claim that state welfare has become essential to the survival of capitalism and cannot be dismantled. Maturity theses claim that, after a period of rapid development, most welfare states have no need for further growth and can be expected to consolidate. Pluralist theses claim that, in the process of surviving the crisis, the tendency has been for welfare states to adapt and to restructure their commitments away from direct services in favour of the funding and regulation of welfare provision in the household, voluntary and market sectors. The suggestion implicit in all such theses is that there is a natural level of state welfare activity to which most developed countries will tend to approximate.

This, I would argue, is not the case. The form of the welfare state and the substance of social rights are likely to vary widely, though they may be subject to pressures to conform not to a single model, but to one of two: a Western European model in the corporatist tradition or an American model in the constitutionalist tradition.

The Europeanisation of social rights

The part of the world where the impetus for convergence is greatest (but the direction of convergence is least certain) is Western Europe. This is a consequence of the 'widening' and 'deepening' of the European Union (EU). The incorporation into the former European Community (EC) in 1986 of the 'Latin Rim' countries –

Greece, Spain and Portugal – brought into the largely corporatist fold three so-called 'rudimentary welfare states' (Leibfried 1993), while the accession to the EU in 1995 of Sweden, the leading Scandinavian welfare state, in many way reflects the erosion under international pressure of democratic socialism's quest for a 'middle way' (Gould 1993). Additionally, ex-communist Eastern European nations have expressed an interest in further widening the EU's membership; however, the prospects of their being able to do so remain uncertain. The EU is primarily an economic alliance of rich nations and, arguably, the gap between Western and Eastern Europe will remain too wide to permit convergence in economic or social terms (Simpson 1993). A widely prophesied scenario is of a 'fortress Europe' shoring itself up economically against the USA and Japan and against the interests of the Third World, while developing an introspective and exclusionary approach to social citizenship (*ibid.*).

The sense in which the EU is also to be 'deepened' reflects a desire that the union between member states should extend beyond the economic level to the monetary and political levels on the one hand and into the 'social dimension' on the other. Since 1957 and the Treaty of Rome it had always been envisaged that European integration should have a social as well as an economic dimension, although in practice this was seen to relate largely to labour market issues and, for example, to the application of modest levels of structural funding to help improve the economic infrastructure of disadvantaged regions. In 1989, however, the Social Charter was signed by all members of the former EC except Britain. In anticipation of the final completion of the Single European Market this declaration sought to establish a set of fundamental social rights which would apply not only to workers, but to all citizens of member European states. Implementation of the Charter was to be achieved, initially, through a Social Action Programme and subsequently through the addition of a 'Social Chapter' to the 1992 Maastricht Treaty. In the event, such binding directives as emerged as a result of the Social Action Programme were principally confined to employment-related rights. The Social Chapter, having first been diluted in scope to apply by and large to workers' rather than to citizens' rights, was finally consigned to the status of a protocol to the Maastricht Treaty, because Britain refused to be bound by its terms (for a useful summary see, for example, Simpson and Walker 1993). There was probably never any prospect of the pan-European harmonisation of policy in areas such as social security provision, although this does not rule out a 'convergence of objectives' and the use of EU institutions to achieve over time a general levelling of social security standards (see Berghman 1991; Keithly 1991).

The significance of the EU's concern for the social dimension is that this lies classically within the conservative/corporatist tradition with its central concern for workers, rather than citizens as a whole, and with its perception of social rights as an extension of civil (i.e. economic) rights, rather than as a component of full citizenship. The former EC's low-key anti-poverty programmes were primarily concerned with research into what was defined as 'exclusion' or 'marginalisation'. These terms were used loosely or even synonymously to refer, not to social exclusion in a wider sense, but to processes by which individuals, communities or regions are excluded or marginalised from labour markets and employment opportunities (Cross 1993). To the extent that the EU has a social policy it is directed to the social consequences of economic integration. Whether it is remotely adequate to assuage the scale of social polarisation and impoverishment which could result can be seriously questioned (see, for example, Townsend 1992). The thrust of the EU's social dimension is not to relieve poverty but to complement the 'negative integration' measures by which to remove barriers to the single market with 'positive integration' measures. The purpose of enhancing the rights and conditions of employees is to increase economic efficiency, without risking social cohesion (Gold and Mayes 1993). The British government in the late 1980s and early 1990s sought to disengage from this process and to sustain the distinctive ambiguity of Britain's welfare state regime.

With or without Britain's participation, the future of an expanding EU will bring changes to the form which welfare rights and social legislation take. Stephan Leibfried (1993) has suggested there are two ways in which this might happen. The first he defines as the 'Europeanisation' of poverty policy 'from the top down' (*ibid.*: 148 and 143). This would entail the institutions of the EU securing convergence between welfare systems by, for example, the imposition of a European formula for minimum income protection. This Leibfried characterises as a Bismarckian or Napoleonic solution. Provisions would be centrally dictated before or even without the development of individual political or democratic rights in the institutions of the EU. To the extent that the protections guaranteed by such interventions might extend to citizens beyond the labour force, Leibfried foresees a danger that protection might be restricted to groups such as older and disabled people, but would not be extended to groups attracting little popular sympathy, such as unemployed people and lone parents, whose fate would remain dependent on nationally determined priorities (see also Room 1991).

The Americanisation of social rights

The second way in which European poverty policy might develop Leibfried describes as 'Americanisation from the bottom up' (1993: 143). Current EU social legislation is mainly procedural rather than substantive, leaving the implementation of welfare policy at the level of the nation-state. This makes it possible for the EU to develop as a United States of Europe, in a manner which constitutionally would be similar to the USA. In the USA social rights of citizenship developed only after political citizenship had been fully established and to a much lesser extent than in Western Europe. Leibfried argues that with the development of EU citizenship it will in time be possible and indeed necessary to develop procedural legislation which enables citizens from one European state to claim poor relief or medical treatment in any other European state. To an extent, this is already beginning to happen but, ultimately, it could progress beyond the present limited reciprocal funding arrangements to the provision of automatic EU-wide rights for all EU citizens and for the setting of minimum standards of provision. As happened in the USA, the assertion of individual rights to free movement might eventually draw concessions at federal government level so as to create new kinds of rights and new (generally minimal) duties for member states.

As we approach the twenty-first century, there are other reasons which can be advanced for supposing that the liberal/selectivist welfare state regime characteristic of North America may represent a more dominant paradigm than that of the conservative/corporatist regimes of Western Europe. This is a possibility consistent with Ramesh Mishra's diagnosis of the predicament of the 'post-crisis'

welfare state (1990) and the nature of postmodernity (1993). Mishra
is prepared to acknowledge the claims by Lyotard (1984) and others
that the old 'meta-narratives' are spent. He concedes the demise of
the Marxism which informed the communist alternatives of Eastern
Europe; the democratic socialism which informed the reformist
road of the Scandinavian welfare states; and the neo-conservatism
which informed the New Right's attempts to roll back the welfare
state in the 1990s. These three perspectives, he argues, have only
one thing in common:

> in different ways they all see the hybrid of welfare capitalism as a
> transitory phenomenon . . . [T]he persistence of the hybrid of welfare
> capitalism, at variance with the predictions and prescriptions of both
> left and right, appears to confirm the postmodern notion of a decline
> in the credibility of historicism and social Utopias. (Mishra 1993: 24)

What also characterises postmodernity is the end of full
employment, the decline of the tripartism which had characterised
the corporatism of Western Europe and Scandinavia, and a
transition from class politics to plural politics and new social
movements. Since the 1970s, according to Mishra:

- the new technologies, which have made possible jobless growth,
  and the globalisation of capital, which has made possible an
  international division of labour, now mean it is beyond the power
  of national governments to secure the full employment on which
  the old Keynesian welfare state depended;
- the consequent restructuring of both capital and labour and the
  decline in trade unionism have undermined the scope (and from
  capital's point of view the necessity) for the tripartite negotiation
  of social policy;
- the contraction of the traditional (i.e. manual) working class, the
  emergence of new social cleavages based on consumption rather
  than occupational patterns and the emergence of movements
  (such as feminism and environmentalism) which cut across class
  lines have removed the collective basis on which demands for
  universal social policies were once based.

These developments will certainly have had a greater impact on
Western Europe than North America, but they are also likely 'to
bring the political economy (though *not necessarily* the social
policy) of European welfare states somewhat closer to that of North

America' [emphasis added] (Mishra 1993: 28). However, it remains to be seen whether social rights in capitalism's First World will conform to a European or an American model, or indeed whether social rights in the Second and Third Worlds will conform to either.

Conclusion/summary

Welfare rights and social legislation are by no means the automatic outcome of capitalist development. This chapter has sought to illustrate this in four ways.

First, we have discussed the extent to which social rights have or have failed to develop in the so-called 'Third' (or 'developing') World. Particular attention has been drawn to the way in which notions of 'rights', founded in Western Judaeo-Christian tradition, may be culturally inappropriate to some parts of the Third World and to the possibilities that welfare provision may be developed without 'rights' in the sense that they are understood within the traditions of the First World.

Second, we have discussed the extent to which social rights in the 'Second' (or 'ex-communist') World are in retreat. The efficacy of social rights under former communist regimes may have been impaired by the absence of a complementary framework of civil and political rights, but as the countries of the former Soviet Union and its Central and Eastern European neighbours struggle to adopt capitalism, the evidence is clearly that this has been at the expense of social rights.

Third, we have discussed the different ways in which the welfare states of the First World have been formed. The social rights of citizenship provided in the former absolutist monarchies of Western Europe tend to differ in character from the social rights provided in constitutionalist Anglo-Saxon countries. What is more, the social democratic ideal embodied in Marshall's notion of 'democratic-welfare-capitalism' has best been exemplified in the Scandinavian countries, although the character of these appears to be changing.

Finally, this chapter has considered the idea that social rights may in time converge towards a universal, globalised form. The future of welfare rights and social legislation both in Britain and throughout the world will be subject to global influences, but the outcome remains uncertain and the likelihood that a single type of welfare state will emerge as ascendant seems remote.

Having therefore underlined the point that the British form of social rights is far from being the only or an inevitable form, the next chapter will consider the extent to which social rights are necessarily an unambiguous good.

Recommended additional reading

Esping-Andersen, G. (1990) *The Three Worlds of Welfare Capitalism*, Polity Press, Cambridge, Chapters 1 and 3.
George, V. (1988) *Wealth, Poverty and Starvation: An international perspective*, Harvester Wheatsheaf, Hemel Hempstead, Chapters 1, 3 and 4.
Jones, C. (ed.) (1993) *New Perspectives on the Welfare State in Europe*, Routledge, London, Chapter 2 and Part III.

Questions for reflection

Just how might it be possible to have, on the one hand, social development without economic development, and on the other, 'welfare' without 'rights'?

The 'American'/constitutionalist and 'European'/corporatist models of social rights reflect different historical roots and ideological traditions which may militate against their convergence, but, in the light of recent global developments, to what degree are the conflicts between these models still relevant?

CHAPTER 4

SOCIAL RIGHTS AND
SOCIAL CONTROL

It will be clear from the preceding chapters that this book treats welfare rights and social legislation as ambiguous phenomena. T. H. Marshall, whose concept of social rights was discussed at length in Chapter 1, looked on social rights as a civilising influence, a form of 'class abatement' with consequences for the stability of society and for the structure of social equality. Implicitly, this civilising influence would not only tame the excesses and redress the diswelfares of the capitalist system, but it would also temper or refine the conduct of the working class. The nature of this inherent ambiguity is most clearly brought out by Ian Gough, who has written of the welfare state:

> It simultaneously embodies tendencies to enhance social welfare, to develop the powers of individuals, to exert control over the blind play of market forces; and tendencies to repress and control people, to adapt them to the requirements of the capitalist economy. (1979: 12)

In so far as modern welfare state and social security provisions have their historical origins within discretionary systems of poor relief, the extension of social rights can quite easily be portrayed as an extension of the crude controls exercised against the poor during capitalism's earlier stages (see Piven and Cloward 1974; Novak 1988). However, even allowing for the cross-national variations discussed in Chapter 3, the social rights which characterise the welfare systems of advanced capitalism differ significantly from the discretionary forms of poor relief which they have superseded, in their form and scale on the one hand and in their substance and sophistication on the other. Social rights are still associated with correlative duties and conditions of entitlement, but the nature of these is different in character. Challenges to the idea that citizens can have 'rights' to welfare and as to the nature of such rights have issued from several quarters; this chapter will explore certain of these.

Giving citizens rights is ostensibly one way of protecting their liberties, of safeguarding them from arbitrary power. This was fundamental to the strategy by which the property-owning bourgeoisie, in their bid to wrest power from the crown and the feudal aristocracy, sought to displace conceptions of 'natural' rights with laws which were 'man-made' (see Chapter 1 and, for example, Thompson 1975). For precisely this reason, conservatives in the mould of Edmund Burke have been mistrustful of any extension of human rights, since the only common right which they would recognise is the 'right to adjudication'; that is, the right to be governed by the decisions of established authority with the power to translate imagined rights into realities (see Scruton 1991: 16–18). Rights are an explicit challenge, not only to traditional paternalistic authority, but also to newer forms of administrative authority. Fabian academics like Richard Titmuss (1971), for example, have expressed themselves to be in favour of 'creative' or 'individualised' justice administered by compassionate experts, rather than the crude 'proportional' justice bestowed by rights which are legally prescribed. There are therefore those on both the left and right of the political spectrum who would question the need for rights which might impair the exercise of benevolent authority in the interests of the welfare of the people.

The history of the welfare state is a story of transition from relief based on charity and discretion to benefits based on legislation and entitlement. While conservatives resisted the welfare state and Fabians championed it, the common ground they shared was an attachment to the value of discretionary decision-making. The compromise which both were prepared to strike with the liberal ideal of 'rights' can best be understood when it is realised that rights need not extinguish the scope for discretionary decision-making. Dworkin (1977) makes the point that administrative institutions in advanced capitalist societies function in a discretionary 'void', surrounded like the hole in a doughnut by legal rules and principles.

Rights created by legislation require the exercise of administrative discretion for the interpretation and application of those rules. The creation of rights to welfare extended rather than diminished administrative power, and the expansion of the discourse of rights into the realm of welfare has generated new theoretical and practical concerns about the relationship between state authority and the individual citizen. Challenges to the nature and effects of social rights have come from the radical wings of both the political Right and the political Left and from a range of new intellectual and social movements.

The neo-liberal challenge

In seeking to recapture and revitalise the classical doctrines of economic liberalism so-called 'neo-liberals' would seek to restrict the rights of citizenship to civil and political rights, and primarily to the negative liberties by which the free play of market forces may be guaranteed. Though the distributive outcomes of impersonal market forces may be unequal, this is neither intended nor foreseen and cannot therefore be unjust. According to Hayek (1976), the very idea of social justice and of social rights which might compensate for such injustice is no more than a mirage. If the rich and successful have moral obligations, how and to whom these may be discharged is a matter of choice: such obligations are not enforceable and give rise to no implication that those who fail to prosper have rights against those who succeed. Translating wants and needs into rights has been described by Enoch Powell as 'a dangerous modern heresy' (1972: 12).

Among the things that neo-liberals condemn have been the substantive development since the Second World War of welfare states in countries like Britain and, for example, the United Nations' largely symbolic Universal Declaration of Human Rights, signed in 1948. The significance of the latter was that it encompassed not only civil and political rights (the right to life, freedom of movement, a fair trial, universal enfranchisement, etc.), but also social and economic rights, including the right to social security, to work, to education and even to leisure. Article 24 states:

Everyone has the right to a standard of living adequate for the health and well being of himself and his family, including food, clothing, housing and medical care and necessary social services, and the right to security in the event of unemployment, sickness, disability, widowhood, old age or other lack of livelihood in circumstances beyond his control.

At the level of rhetoric at least, welfare rights enjoy internationally recognised status as basic human rights (see Watson 1980: ch. 10). This gives rise to two kinds of objection, the first characterised by Nozick who claims that welfare rights violate property rights; the second from Cranston, who claims that welfare rights do not meet the conditions necessary to qualify as basic human rights.

Turning first to Nozick (1974), his argument is based on an interpetation of Kant's alternative formulation of the 'categorical imperative', namely that respect for other persons depends on their being regarded as ends in themselves and not as means. This he uses to build a case against any form of social rights requiring redistribution. For Nozick, the inviolability of the individual is synonymous with the inviolability of the property in which his/her rights are vested. To redistribute any portion of that property to another is to treat that person as a means and not as an end. We may not violate persons for the social good because, says Nozick (in words remarkably similar to Margaret Thatcher's infamous 1988 declaration that 'there is no such thing as society'), 'there is no *social entity* with a good which undergoes some sacrifice for its own good. There are only individual people with their own individual lives' (1974: p. 32). Individuals may choose to undergo some sacrifice for their own or somebody else's benefit, but they should not be compelled to do so in the name of some other person's 'right'. Such compulsion does not create social rights but rights of the state over the property of its own citizens; rights which violate the principle of respect for persons.

Second, there is Cranston's denial that social rights can be human rights (1973; 1976). More in the tradition of legal positivism than neo-liberalism Cranston draws a distinction between legal rights (which are 'positively' defined) and human rights (which are 'morally' defined). Human rights pertain to a human being by virtue of his/her being human and, according to Cranston, they have three tests of 'authenticity': practicability, paramount importance and universality. Civil and political rights by and large meet these

criteria in so far as they are relatively easily secured by appropriate
legislation, they are fundamentally necessary to the just functioning
of capitalist society and they may be applied genuinely to
everybody. Social and economic rights, however, are of a different
order. The resources required for a social security system, for
example, may be beyond the command of Third World governments; social services and economic security may represent an
ideal, but they are not essential; and the needs which social rights
address are relative, not universal. Therefore,

> the effect of a Universal Declaration which is overloaded with
> affirmations of so-called human rights which are not human rights at
> all is to push *all* talk of human rights out of the clear realm of the
> morally compelling into the twilight world of utopian aspiration.
> (1976: 142)

Objections to these views are rehearsed elsewhere (Plant *et al.*
1980: ch. 4; Plant 1992, which we shall discuss in Chapter 10;
Watson 1980: ch. 10). The two points which need to be drawn out
are that what is here characterised as the neo-liberal case against
social rights rests first, on the costs of achieving social rights and in
particular the role this affords to the state; and second, that social
rights do not supplement but undermine the liberties necessary to
the perpetuation of capitalism.

The neo-Marxist challenge

From the opposite end of the ideological spectrum comes a
contrasting set of arguments, but arguments which can be just as
sceptical about the value of social rights. First, there is a group of
academic writers who have sought to interpret Marxist principles
in relation to the role which social rights play in regulating labour
and sustaining rather than undermining capital. Second, there are
theorists who have developed the Marxist critique of the form of
individual legal rights in order to demonstrate the capacity of social
rights for ideological mystification and control.

Turning to the first of these approaches it is necessary to be clear
that there are different strands of thought within neo-Marxism.
There is an *instrumentalist* strand, which adopts from Marx's earlier

writings the idea that the state under capitalism acts as no more than 'a committee for managing the common affairs of the whole bourgeoisie' (Marx, 1848: 69). There is also a *structuralist* strand deriving from Marx's later writing, which analyses state forms as an expression of the immanent logic of the capitalist system and its class antagonisms. When neo-Marxists have come to analyse the twentieth-century welfare state and the significance of the development of social rights, both these strands have become to some extent intertwined.

The first kind of critique was developed by Saville (1958), O'Connor (1973) and Gough (1979). They began to forge an account of how the welfare state had developed, claiming in essence that it was the product of three interacting influences. The first of these was the struggle by the working class for better living conditions. The social policy reforms obtained in this way had the effect of increasing levels of social consumption and general living standards; but they also benefited capital by furnishing an element of 'quantitative regulation' over labour-power – partly by reducing the direct costs of labour and partly by having the state look after people whose labour was not required. The second influence was capital's growing need for an efficient environment and a productive workforce. The reforms resulting from this influence amounted to the investment by the state of 'social capital' and the necessary 'modification' of labour-power through the provision of health and education services so as to produce better workers. The third influence was a concern for political stability. The policies resulting from this influence involved the discharge of the 'social expenses' necessary for the 'qualitative regulation' of labour-power; or, more crudely, for the production of contented workers through the provision of those benefits and services required to secure social order and a degree of ideological control.

The neo-Marxist writer to engage most directly with the idea of social rights was Claus Offe. One of his central arguments was that 'the owner of labour power first becomes a wage labourer as a citizen of a state' (1984: 99). Industrial capitalism required more than the passive compulsion of economic forces in order to get people to accept the burdens and risks associated with wage labour and a market economy. To make people actively participate, it was necessary to have what Offe described as 'flanking sub-systems', namely systems of political-administrative and normative control.

Social policy is 'the state's manner of effecting the lasting transformation of non-wage labourers into wage labourers' (*ibid.*: 92). This is the basis on which Offe challenges Marshall's account of social rights (see Chapter 1). Social rights were not an optional extra or final refinement to citizenship under capitalism; they are, according to Offe, a necessary part of it. Without such rights citizens would not 'muster the *cultural motivation* to become wage labourers' (*ibid.*: 94). Within Offe's account, social rights were necessary first, as a precondition for the suppression of begging and modes of subsistence which might undermine the wage labour system; second, as the medium through which to justify the provision of facilities for improving the quality of labour-power (in ways which individual self-seeking capitalists are incapable); and third, as a mechanism by which potentially or conditionally to exempt certain parts of the population from labour force partici- pation (mothers, children, students, disabled people, old people). Social rights are as important as civil rights as a device for articulating labour-power with the market.

Turning now to the second kind of neo-Marxist critique, this is concerned less with the substance or effects of social rights than with their form. Marx (1859) himself argued that law and state apparatuses are no more than 'superstructural' phenomena, supported and indirectly shaped by the economic 'foundations' on which they are constructed. In *Capital* (1887), however, he went further and sought to demonstrate that the form of individual rights within bourgeois liberal ideology is a logically necessary conse- quence of capitalist production and market exchange. Because under market conditions goods must be exchanged as commodities, the producers and owners of such commodities must recognise in each other the rights of private proprietors and relate to each other on the basis of legal and contractual rules. Under capitalism it is not only materials and products which are traded but, following the destruction of feudal land tenure, real estate and even human labour are 'freed' to enter the market as commodities. Rights in ownership – of goods, land or labour-power – become the universal foundation of human relationships. Unlike Hegel (whose account of rights was similar – see Chapter 1), Marx dismissed rights in ownership as an illusion, a 'fetishised' form which obscures the fundamentally exploitative substance of the social relations of production under capitalism.

In the course of the twentieth century these ideas have been taken up by other writers, foremost of whom was Pashukanis (1978). Writing in the 1920s Pashukanis argued that, since it is the exchange of commodities which forms the very basis of social life, even such fundamental legal concepts as equity, restitution and entitlement are all derived from the commodity form. Just as 'value' is a concept which fundamentally defines our understanding of the nature and capacities of commodities, so 'right' is a concept which fundamentally defines our understanding of the nature and capacity of human beings. The individual juridical subject or citizen, as the bearer of rights, is the 'atom' – the simplest irreducible element – of legal and administrative theory. Pashukanis argued that this private form of possessive individual right has been rendered universal by being appropriated into the sphere of public and administrative law. This highly abstract line of reasoning has been developed by later theorists (see Holloway and Picciotto 1978), who have claimed that the form of the state – and the form of welfare rights and social legislation – is 'derived' from capitalism's characteristic commodity form and from the nature of the wage relation as the most exploitative expression of that commodity form (see H. Dean 1991: 14–16). The challenge here is that social rights are not all they seem. To cloak human welfare in an ideological discourse of 'rights' conceals the fundamental nature of relations of power under capitalism. It is nonsense to suggest that civil rights will guarantee that individual employees may bargain on equal terms with corporate employers, and it is nonsense to suggest that social rights will guarantee unemployed people, pensioners or disabled people power to negotiate their claims with departments of state. Social rights give expression to the ultimate dominance of capital over labour and serve to extend or permeate that dominance beyond the immediate sphere of the wage relation, into the sphere of state–citizen relations, and into everyday life.

This is the basis on which writers like Bankowski and Mungham (1976) have attacked the mystificatory form of welfare rights and social legislation, the effect of which, they say, is to channel or co-opt working-class resistance into bureaucratic and legal modes of participation. Bankowski and Mungham are especially critical of so-called 'radical' lawyers and welfare rights specialists because, while they may undermine the 'high bourgeois image' of the law, they also succeed in bringing it closer to people. In so doing, radical lawyers and welfare rights workers dehumanise their clients by negating people's own understanding and experience of how problems might be solved. According to Bankowski and Mungham, the promotion of social rights should not be considered as a technical or rational means to achieving reformist ends, since this is to divorce the apparent benefits of social rights from any understanding of their overarching form and function.

Once again, objections to these views are rehearsed elsewhere (we shall return to these views in Chapter 10, but see Campbell 1983; or more generally, Hall and Held 1989). However, in spite of differences between them, the essence of the neo-Marxists' case against social rights is first, that in ameliorating the exploitative impact of capitalism they help ensure its survival; and second, that social rights provide a powerful mechanism for state/ideological control.

The challenges of 'postmodernity'

As we approach the *fin de siècle* it is tempting if perhaps facile to suppose that the world is entering a new age of 'postmodernity'. In Chapter 3 it was noted that the global trends which allegedly characterise postmodernity are first, the exhaustion of 'grand narratives' such as liberalism and Marxism; second, far-reaching cultural changes resulting from technological, economic and social changes; third, political pluralism and the growth of new social movements. Such trends, it is claimed, pose a threat to the notions of universalism and progress on which democratic-welfare-capitalism is founded (for succinct accounts, see Williams 1992; and Hewitt 1994). Against such views Habermas (1985) and Giddens (1990), for example, argue that modernity continues to evolve and that the great Enlightenment project is not yet complete.

With regard to the first of the above-mentioned trends, Taylor-Gooby (1994) has retorted that the world is witnessing not a global disillusionment with all grand narratives, but the ascendancy of just one of them. The spreading influence of New Right thinking in the First World, the collapse of communism in the Second World and the far-reaching effects of the monetarist policies of the IMF and World Bank in the Third World signal a near-global triumph of a classical or neo-liberal version of the capitalist project and of the patterns of poverty and inequality which such an ideology is prepared to tolerate. The full significance of this, says Taylor-Gooby, is obscured by the 'ideological smokescreen' (*ibid.*: 385) of postmodernism.

None the less, the second and third of the trends attributed to postmodernity are of undeniable importance, not least because they have fomented alternative insights, theories and critiques concerning the nature of *modernity* rather than 'postmodernity'. To the extent that these bear on the 'modern' notion of social rights, it is to these that this chapter now turns. I shall first discuss what are sometimes called poststructuralist critiques of modernity; second I shall examine 'emancipatory' critiques associated with new social movements (specifically, feminism and anti-racism); and finally, I shall touch on some of the 'defensive' critiques emanating from the new political pluralism (the distinction between emancipatory and defensive social movements is drawn from Habermas 1987: 393).

Poststructuralist critiques

Theorists of postmodernity have called into question whether the eighteenth-century Enlightenment which gave birth to 'modernity' was ever a dispassionate quest for truth and reason. On the contrary, according to Bauman (1987), it was an exercise in two parts:

> First, in extending the powers and ambitions of the state, in transferring to the state the pastoral functions previously exercised by the church, in reorganising the state around the function of planning, designing and managing the reproduction of social order . . . secondly, in the creation of an entirely new and consciously designed mechanism of disciplinary action, aimed at regulating and regularising the socially relevant life of the subjects of the teaching and managing state. (p. 80)

What was obscure under modernity is more transparent within the postmodern world of information technology and new managerialism in which, for example, scientists are hired 'not to find truth, but to augment powers' (Lyotard 1984: 46). Bauman and Lyotard are echoing here the arguments of Michel Foucault, whose claim had been that modernity was based not on scientific reason and rationality but the 'will to power'; that the legitimacy of modern governance was an effect of power and not truth or justice; that the reality behind the veil of democratic-welfare-capitalism is that of an inherently 'disciplinary society' (see especially Foucault 1979).

Foucault's general arguments have also influenced some particular critiques of the disciplinary aspects of social policy (Squires 1990; H. Dean 1991). The basis for such approaches has been a re-examination of the history of the welfare state and of the increasingly sophisticated surveillance and disciplinary processes associated with the administration of welfare rights and social legislation. These approaches invoke a relational theory of power which holds first, that the shift from feudalism to capitalism was associated with a shift from coercive to administrative (welfare) state power. Administrative state power has had as much to do with the regulation of human behaviour as the 'dull compulsion' of economic forces. The development of state welfare and social rights has involved new *technologies of power* and pervasive new *disciplinary techniques*. The characteristic of these technologies and techniques is that, unlike class power, they bear on *individual difference*. In place of the uncontrollable mass is the controllable individual subject.

My own account (H. Dean 1991) has concentrated on three intersecting processes by which citizens of the modern welfare state have been constructed. First, there has been an historical process of transition 'from begging bowl to social wage' (*ibid.*: 37). In place of the indiscriminate giving of alms to the anonymous poor there has been erected the complex panoply of the welfare state which scrutinises and documents each individual 'client' or 'case'. In place of careless humanitarianism there has been inserted meticulous paternalistic control. Second, there has been a historical process of transition 'from corporal to pecuniary sanctions' (*ibid.*: 43). In place of such practices as the public whipping and branding of vagrants there have emerged more discreet and less violent forms of coercion based on benefit penalties and disqualifications. In place of an explicit Malthusian desire to punish the poor there have developed more subtle forms of containment. Third, there has been an historical process of transition 'from oppression to discipline' (*ibid.*: 51). In place of crude processes of classification and surveillance associated with the workhouse and the Poor Laws there have been constructed administrative systems based on legal definitions and regulations to which citizens must submit in order to exercise their 'rights'. In place of the prying concern and moralistic edicts of philanthropists and utilitarians there has emerged a voluntaristic discourse based on the idea that citizens of the welfare state are juridical subjects with the freedom to exercise their rights and a responsibility to abide by the rules.

The history of the welfare state is therefore seen not as a story of progress towards the development of universal social rights, but as a story of developing state power and increasingly sophisticated methods of social control. It is additionally argued that, far from dismantling state power, recent policies of welfare retrenchment have often involved subtle refinements to the disciplinary mechan isms which underpin our rights to welfare (*ibid.*: ch. 7; H. Dean 1988/9).

Feminist critiques

In the sphere of social rights – as in the sphere of civil and political rights – women are 'second-class citizens' (see, for example, Lister 1990). Past generations of feminists have campaigned against limitations on property rights (not redressed until 1882) and voting rights (not fully redressed until 1928), yet women remain by and large economically and politically disadvantaged. In the 1940s feminists campaigned for social rights (Dale and Foster 1986) and against the limitations on women's social rights which the Beveridge Report portended (see Abbott and Bompas 1943).

Feminism's most recent 'wave', however, has challenged in ways which past generations did not the underlying form as well as the substance of their 'rights'. The problem with the universalistic liberal conception of equal rights is that, even where it acknowledges that men and women should be treated the same,

> treating people as though they are the same is quite different from treating them as equals. This approach neglects crucial differences, for example, the fact that in a market economy being a parent means being less 'free' and hence less 'equal' in the labour market than a single person; a mother is significantly less free and equal than a father. (Langan and Ostner 1991: 139)

While there remains a liberal feminist strand whose concern is to promote equal opportunities legislation (Williams 1989: 44–9), the 1970s and 1980s witnessed the birth of socialist and radical strands of feminism whose resistance to women's oppression is founded in an analysis of patriarchy. Patriarchy is regarded as a structural characteristic of human society and, in spite of important differences between the newer strands of feminism, their central theoretical insight relates to the distinction which can be drawn between society's public and private spheres (see especially Pascall 1986). The public sphere is where civil and political rights reside; it is the domain of the market and the state; it is the site of productive and administrative activity which is dominated by men. The private sphere, in contrast, is not inhabited by rights; it is the domestic domain of hearth, home and family; it is the site for the reproduction of social life, a process to which women are confined. The public/productive sphere is separated from yet dominates the private/reproductive sphere. Social rights have been immensely important to the articulation between the two. As Pascall (1986) puts it, the welfare state was created 'in the void between the factory and the family'.

Welfare rights and social legislation have succeeded in redistributing resources from men to women but, for all that, the development of the social rights of democratic-welfare-capitalism have failed women on two counts: first, because they have been instrumental in the supervision and enforcement of women's dependence in the private sphere; second, because they have not compensated women for their disadvantaged position in the public sphere.

Women and the issue of women's dependence have been ignored and rendered invisible in most mainstream (or 'malestream') analyses of social rights. Certainly, this was true of Marshall (see Lister 1990: 56). While social rights may have ameliorated the effects of class differences, their effects on gender differences were not even considered. Such architects of the welfare state as Beveridge were so inured to patriarchal ideology that it was explicitly assumed that married women would be financially dependent on their husbands. While such directly discriminatory features have since been removed (albeit in Britain largely as a result of Equal Treatment Directives from the EU), the structure of social security benefits, for example, remains indirectly discriminatory. In practice it is predominantly male heads of household who claim benefits on behalf of predominantly female dependants. As Lister puts it, for such women 'rights mediated by their partners cease to be genuine rights' (*ibid.*: 58).

Similarly, the systematic disadvantage of women in the public sphere, and particularly in the labour market, has been ignored. For example, Esping-Andersen's influential account of the role of social rights in 'decommodification' (which I outlined in Chapter 1) has been criticised by Langan and Ostner (1991) because, although it recognises the importance of women and families at the empirical level, it fails to confront their theoretical significance:

> Men are commodified, made ready to sell their labour power on the market, by the work done by women in the family. Women on the other hand, are decommodified by their position in the family. Thus men and women are 'gendered commodities' with different experiences of the labour market resulting from their different relationship to family life. The role of social rights in decommodification differs according to gender, in general protecting men's position in the labour market while disadvantaging women by restricting their access to certain areas of employment. (p. 131)

Once again, the issue is not only one of direct discrimination (though the strategies of employers for excluding women from higher-paid men's jobs are important), but also of the failure of social rights to redress the unequal burden of (unpaid) caring and domestic work which women carry. As Smart has put it, 'the acquisition of rights in a given area may create the impression that a power difference had been "resolved"' (1989: 144). Social rights, especially in countries like Britain, have not done enough in terms of guaranteeing care provision (for example, for pre-school children or disabled relatives) to allow women independent access to the labour market; and they have done nothing at all to guarantee a more equitable sexual division of labour within the ideologically constructed family. Additionally, some feminists advance arguments similar to those of poststructuralists and point out that, historically, seeking refuge in claims to 'rights' has resulted for women in their being subjected 'to more refined notions of qualification . . . more centralized knowledge of sexual relationships, child care organization, and so on . . . the possibility of greater and greater surveillance' (Smart 1989: 142).

To the extent that 'family' policy may afford 'social' rights it serves to reinforce what Dominelli (1991) calls 'patriarchal conjugality'. The feminist case is that the lack of public alternatives to private care for dependent children and disabled adults, the systematic disadvantage of women in the labour market, and their difficulty of independent access to such things as cash benefits, pensions and housing are all calculated to ensure 'the preservation of the dependence of women in families and the discouragement of their independence from men' (Pascall 1986: 163).

Anti-racist critiques

Like the feminist critique, the anti-racist critique of social rights claims that 'black' people or people from ethnic communities in countries like Britain remain 'second-class' citizens (see Lister 1990: 52). As a social movement (rather than as an intellectual critique) anti-racism has not had the same profile as feminism, but just as contemporary feminism is organised around a theoretical critique of patriarchy, so anti-racism has been organised around a theoretical critique of racism. There are differences between anti-racist theorists concerning the degree to which racism is autonomous of other forms or dimensions of oppression (Williams 1989: ch. 4), but what distinguishes the anti-racist critique from 'liberal' concerns about racial discrimination is that it regards racism as an ideology. Racism is seen not as a set of attitudes held by white people about black people, but as a set of outcomes arising from a system of legal, policy, institutional and discursive practices. Just as the sexual division of labour is rooted historically in the ideological construction of 'the family', so there is a racial division of labour that is rooted historically in the ideological construction of 'the nation' and, in Britain's case, its rise and fall as an imperial power (Miles and Phizacklea 1984).

The rights of citizenship enjoyed by black British citizens have not prevented their being twice as vulnerable to unemployment as white citizens (Oppenheim 1993) and, when in employment, having lower average earnings (see, for example, Breugal 1989). The incidence of poverty is higher among Britain's black population than among the white population (Amin and Oppenheim 1992) and yet there is evidence that the take-up of social security benefits is lower among the former than the latter (see, for example, NACAB 1991; Cook and Watt 1992). Inclusionary notions of citizenship and the rhetoric of universal social rights are contradicted by exclusionary practices towards black people and their differential access to welfare. The 'racialisation' of politics in post-war Britain has revolved around two contradictory movements: on the one hand, the extension of 'black' immigration control and restrictions on the definition of citizenship; on the other, the development of race relations legislation and measures supposedly to guarantee the civil rights of black minorities (see, for example, Solomos 1989). The former has had both real and symbolic significance for the extent to which black people can become or consider themselves to be British citizens; the latter has been limited in its effects and has failed to secure substantive equality of access to welfare benefits and services. Both movements have a common tulcrum. As was pointed out by Cranston in his polemic against social rights (see above), civil and political rights are relatively easy to secure, but social rights do not come cheap. To guarantee employment, social security or housing requires resources. If such resources are constrained (whether for economic or political reasons), one way to limit demand is to adopt a restrictive definition of who shall be a citizen; another is to ration public resources and, while it is possible formally to guarantee equality of opportunity for *individual* citizens, administrative rationing may tend substantively to exclude those *groups* of citizens who are already subject to systematic disadvantages.

Since the first Aliens Order of 1905, the preoccupation of British immigration controls has been to prevent poor racial minorities from obtaining any right of citizenship which might entail an expenditure of public funds. The original legislation had been fuelled by anti-Semitic sentiment following an influx in the late nineteenth century of Jewish migrants from Eastern Europe. Its effect was to exclude from Britain any 'alien' not having adequate means of assistance and to provide for the expulsion of aliens found to be in receipt of poor relief. This precedent has informed all subsequent immigration controls, including those introduced in the 1960s and early 1970s to restrain Commonwealth immigration. The latter controls had been fuelled by racist sentiment directed against black immigrants from former British colonies who had been enticed to Britain during a period of labour shortage in the immediate post-war period. The principles on which such immigration controls were built were enshrined in nationality law in 1981, effectively excluding from citizenship all but those with a link by direct descent to the UK. As recently as 1988, the right of British citizens to be joined by a non-European spouse was made subject to the condition that they must be able to maintain that spouse without recourse to public funds. It is black people (especially those of Asian and African-Caribbean ethnic origin) who have been most systematically excluded from British citizenship and, to the extent that social rights are synonymous with 'recourse to public funds', it is from the social rights of citizenship that they are most rigorously excluded.

Because access to social security benefits, housing and other forms of welfare provision can therefore be conditional on immigration status, 'it has become legitimate for a range of officials to question claimants and others about their status and thus to act as agents of immigration control' (Gordon 1989: 7). This can act as a deterrent, even for black people who are legitimately settled in Britain. What is more, access to social rights is often dependent on citizens' capacity – in terms of knowledge and linguistic skills – to exercise their rights, and/or on their past employment record (in the case of state pensions, for example). Race relations legislation which provides only a limited right of individual redress, is unlikely to be strong enough to guarantee equality of access to all. It will be of little value to those whose difficulties stem from a lack of information or language skills, and no value at all to those who are excluded from rights by the structural features of state provision.

The emancipatory claims of feminism and anti-racism are based on an analysis of relations of power or oppression other than class and on dichotomies other than those between the market and the state. Fiona Williams (1989; 1992) emphasises the importance of the intersections between class, gender and 'race' and argues for social policies which can resolve the tensions between universal prescription on the one hand and the recognition of social diversity and difference on the other. Rather than argue on the basis of universal or general conceptions of need, emancipatory critics argue from particular needs (of women and black people) to general needs. There is a sense in which they attempt on behalf of particular constituencies to redeem the universal promises offered by the 'liberal' conception of rights (see M. Hewitt 1993).

Defensive critiques

The 'defensive' critiques to which I finally turn offer a different kind of challenge to the Marshallian conception of social rights. The examples which will be cited, while not necessarily representative of new social movements, have in common the twofold characteristic attributed to such movements by Scott (1990) in that they are concerned on the one hand, to promote an expansion of citizenship and on the other, to insert excluded groups within the polity. I propose very briefly to outline three complementary lines of argument in favour of a democratisation of the welfare state and a rethinking of the basis for social rights.

First, perhaps a seminal formulation of the pluralist critique of the welfare state was that provided by Hadley and Hatch (1981). It was a critique informed in some respects by the community development movement of the 1970s and prefigured in others by the writing of Illich *et al.* (1977) and Lipsky (1976). Hadley and Hatch's quarrel was with the centralised nature of the welfare state and the character this afforded to the administration of social rights. Unitary government, they claimed, is an inheritance which has suited parties of both Left and Right and has now become entrenched by virtue of its own internal momentum. The result is bureaucratic, unaccountable and inefficient. It gives to professionals and officialdom unwarranted power to control the behaviour of clients and service users. The solution which Hadley and Hatch recommended was a shift to welfare pluralism with a greater role for the voluntary and informal sectors (reforms which have since in some measure been achieved) and the development of 'participatory alternatives' to centralised social services (an objective which can hardly be said to have been realised at all). The nature of such participatory alternatives would have been such as to give clients or service users the right to an active role in negotiating the nature of the services they received. What is more, the performance of such services would be judged with reference to outputs, rather than inputs.

This emphasis on results rather than resources or 'rights' represents a theme espoused in common with my second example, namely Waltzer (1983). Waltzer has contended that *justice* is more important than 'rights', since distributive justice or equality represents outcomes (which can be assessed) rather than objectives (which cannot). Justice itself, however, 'is a human construction, and it is doubtful whether it can be made in only one way' (*ibid.*: 5). Equality, Waltzer argues, does not require the elimination of difference and what justice must entail is egalitarianism 'without the Procrustean bed of the state'. The bed in the Procrustean legend was one to which victims were fitted by being forcibly stretched or shrunk and Waltzer's case is that human beings need not be so manipulated; it is social goods, not citizens which should be controlled or made to fit. What is required is not universalism, but a form of 'complex equality'.

The notion of complex equality chimes with the last of my examples, namely that of eco-socialism. Though the deep-ecology strand within the Green Movement is not concerned with social rights (Ferris 1991), social ecologists and eco-socialists clearly are. Writers like Keane (1988) advocate a form of 'civil society socialism' in which human co-operation would be governed neither by the compulsion of market forces, nor by the administrative power of a *dirigiste* state. The state would be accountable to civil society (the sphere of voluntary co-operation) and would act as guarantor of social needs only to the extent that such needs were identified or generated in the course of ecologically sustainable production and consumption. Such thinking had in part been influenced by Claus Offe, the neo-Marxist theorist, who is mentioned above and whose later thinking I shall return to in Chapter 10. Offe had been a prominent member of the German Green Party and would seem to have become a recent convert to the idea of a Basic Income Guarantee (a universal cash benefit which would replace all existing social security benefits and tax allowances) (Offe 1992). The Basic Income Guarantee is supported (but was not conceived) by social ecologists, because it would supposedly guarantee the autonomy of the citizen – both from the market and the state (see, for example, Kemp and Wall 1990). The existing pattern of welfare entitlements, which seek for example to maximise work incentives, is tied to the logic of capitalist production. Eco-socialists and social ecologists seek an alternative role for social rights in facilitating more diverse, yet more sustainable patterns of human existence.

The common theme of these defensive critiques is a rejection of the generality of the centralised state and social rights based on prescription, and an insistence on the particularity of civil society and the importance of participation in need satisfaction.

Conclusion/summary

This chapter has considered several critiques of the ideological notion of welfare rights and of the practical consequences of social legislation. These critiques are diverse. The element which they seem to have in common is a recognition that social rights of citizenship must inevitably involve some propensity for social control. Where the critiques differ is in the reasons why they regard such a propensity to be problematic.

The neo-liberal objection is that rights involving the redistribution of income or property are corrupting. They are not rights at all; on the contrary, they are an infringement of real (i.e. property) rights or a distraction from properly enforceable (i.e. civil and political) human rights. The neo-Marxist objection is that social rights, in spite of the advantages they have brought the working class, are exploitative. They are a necessary component in the process by which labour-power is reproduced and articulated with the capitalist market system and they are a source of ideological mystification. The poststructuralist objection is that the extension of social rights is constituted as an extension of administrative state power, based on an increasingly sophisticated array of disciplinary techniques for the definition and control of individual subjects.

Feminist and anti-racist critics of social rights complain that women and black people are systematically excluded from social rights. Social rights function to the advantage of men and white society. There are also related defensive critiques whose concern is with the undemocratic nature of social rights and their capacity to impose conditions of social uniformity and/or to reinforce ecologically destructive behaviour.

Inevitably, this complex spectrum of arguments has been somewhat simplified, but the purpose of this chapter has been to demonstrate that social rights are controversial. In Chapter 10 I shall return to some of these controversies and shall attempt to argue that, for all their negative and controlling propensities, social rights are important and should be defended. First, however, it is important that the theoretical and often abstract approach adopted in Part I of this book should be grounded in some practical accounts of welfare rights and social legislation in a specific context, namely Britain. It is to this task that Part II now turns.

Recommended additional reading

Dean, H. (1991) *Social Security and Social Control*, Routledge, London, Chapters 2, 3 and 7.
George, V. and Wilding, P. (1994) *Welfare and Ideology*, Harvester Wheatsheaf, Hemel Hempstead, Chapters 2, 5, 6 and 7.
Williams, F. (1989) *Social Policy: A critical introduction*, Polity, Cambridge, Part II.

Questions for reflection

To what extent do neo-liberals and neo-Marxists, from their respective extremes of the ideological spectrum, share common assumptions about the nature and origins of rights? Does this help us understand what may be problematic about social rights?

Welfare rights are created through the legislative power of the state. Is it inevitable that such power will be used to control people's behaviour, or to the disadvantage of particular groups of people?

PART II

CHAPTER 5

RIGHTS AND SUBSISTENCE

The Universal Declaration of Human Rights speaks of a right to social security (UN 1948: Article 22) and, more particularly, a person's 'right to security in the event of unemployment, sickness, disability, widowhood, old age or other lack of livelihood in circumstances beyond his control' (*ibid.*: Article 25). In different parts of the world and at different moments in human history people have achieved social security by different means. Human subsistence may after all be sustained by more than one form of social organisation. Social security may be ensured through the simple exchange of goods and services, or by the organised distribution of benefits in kind or in cash. A defining feature of democratic-welfare-capitalism is that everyday subsistence is conditioned by a cash nexus. However, cash benefits can be organised in accordance with a variety of principles, not all of which provide the same degree of security. This chapter is concerned very specifically with what in Britain is called the social security system, though the rights which that system provides are in fact qualified rights to income maintenance. These are rights guaranteed by social legislation, but whether they provide social security will be left to the reader to judge.

Carried with any right to social security are conditions and duties. Social policy in the area of income maintenance is driven as much by the conditions and duties which it imposes on the recipients of cash benefits as by the rights which it creates. With or without a welfare state, the social organisation of human subsistence requires that individuals co-operate. Social guarantees of income maintenance are therefore based on particular normative assumptions about the way that individuals should behave. In democratic-welfare-capitalist societies this entails assumptions about individuals' liabilities to maintain themselves through paid employment and to maintain each other within families. As has been discussed in Chapter 4, social rights are inseparable from the enforcement of socially constructed duties.

This chapter is divided into five sections. The first outlines the structure of the British social security system not least because this will be necessary to aspects of Chapters 6 and 7. The second section considers the main subsistence benefit which that system provides, while the third discusses the ways in which the welfare state enforces the responsibilities of family membership. Finally, the fourth and fifth sections respectively will examine the rights of older people, and people with disabilities and their carers.

A hybrid system

The unusual complexity of British income maintenance arrangements reflects the fact that they constitute a hybrid system, combining elements of at least three different principles of social security: social assistance principles, social insurance principles and universal/contingency principles. What is more, as Titmuss remarked in his seminal essay *The Social Division of Welfare* (1958), such income maintenance arrangements coexist with parallel systems of fiscal and occupational welfare. The social security system has complex and changing interrelationships with the tax system and tax allowances on the one hand, and with occupational pension and benefits schemes and private insurance based schemes on the other. Not all these complexities can be satisfactorily encompassed within this chapter, but it is important to set the explanation which follows in the wider context illustrated in Table 5.1.

Social assistance

The modern British social security system has its origins in the

Table 5.1 The British income maintenance system

Social Security System		
Social assistance benefits (selective/means-tested)	**Social insurance benefits** (contributory)	**Universal/contingent benefits** (non-means-tested and non-contributory)
Income Support		Child Benefit (and One Parent Benefit)
Jobseeker's allowance (means-tested)	Jobseeker's allowance (contributory)	Severe Disablement Allowance
Means-tested 'in work' benefits (Family Credit and Disability Working Allowance)	Incapacity Benefit	Disability Living Allowance
	Basic retirement pension and SERPS	Attendance Allowance
Housing Benefit		Invalid Care Allowance
	Widow's Benefits	Industrial Injuries Scheme
		War Pensions Scheme

Social Fund (discretionary) (regulated)

Fiscal welfare (tax concessions)
Personal allowances
Mortgage interest tax relief
Pension fund tax exemptions

Occupational/private welfare (employer-provided or privately organised)	
Statutory	**Non-statutory**
Statutory sick pay	Occupational sick pay/health insurance
Statutory maternity pay	Occupational and personal pensions

Note:
1. This table illustrates the principal benefits by which personal income may be maintained in relation to the principles which inform their operation.

Elizabethan and Victorian Poor Laws (deSchweinitz 1961; George 1973; Novak 1988; H. Dean 1991: ch. 3). The underlying principle of relief under the Poor Law has provided the basis of what is now called social assistance. Poor relief was never a right. The local parish, the Poor Law Unions and the Public Assistance Committees which succeeded them were charged with responsibility for controlling vagrancy and relieving destitution. The means by which they did so was left in part to their discretion, though such discretion became subject increasingly to central government direction. Social assistance emerged from the Poor Law as a result of two developments: first, a gradual erosion of the infamous nineteenth-century workhouse test in favour of 'out-relief' (money payments to paupers in their own homes); and second, the development of systematic means testing (standardised methods of calculating relief by comparing people's subsistence needs with their assessed means).

Nationally administered means-tested benefit schemes were developed separately from the Poor Law for old people in 1908, and for uninsured able-bodied unemployed people in 1934. The final repeal of the Poor Law came in 1948 as part of the post-Second World War Beveridge reforms. Those reforms retained a nationally administered means-tested benefit called national assistance as a residual safety-net for those who might not be adequately provided for by new social insurance and universal benefit provisions (see below). In the event, national assistance became anything but residual and was itself reformed in 1966 to become supplementary benefit. The new benefit retained a means test, which was in principle no less selective than that which had applied before, but the legislation which introduced it contained a symbolic declaration that people who satisfied the means test conditions were entitled to their benefit as a 'right'. In 1988 the supplementary benefit scheme was in its turn reformed to become income support, the benefit that is arguably now the mainstay of the British social security system. At the end of the 1980s, one in six people in Britain were dependent in whole or in part on income support (SSC 1992a).

There are in addition to income support other benefits which function in accordance with social assistance principles; that is to say, which are selective or 'targeted' through the use of a means test. First, there are certain 'in work' benefits, namely family credit and disability working allowance, which may in certain circumstances be claimed by low-paid employees: these will be discussed in Chapter 6. Second, there are housing benefit and council tax benefit, local authority-administered benefits which may be claimed by people on low incomes in order to help meet their rent or council tax liabilities: these will be discussed in Chapter 7. The means test on which these other benefits are based has key elements in common with income support. Additionally, the calculation of entitlement to the means-tested element of jobseeker's allowance is substantially the same as for income support.

Recipients of means-tested benefits are also entitled in certain circumstances to make applications to the social fund. This fund was created in 1988, replacing provisions which had previously been made under the national insurance scheme (see below) for maternity and death grants, and under the supplementary benefits scheme for single payments or grants to meet exceptional need. The social fund has two distinct elements. The regulated social fund provides payments – subject to a maximum ceiling – towards maternity and funeral expenses for applicants who are in receipt of income support, family credit or disability working allowance, and cold weather payments to members of certain vulnerable groups who are in receipt of income support. The discretionary social fund is available only to income support claimants and provides community care grants (intended to assist people in leaving or avoiding institutional care), budgeting loans and crisis loans on a strictly rationed basis. While the regulated social fund represents a form of social assistance, the discretionary social fund sits in a sense outside the established principles of the social security system: first, because the nature, extent and urgency of need is determined by officials on an entirely discretionary basis; second, because the scheme is budget-limited and officials must prioritise applications in accordance with available resources; and third, because much of the expenditure is made by way of loans, which applicants must repay through deductions from their income support entitlements (for a fuller discussion see, for example, Craig 1992).

Finally, the recipients of social assistance may also be entitled to a range of incidental benefits in kind. Income support recipients are entitled to free school meals for their children. Recipients of income support and family credit are exempt from certain health service charges, including charges for prescriptions, dental treatment and spectacles (which, subject to a means test, other people on low incomes may also obtain free or at reduced cost).

Social insurance

Social insurance may be remembered as one of the big ideas of the twentieth century. The concept has exerted considerable influence over social policy (Gilbert 1966; Peden 1991), yet in Britain in the 1990s it has been partly eclipsed, leaving behind within the social security system some obsolete and arcane administrative features.

The principle of social insurance is that all workers compulsorily contribute to a national insurance fund and, in the event of sickness, unemployment or retirement, they are entitled to claim on that fund. The attraction of such a scheme in a democratic-welfare-capitalist society is obvious. It creates social rights based on a collective sharing of risks, but it does so without undermining the free play of market forces or the responsibility of individuals to provide for themselves. In so far as insurance-based social security benefits give to their recipients a sense of entitlement, it has been a popular concept. Unfortunately, however, the practical and political difficulties of maintaining a national insurance fund in accordance with actuarial conventions have never been surmounted and the popular credibility of the concept has progressively been undermined by fears about its alleged unsustainability. Unfortunately too, social insurance schemes protect workers as employees, not as citizens. Social rights based on insurance principles are enjoyed by those who 'earn' their entitlements in the labour market, while citizens who have been excluded from the labour market can benefit only as dependants of those who have contributed or, alternatively, if the insurance principle is broadened (some might say compromised) so as to admit those who are excluded by giving them 'credits' or notional contributions. In particular, as will be discussed below, social insurance has systematically disadvantaged women.

The first National Insurance Act of 1911 provided limited unemployment and sickness insurance, schemes which all but collapsed during the 1920s and 1930s. The National Insurance Act 1946, however, represented the centrepiece of what Beveridge had intended should be a comprehensive social security system. The

1946 Act provided that all workers should pay a flat-rate weekly contribution in return for which there would be an entitlement to flat-rate weekly benefits, pensions or grants covering sickness, invalidity, unemployment, maternity, widowhood, retirement or death. It was believed that – together with family allowances (see below) and free health care – such a scheme would supersede the need for stigmatising forms of social assistance. In the event, successive governments failed to underwrite national insurance at a level which would have made this possible.

In the course of the 1960s and 1970s the flat-rate principle was abandoned in favour of graduated national insurance contributions and earnings-related benefits and pensions. In this way, it was hoped, benefit and pension levels for the majority could be raised above poverty levels. In the 1980s, however, a radical Conservative administration effected a number of changes which have relegated social insurance as a principle to the sidelines. Earnings-related additions to short-term benefits were abolished and the value of pension additions under the state earnings-related pension scheme (SERPS) were halved. The convention by which basic pensions were uprated annually in line with general earnings was also abandoned, so as to link pensions to price inflation only, the effect of which will be to render the value of retirement pensions in the twenty-first century 'nugatory' (Portillo 1993). Certain short-term national insurance benefits – sickness benefit and maternity allowance – were largely 'privatised' through the introduction of statutory sick pay and statutory maternity pay (see Chapter 6). The widow's benefit scheme was 'streamlined' by substituting lump-sum payments for pensions for younger widows. In the 1990s, incapacity benefit and jobseeker's allowance have been introduced: the former replaced the sickness and invalidity benefit schemes and reduced their scope through the application of stricter medical tests; the latter merged the administration of contributory unemployment benefit with that of means-tested income support.

What remains of social insurance is not inconsiderable. The cost of basic retirement pensions remains the biggest single charge on the social security budget. None the less, the application of the insurance principle has been effectively hobbled. It is no longer supposed that basic retirement pensions, widows' benefits and the incapacity benefit scheme should provide adequate replacement incomes. Benefits like maternity allowance (which may still be claimed by a small number of women who have paid national insurance contributions but are not currently employed) and a range of abolished benefits to which contributors may still be entitled until they are phased out remain as an anomaly.

At the core of any social or national insurance scheme lies the contributory principle: the idea that people must pay something in before they can get anything out. If social insurance is to survive as a credible component of the British social security system, it will be necessary to modify the contributory principle so as to recognise more fully the various kinds of non-monetary and social contributions which citizens may make to national well-being. Such ideas are advanced, for example, by the Commission on Social Justice and will be discussed in Chapter 10. In the meantime, the contribution rules are arcane. Detailed accounts are provided elsewhere (for example, Poynter and Martin 1994: ch. 12) and what follows is a bare outline. Members of the national insurance scheme may establish a contribution record in the following ways:

- Employees contribute a percentage of their earnings (subject to a lower and an upper limit) and their employers are separately liable to pay a percentage of each employee's earnings (subject to the same lower, but no upper limit). Employees and employers pay reduced contributions if the employee has contracted out of SERPS (the state earnings-related pension scheme).
- Self-employed persons, provided their incomes exceed a certain minimum, pay a flat-rate contribution and they must additionally pay a percentage of any profits falling within set limits.
- People who are non-employed may make voluntary contributions at a flat rate, though these give rise to limited entitlements.
- People who are registered as 'job-seekers' (i.e. as unemployed), who receive incapacity benefit or invalid care allowance or who are on approved training courses receive 'credits' towards their national insurance records.
- Since 1977 limited forms of 'starting credits' have been available for young people staying on at school after the minimum school leaving age.
- Since 1978 a form of home responsibilities protection or credit has been available for people who have spent periods looking after dependent children or adult invalids.

To receive benefits, contributors (or, in certain circumstances, their spouses) must have paid and/or been credited with contributions to a specified level for a requisite period of years. The rules for each benefit are different, but for all benefits there is a requirement that certain of the contributions giving rise to an entitlement shall have been actually paid, rather than merely credited.

Universal/contingency benefits

The principle underlying universal benefits comes closest to a pure form of a social right. Universal benefits are payable to citizens without a means test and without contribution conditions, but subject in practice to a particular contingency, such as parenthood or disability.

The first universal benefit in Britain was family allowance. The family allowance scheme was introduced in 1948, though it was further developed in 1978 through the effective incorporation of child tax allowances so as to produce the child benefit scheme, which provides a weekly non-taxable benefit, payable to parents (almost invariably mothers), for each co-resident dependent child. When family allowance was first introduced it was not payable for a first child, only for second and subsequent children. Child benefit has always been payable in respect of each child up until s/he leaves school or until the age of 19 if s/he remains at school or in full-time further (not higher) education (or more recently until the age of 18 if s/he is registered unemployed but not receiving benefits). Since 1991 child benefit has been payable at a higher rate for the first child in a family than for second or subsequent children.

The level at which family allowance and subsequently child benefit was paid was never intended to be sufficient to meet the actual subsistence needs of a child. It symbolised none the less a contribution by the state on behalf of the wider community towards the costs of bringing up children and to the needs of the next generation. It was also regarded as a key component of the 'social wage'; that parcel of state benefits which can function to reduce the extent to which 'real' wages must include provision for workers' families (Land 1975; 1992). Universal child benefit is often ridiculed because it is paid to all parents, even the most affluent (Boyson 1971; Dilnot *et al.* 1984). From 1987 to 1991 the value of child benefit was frozen, on the explicit premiss that resources should be diverted from inefficient and expensive universal provision to means-tested benefits such as family credit which is 'targeted' on the families which most need help (DHSS 1985). The fact that the government subsequently relented and resumed the annual up-rating of child benefit is a reflection of pressures exerted partly by the sheer logistics of (by Western standards) a relatively low-wage economy (H. Dean 1993), and partly by the considerable measure of popular support which child benefit enjoys (Walker *et al.* 1994). It remains possible, however, that child benefit may yet become means-tested and/or taxable.

Also administered with child benefit is guardian's allowance (which is payable on a similar basis to people looking after children who are effectively orphans) and one parent benefit. One parent benefit, which was introduced in 1978, is a small addition paid with child benefit to lone parents, and represented a partial and belated concession to the Finer Committee's (1974) recommendations for a 'guaranteed maintenance allowance'.

Universal provision within the Beveridgian social security system was comparatively limited in scope precisely because the system was primarily informed by social insurance and not universalist principles. However, a non-contributory industrial injuries scheme was also incorporated into social security to provide benefits and pensions for people who were injured and/or disabled in the course of their employment, whether as a result of an accident or an industrial disease. The scheme replaced the provisions of the Workmen's Compensation Act 1897, under which injured employ-ees were obliged to seek compensation from their privately insured employers. The original scheme of 1946 established an industrial injuries fund, separate from the national insurance fund, on which injured employees could claim, although this was abolished in 1973 as administration of the scheme was progressively absorbed into the mainstream of the social security system (Ogus and Barendt 1988: 250–3). The main benefit under the scheme is disablement benefit, the amount of which is determined on a tariff basis in accordance with the extent of disablement incurred. Disablement benefit may be supplemented with various allowances, including constant attendance allowance and exceptionally severe disablement allowance, though other allowances (such as unemployability supplement and reduced earnings allowance) were abolished in the

1980s or are being phased out. The scope of the scheme has lately been eroded in other ways. The benefits originally provided included a short-term injury benefit and an industrial death benefit: the former has now been incorporated into statutory sick pay and incapacity benefit provisions and the latter into the widow's benefit scheme. What remains of the scheme is universal to the extent that it is neither means-tested nor contributory, but it remains strictly contingent on accidental injury or the onset of a prescribed industrial disease. A very similar war pensions scheme survives to provide benefits and pensions for service personnel and others disabled in the course of war or armed conflicts.

In the post-Second World War social security system, therefore, universal provision was made for children until such time as they could become social insurance contributors (and/or – in the case of females – until they could obtain dependence on a social insurance contributor through marriage) and for people whose capacity as a social insurance contributor was impaired through disablement in the course of their employment or in war. No provision was made for people who might never become (or might never marry) a social insurance contributor. People who were disabled from birth or since childhood, people with severe learning difficulties, and people who provided full-time care for dependent adult relatives, might never obtain membership of the national insurance scheme. For these people, the only provision that existed was through means-tested benefits. From the 1970s onwards, to remedy this omission, a range of new benefits was developed for disabled people and carers and these will be described later in this chapter. The benefits in question are universal, though all are once again strictly contingent on disability as defined by medical tests and criteria.

Security through means testing?

Depending on one's view, means-tested social assistance benefits represent either the 'safety-net' of the social security system, or its most efficient component. This section will outline the workings of income support, the main British social assistance benefit. (Note: unless otherwise stated, references to income support may be taken to apply also to the means-tested element of the jobseeker's allowance.) The object of a means-tested benefit is to guarantee a minimum standard of subsistence. In practice, however, income support guarantees different standards for different groups of people and excludes some groups from any right to subsistence.

The details and even the terminology used in connection with social assistance schemes are subject to continual revision by governments. However, at the heart of any means test lies a comparison between a claimant's needs and her/his means – a calculation which in its simplest form 'tops up' a person's means to meet her/his needs (see Figure 5.1). Translating this principle into practice requires elaborate processes of definition (for a full account see, for example, Webster *et al.* 1994).

Under income support, a person's needs are determined with reference to an 'applicable amount'; the weekly amount of money which is deemed under the legislation to be needed for a person and her/his family to live on. The applicable amount has up to three components:

● A personal allowance, which varies according to the claimant's age, whether s/he resides with a partner, and the number and ages of any children in her/his family. The monetary value of personal allowances derive from scales which are reviewed annually but which owe their origin to research on budget standards conducted in the 1930s (Rowntree 1937). Since these scales were first applied in 1948, they 'have been uprated on the basis of historical precedent, opportunism and political hunch' (Bradshaw 1993b: xiii). The basic personal allowance for a single person aged 25 or over currently stands at rather less than one seventh of average male earnings, while provision made through personal allowances for a child under 11 in a two-adult, two-child family claiming income support stands at around three-fifths of the weekly sum which recent research indicates to be required

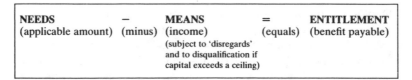

Figure 5.1 'Top-up' means test calculation.

to maintain such a child even on a 'low-cost' budget (Bradshaw 1993a; Oldfield and Yu 1993).

● A premium which will apply only if the claimant (and/or a member of her/his family) is a member of a particular 'client group'. The client groups which attract premiums are families with dependent children; people who are caring full-time for an invalid; people who are disabled and in receipt of other 'qualifying' benefits; and pensioners. Higher-level premiums apply if the claimant's family is a lone-parent family, or if it includes a disabled child; if a severely disabled claimant or family member has no one to look after them; for pensioners who are above certain ages and/or who are also disabled. The rules which govern eligibility for premiums are often complex, and in the case of disability-related premiums often depend on a claimant or family member's eligibility for some other qualifying benefit.

● Housing costs, but only in instances where these are not met by housing benefit. Generally, this will apply to the cost of mortgage interest payments faced by home owners. This is discussed in more detail in Chapter 7.

For income support purposes a person's means are assessed with reference to her/his income (including income from other social security benefits) and her/his savings or capital. Certain income may be disregarded in whole or in part, although these 'disregards' are limited. The disregards which apply in the case of income from child maintenance or disability benefits are discussed later in this chapter, while those which apply to income from earnings are discussed in Chapter 6. Certain savings or capital may also be disregarded, though generally this will only apply to the value of the claimant's own home. Unless it is disregarded, the possession of savings or capital which exceed a certain modest value will disqualify the holder from income support. The calculation of a claimant's means requires the claimant to disclose exhaustive details, not only of her/his own personal resources, but also (as will shortly be seen) of any person(s) who are deemed to be members of her/his 'family'.

The complex form of this means test is such that it privileges certain groups in the population at the expense of others. This results partly from the effect of premiums. The highest premium (severe disability premium) is currently almost as much again as the appropriate personal allowance, but this applies only in the most rare and extreme circumstances. The premium applicable to an ordinary pensioner couple is a little more than a third of their personal allowance, while that of a working-age couple with two children aged under 11 is only about a tenth. In relative terms, pensioners are more generously treated than adults of working age and families with children. It must none the less be borne in mind that, at the time of writing, a pensioner couple's basic contributory retirement pension is around 7 per cent less than their applicable amount for income support purposes: for pensioners without any other source of income, it is social assistance levels which effectively determine their maximum standard of subsistence.

Under income support, young people fare even worse than other working-age adults. The personal allowance for people aged 18–24 (unless they are lone parents) is around one fifth less than that for those aged 25 or over. Personal allowances for 16 and 17 year olds are even lower, but most 16 and 17 year olds in fact have no entitlement to income support at all: they represent just one of a number of groups who are subject to special rules or who are excluded from entitlement altogether. The social security system at present assumes that people aged 16 and 17, if they are not in employment, should be in full-time education or training and usually it is only if they are lone parents, if they are sick or disabled, or if exceptionally they might otherwise suffer hardship that they may claim.

In general, no one may receive income support if they or their partner are in full-time employment (currently defined as employment of more than 16 hours per week). People who are employed for more than 16 hours per week may be entitled to other means-tested benefits (calculated none the less on a similar basis to income support). People who are employed but are on strike or locked out as a result of a trade dispute may claim income support, but subject only to special rules. People who are unemployed must claim means-tested jobseeker's allowance rather than income support which, although it is in other respects identical with income support, is subject to additional conditions concerning the claimant's jobseeking and availability or work (including, for example, rules which exclude students from claiming benefits, and special provisions for people on government training schemes). All these matters will be discussed in Chapter 6. Otherwise, the only people who may claim income support without being subject to such conditions are those who satisfy the incapacity for work test (also discussed in Chapter 6) or who are mentally or physically disabled, and those who are over 60 years of age or who are lone parents. Special rules apply to income support claimants who are resident in residential care or nursing homes, to people going in or coming out of hospital or prison and to people with no settled accommodation.

Special rules also apply to 'persons from abroad'. These rules are especially significant because of the wider implications they have for social citizenship. In this regard, entitlement to income support (and related means-tested benefits) is subject to three tests. The first, the immigration status test, excludes from benefit anyone who under immigration law has entered or remains in the UK illegally or subject to a condition that they shall have no recourse to public funds. The second, the residence directives test, relates to nationals from European Economic Area states, and excludes them from benefit unless they are economically active, so excluding students, retired people and lone parents, but giving certain rights to workseekers (who may none the less be directed to leave the UK after 6 months). The third, the habitual residence test, was introduced in 1994 to prevent alleged 'benefit tourism' (Lilley 1993) and denies benefits even to EU and returning UK nationals if they cannot establish that they are habitually resident: the test may take account of a claimant's past residence, employment and family ties, but also their future intentions and prospects. Those who fail the above tests may in certain limited circumstances be able to claim reduced benefits, for example, pending the outcome of immigration appeals or applications for asylum. The scope for discriminatory application is self-evident. One particular effect is to implicate the social security system in the application of immigration policies which are inherently racist (Amin and Oppenheim 1992). What is more, the additional checks entailed in administering such tests engender a climate of suspicion and uncertainty which deters many claimants from ethnic minorities from claiming benefits to which they are legally entitled (see NACAB 1991). There are in fact various kinds of more basic 'residence test' attaching to all social security benefits.

Enforcing family responsibilities

Earlier in this chapter it was remarked that social security provision rests on assumptions about people's liabilities to maintain each other within families. This has consequences for the mutual interdependence of adults, as well as for the basis on which financial support for children may be secured. This section will first consider the particular significance of social insurance and social assistance regimes for women, before turning to the issue of child support.

The Beveridgian model of social security assumed that married women would (and should) by and large be dependent on their husbands. The nature of a social insurance-based system of social security is such as to make entitlement conditional on labour market ties in a context in which labour markets systematically disadvantage women. This continues to be the case in spite of the introduction of equal opportunities provisions within employment law and equal treatment provisions within social security law (Glendinning and Millar 1992). Female labour force participation has risen dramatically and continues to do so, yet women tend to remain in less well paid, less secure employment and remain less likely than men to establish national insurance records which will entitle them independently to benefits and pensions. Feminists argue that this reflects more than a failure of the labour market; it is also a failure of the social security system to redress the unequal burden of unpaid caring and domestic work which women carry in their families (see discussion in Chapter 4).

With social insurance benefits, assumptions about family dependence are implicit, but with social assistance benefits they become quite explicit. Contribution tests are applied on the basis of an individual worker's insurance record; means tests, on the other hand, are applied directly to households or families. In the jargon of the old supplementary benefit scheme, a claimant and the members of her/his immediate household were referred to as a 'unit of assessment'. The income support scheme uses the cosier term 'family'. The assumption, none the less, is that the needs and means of a cohabiting man and woman and any children for whom they are responsible should be shared or 'aggregated'. The computation of 'applicable amounts' and of income resources extends so as to include a claimant's 'partner' and child dependants. In so doing mean-tested schemes pay no regard to the dynamics of family relationships and the ways in which these are in practice negotiated (see Finch and Mason 1993). Instead, such schemes impose their own rules and definitions.

For social assistance purposes the rule is that people must claim as a 'couple' and will be treated as 'partners' if they are married and living in the same household, or if they are not married but 'living together as husband and wife'. This, the so-called 'cohabitation rule', has several implications and effects:

- It assumes the normality of heterosexual relationships and marriage. The relationships of gay and lesbian couples are not recognised and stable heterosexual relationships are characterised in terms of their semblance to marriage.
- It compels men and women who share a household and have a stable relationship to be financially interdependent whether or not they may choose to be so.
- It seriously prejudices the position of a non-claiming partner in situations where 'family' resources are not equitably shared in practice.
- It excludes from benefit anybody whose partner's resources are adjudged sufficient for her/his 'family' as a whole, so depriving that person of any independence s/he may have previously enjoyed.
- Because the applicable amount for a couple is less than that for two independent adults, it reduces the income potentially available to the 'family' as a whole.

It is women rather than men who are most likely to be disadvantaged. So far as women in two-parent families are concerned, they are likely to exercise less control over 'family' income than men (Pahl 1989), yet it is usually they who must bear the burdens of daily household management and the brunt of the sacrifices entailed in doing so on a low income (Bradshaw and Holmes 1989). Additionally, aggregated means-tested entitlements stand to be reduced on account of any part-time earnings belonging to a claimant's partner, which may outweigh the advantage of the partner continuing in such employment: it is characteristically women in families on benefit who are obliged to surrender the independence which part-time work may have given them (McLaughlin *et al.* 1989). So far as lone parents are concerned, 90 per cent of whom are women (Burghes 1993), the existence of a cohabitation rule subjects them to a degree of surveillance, whether actual or implied. Elements of the rule also apply to the receipt of contributory widow's benefits and non-contributory one-parent benefit. Lone parents lose their particular independent entitlement to benefit if they should take a 'partner'.

Over and above the aggregation of needs and means within families for the purposes of social assistance, social security law also imposes a specific duty to maintain one's spouse and/or children so long as income support is being paid for them. This applies regardless of whether one lives with one's spouse or children, though it ceases to apply following divorce and/or when children reach the age of 16 (or in some circumstances 19). A similar provision applies in the case of anyone who under immigration law is a 'sponsor' of a 'person from abroad' who may have had recourse to income support. The government has power to pursue 'liable relatives' for the recovery of benefits paid for their legal dependants and to enforce or seek court orders for periodic maintenance. In the case of maintenance for children, such powers were enlarged and passed in 1993 to the Child Support Agency (CSA). Powers in respect of maintenance for spouses and sponsored immigrants remain with the Social Security Benefits Agency.

The most significant and widely used powers are those which now vest in the CSA. The assumption which underlies the child support scheme is that biological parents have an inviolable duty to support their children financially, regardless of any changes or breakdown in family or living arrangements. The scheme provides a formula by which to calculate the liability of 'absent parents' (mainly fathers) for the maintenance of dependent children with whom they do not co-reside and machinery by which to enforce the payments of such maintenance to the 'parents with care' (mainly mothers) of the children concerned. The scheme is therefore concerned to guarantee the subsistence needs of children, but it seeks to do so by defining rights for parents with care. What it creates, however, are not strictly social rights, but personal rights which are mediated by the state. The CSA assumed powers as to the making of maintenance orders which had previously been vested in the courts and which had for the most part been exercised only in the course of legal proceedings between private individuals. The intention had been generally to increase the level and consistency of maintenance payments by absent parents (DSS 1990), but specifically thereby to diminish the cost of social assistance benefits for lone parents (see Garnham and Knights 1994b).

Because child support payments count as income for the purposes of means-tested benefit entitlement, the effect is to substitute a private entitlement for a social entitlement. The way in which child support payments count as income is significant in so far as the amount of child support that is 'disregarded', though small, is higher for parents with care who are receiving family credit (and are therefore in full-time employment – see Chapter 6) than it is for parents with care who receive income support. At the time of writing, parents with care have child support payments counted in full for income support purposes, but from 1997, it is proposed, they will be entitled notionally to a weekly 'disregard' (lower than that to which family credit claimants are entitled) which, though it will be withheld from benefit, will be 'rolled up' as an accumulating credit which may be paid to the claimant in a lump sum if and when the parent enters or returns to full-time employment (DSS 1995). The explicit intention is to provide incentives for lone parents to obtain full-time employment.

While some parents with care of a qualifying child under the child support scheme may choose whether to avail themselves of the CSA's services, any such parents who receive income support, family credit or disabled working allowance have no choice. They are required to make an application for child support and, unless they can show 'good cause', they are subject to a 'benefit penalty' (a temporary reduction in benefit entitlement) for failing to co-operate.

The child support formula is itself byzantinely complex (for a full account see, for example, Garnham and Knights 1994a). In essence the formula compares the maintenance requirements of the child(ren) concerned with the assessable income of their absent parent (characteristically, their natural father). The child(ren)'s requirements and the amount of the absent parent's income that is exempt from assessment are each based on prevailing income support personal allowance scales. Controversially, the child(ren)'s maintenance requirement also includes an allowance explicitly for the parent with care, while the absent parent's exempt income does not include provision for the maintenance (other than housing costs) of any 'second family' for which he may be responsible. Absent parents must pay at least half their assessable income towards meeting the qualifying child(ren)'s maintenance requirement, but this liability can be reduced if it would reduce any second family's income below a protected level. Absent parents' liabilities can be increased (subject to upper limits) above the level of the basic maintenance requirement of the qualifying child(ren) if the absent parent's assessable income is more than twice the basic requirement. Changes to the operation of the scheme introduced in 1995 were intended to ensure that no absent parent should pay more than 30 per cent of his overall income (net of taxes) in child maintenance and to provide that account be taken of the value of contributions which parents may have previously made by transferring property to the parent with care.

At the time of writing, legislation is proposed to permit discretionary variations in the application of the child support formula (DSS 1995). Provision exists for the CSA not only to assess an absent parent's liability to child support, but also to collect payments on behalf of parents with care.

Security in old age

Old age is relative. In the mid-nineteenth century average life expectancy in England was around 40 for men and 42 for women. In the late twentieth century, it is 72 for men and 78 for women (Nissel 1987). Retirement in old age, however, is a recent phenomenon. The proportion of men aged 65 or more who were retired from the labour force increased from around a half in the 1930s to well over 90 per cent in the 1980s (Walker 1987). Townsend has argued that, as longevity increases and labour markets tighten, retirement is 'a kind of mass redundancy' (1991: 6). While social security in 'old age' may be a fundamental human right, most people over the age of 65 are not yet frail or physically dependent. The socially manufactured expectation of retirement represents a form of 'structured dependency' (*ibid.*).

Pensionable age in Britain was set in 1946 at 60 for women and 65 for men (although, in order to equalise pensionable ages, between 2010 and 2020 there will now be a phased increase in the pensionable age for women from 60 to 65). Prior to 1989, social security law also specified a 'retirement age' (65 for women and 70 for men) and between pensionable age and retirement age people were obliged to retire in order to receive a state pension. More recently, retirement has not been a condition of entitlement for the basic state pension and any earnings which a pensioner continues to receive will not affect her/his pension, though retirement pension is itself taxable. None the less, the basic contributory pension is still called a retirement pension. Its value, as has been remarked above, by itself is barely sufficient to provide subsistence by contemporary standards. Nor, save for an age addition of literally a few pence per week for people over 80, does the value increase as people become older, when they are in fact more likely to be frail and vulnerable (Henwood and Wicks 1984). Though retirement pension is received by the vast majority of people of pensionable age, for most it is supplemented by other state benefits (SERPS, disability benefits and/or means-tested benefits), or by occupational or private pensions.

To qualify for basic retirement pension, a claimant or her/his late spouse must in the course of a year at some time have actually paid the equivalent of a year's worth of minimum level national insurance contributions (i.e. a sum equivalent to the national insurance 'lower earnings limit') and s/he must have paid or been credited with a year's worth of minimum level contributions for a 'requisite number' of years in the course her/his 'working life'. There are limited circumstances in which divorced people can rely on a part of an ex-spouse's contribution record. Additionally, the requisite number of years' contributions can be reduced by the home responsibility protection provisions, but only up to a certain limit. The system is such as to disadvantage women and indeed anyone with a discontinuous employment record or who has worked in part-time employment at wages beneath the national insurance minimum (below which no contributions are paid). It is possible for people to defer their claim for retirement pension for up to five years after reaching pensionable age and so earn a slightly increased pension. As with most contributory benefits, increases in pension are payable for dependants. Married women who do not qualify for a pension on the basis of their own contributions may claim a reduced pension (at 60 per cent of the basic rate) provided both she and her husband are of pensionable age and her husband is in receipt of a basic pension, and this entitlement substitutes for a husband's entitlement to an increase for his wife as a dependant.

For pensioners aged 80 or more who do not qualify for a basic pension, there is a non-contributory pension (paid at 60 per cent of the basic rate).

In addition to the basic retirement pension, pensioners may also receive a small amount of 'graduated retirement benefit' (based on contributions paid under a scheme which was in place between 1961 and 1975) and, if they have not been 'contracted out', an additional pension under SERPS. When SERPS was introduced in 1978 it was intended that, when the scheme had been in operation for a full twenty years, contributors should expect to retire with an additional pension equivalent to one quarter of the average earnings they had enjoyed during the twenty best earning years of their lives (revalued for inflation). Under the Social Security Act 1986 this provision was reduced so that pensioners in the scheme who retire in or after 1999 may now expect an additional pension of only one fifth of their revalued average earnings, calculated over the whole of their working life. Widows and widowers of pensionable age may 'inherit' one half of their late spouse's additional pension entitlement (though the original SERPS would have allowed them all of it). Up to 1999, interim rules apply for the computation of additional pensions based on SERPS contributions.

Many pensioners, however, will not have contributed to SERPS, but will have contributed instead, either to an occupational pension scheme operated by their employer, or to a private scheme operated by an insurance or investment company. The funds operated by such schemes benefit from substantial tax exemptions on income and capital gains. In order to be able to contract out of SERPS, it is necessary that the schemes to which workers contribute should be recognised by the Occupational Pensions Board, though in practice the degree of regulation which is exercised over pension providers is minimal (SSC 1992b). Prior to 1988, occupational schemes had to offer a guaranteed minimum pension on terms comparable to SERPS, but this requirement was removed in order make way for new kinds of non-state pension based not on a pensioner's earnings at or prior to retirement, but on money purchase principles. New forms of contracted-out occupational money purchase schemes and appropriate personal pension plans were facilitated by legislation and promoted by way of government rebates or incentive payments to the new pension schemes equivalent to 2 per cent of contracted-out employees' earnings. The eventual proceeds of money purchase schemes provide an annuity on retirement, though the value of this will be determined by the performance of investment markets and will not be guaranteed or index-linked in the way that conventional 'final salary'-based occupational schemes are. (A fuller discussion of pension provision is available elsewhere – see, for example, Ward 1990.) It should be emphasised, however, that rights to occupational and 'personal' pensions are individually-based rather than social rights and, although they are governed to an extent by social legislation, they do not purport to guarantee social security.

The spread of occupational pension provision in particular has undoubtedly done much to alleviate poverty in old age but, just as social insurance disadvantages women in particular, so do occupational schemes. Access to better quality schemes is often denied to women because of the hours, the grade or the type of the jobs which they characteristically fill. As Dulcie Groves has argued:

> neither a reformed employers' pension system, nor the new personal pension arrangements, are likely to guarantee an adequate income in old age for anyone (male or female) with a discontinuous employment record and/or a history of multiple job changes. (1992: 205)

As a consequence, substantial numbers of pensioners are also dependent on means-tested benefit provision.

The rights of disabled people and carers

Excepting the specific case of industrial injuries benefits and war pensions, social rights that are directed to the special subsistence needs of disabled people have lagged behind the development of other rights. Benefits that are dependent on a test of incapacity for work (which includes severe disablement allowance) or that assist disabled people who are able to work (namely, disability working allowance) will be considered in the next chapter. This section will describe a clutch of benefits which were first introduced in the 1970s in order to supplement benefit provision for severely disabled people. The benefits originally introduced were called attendance allowance and mobility allowance. These were reformed in the

1990s and, although attendance allowance still exists for people aged 65 and over, a benefit called disability living allowance has incorporated mobility allowance and provision for the attendance or 'care' needs of younger disabled people.

Disability living allowance and attendance allowance are both non-contributory, non-means-tested benefits, which are not taxable and which may be paid in addition to means-tested benefits (except under special rules applying to claimants living in hospitals and local authority homes, and claimants living in residential care and nursing homes where this has been arranged by a local authority). The fact that these benefits are not deducted or set off against other benefits reflects the intention that they should meet the additional costs which disabled people may incur. They are subject, however, to stringent eligibility rules.

Disability living allowance has two separately assessed components: the care component and the mobility component. The care component is payable at three different rates: the highest rate is equivalent to around 80 per cent of the basic retirement pension for a single person, the middle rate to around 60 per cent, and the lowest rate to around 20 per cent. The mobility component is payable at two rates: the higher rate is equivalent to around 55 per cent of the basic retirement pension for a single person and the lower rate is the same as the lowest rate for the care component.

The care component may be claimed by or on behalf of people from birth to the age of 65, provided they have met the relevant 'disability conditions' for three months (unless they are diagnosed to be terminally ill) and are likely to do so for at least a further six months. The disability conditions establish the three levels of disability appropriate to the three rates at which the care component is payable. The conditions define circumstances in which a person is so severely disabled physically or mentally that s/he requires attention in connection with her/his bodily functions or supervision to prevent substantial danger to her/himself or others. If the attention required is frequent and/or the supervision required is continual and it is required both day and night, or if the claimant is terminally ill, s/he will qualify for the highest rate of benefit. If such attention or supervision is required throughout either the day or night, or if in certain circumstances the claimant is a home renal dialysis patient, s/he will qualify for the middle rate of benefit. If the attention required is 'limited' being required for only a period or periods within the course of the day, or if the claimant (provided s/he is aged 16 or over) is unable to prepare a cooked main meal for her/himself, s/he will qualify for the lowest rate of benefit. The scope for dispute regarding the interpretation of conditions such as these is considerable. The bodily functions to which the attention condition relates include such things as going to the lavatory, getting in or out of bed, getting dressed or undressed. The supervision condition extends to include supervision that is merely precautionary such as might be required by a person who suffers from fits, or who is liable to behave violently or unpredictably.

The mobility component of disability living allowance may be claimed by people aged between 5 and 65, provided they have met the relevant disability conditions for at least three months, they are likely to continue to do so for a further six months, and provided they would benefit from enhanced mobility (which might not apply if they are in a coma or cannot safely be moved). To qualify for the higher rate mobility component a claimant must be unable or virtually unable to walk as a result of a physical disability; or be both blind and deaf, or have no feet; or be severely mentally impaired and suffering from severe behavioural problems such that s/he already qualifies for the highest rate care component. To qualify for the lower rate mobility component a claimant, though s/he can walk, must be so severely disabled, physically or mentally, that s/he cannot usually walk outdoors without guidance or supervision.

Attendance allowance is administered in the same way as the care component of disability living allowance, save that it is claimed by people over 65 and with the important difference that it is not available at the lowest rate.

The introduction of the original attendance allowance scheme in 1971 involved a recognition of the care needs of severely disabled people but it was not until 1976 that a benefit expressly for the carers of disabled people was introduced. Invalid care allowance, which is paid at 60 per cent of the level of the basic single person's retirement pension, is a non-contributory, non-means-tested benefit. It is in this sense a universal benefit, unlike disablement living allowance and attendance allowance, but invalid care allowance is taxable and it is taken fully into account for the purposes of means-tested benefit entitlements. The level of subsistence achieved by many carers, therefore, is determined not by invalid care allowance, but by income support (within which provision is made for a carer's premium, the additional value of which stands at just over a quarter of a single adult's weekly personal allowance). In spite of this, invalid care allowance does represent a symbolic recognition of carers as citizens and is valued by those who receive it (McLaughlin 1991). However, when first introduced, the allowance was not made available to women caring for a spouse or male partner, on the assumption that such women would have been available to care in any event. The legality of this discriminatory provision was successfully challenged in the European Court (see Chapter 8). The allowance is now available to anybody providing regular and substantial care for a person who is in receipt of disability living allowance at the highest and middle rates or attendance allowance (or the constant attendance allowances available under the industrial injuries and war pensions schemes). The allowance is not available to people under the age of 16 or over pensionable age, though carers who were receiving the allowance immediately before reaching pensionable age may continue to do so afterwards. The fact that invalid care allowance is not available on fresh claims by pensioners reflects the intention that the benefit is supposed to replace lost earnings. Claimants must demonstrate that they are not gainfully employed and that they are not in full-time education.

Finally, though such assistance is of a discretionary nature and does not represent a social right, severely disabled people may also seek assistance from the government-financed Independent Living (1993) Fund. This fund replaced an earlier fund which had been withdrawn in 1992. The new Independent Living Fund, which is more restrictive than that which it replaced, receives applications from people aged 16 to 65 who are already receiving the highest rate care component of disability living allowance and who either live alone or with someone who cannot help. The fund provides weekly cash payments for the purchase of services to enable applicants to be cared for in their own homes, but subject to a social work assessment and to financial contributions towards such services both by the relevant local authority social services department and by the applicant. The fund is budget-limited and must prioritise demands on its resources.

Conclusion/summary

Any concept of social rights will include a right to the means of subsistence. In advanced capitalist societies this requires the provision of cash benefits. This chapter has discussed the British system of cash benefits, or social security system. The system is peculiarly complex because it employs three different principles of provision. First, the social assistance principle provides for benefits on demonstration of need by means testing. Second, the social insurance principle provides for benefits on the payment of contributions from earnings and in the event of a particular contingency. Third, the universal principle provides for benefits, with neither means tests nor contribution conditions, but as a response to some generally defined contingency.

Though elements of social insurance and universal provision remain important, it is the social assistance principle that has attained particular ascendancy in late twentieth-century Britain. The centrepiece of the social security system is a means-tested benefit, income support, the rules of which also inform means-tested provision for unemployed people, for some who are employed on low wages and for some who cannot meet their housing costs. The essence of a means test is a calculation of the shortfall between a citizen's needs and her/his means. Under income support the needs of different groups are assessed differently and the needs and means of individuals are 'aggregated' with those of their families.

A universal child benefit is payable to all parents as a partial contribution towards the cost of bringing up children. None the less, families are assumed by policy-makers to have a role in providing or guaranteeing the subsistence of their adult members as well as children. Such assumptions are reflected both implicitly in the case of social insurance and explicitly in the case of social assistance. The consequences are such as to amplify the disadvantages of women and to enforce particular patterns of dependence within families. At a time when patterns of family formation have become more fluid, the child support scheme is imposing permanent responsibilities for the subsistence needs of children on biological parents, rather than the state.

This chapter has also paid particular attention to benefit provision for older people and disabled people. Though still based on social insurance principles, basic pension provision for older people has become increasingly inadequate to the subsistence needs associated with the socially constructed status of 'retirement'. Basic state provision must be supplemented. For some people this is achieved through an additional pension from a less than generous earnings-related state scheme, but for many it is achieved privately, through occupational or personal pensions. However, women and disadvantaged groups may have limited access to additional pensions and some may even be denied independent rights to a basic pension: in such circumstances people must fall back on social assistance. Certain universal benefits are available for people who are severely disabled, though such provision is addressed to their special needs, rather than their basic subsistence needs, which will usually still be met from within other parts of the social security system. A universal benefit is also available to those who care for severely disabled people, but at such a level and on such terms that most will also require social assistance.

This chapter has therefore focused on the basic structure of the British social security system and on provision that is made for those who are by and large excluded from the labour market. The next chapter turns to the social rights of people who are actually or potentially economically active.

Recommended additional reading

Current editions of the *National Welfare Benefits Handbook*, the *Rights Guide to Non Means-Tested Benefits*, and the *Child Support Handbook*, all published by Child Poverty Action Group, London (or similar guides or handbooks).

Current editions of the *Disability Rights Handbook*, published by Disability Alliance, and the *Ethnic Minorities' Benefits Handbook*, published by Child Poverty Action Group, London.

For a very full account of the British social security system see Ogus, A., Barendt, E. and Wikely, N. (1995) *The Law Relating to Social Security*, 4th edn, Butterworth, London.

Questions for reflection

The British social security system combines assistance, insurance and universalist principles. In practice, do these principles operate compatibly in parallel with each other, or are there inherent tensions or tendencies within the system?

The particular subsistence needs of children, older people and disabled people are recognised within the British social security system, albeit in quite different ways. What might account for these differences?

CHAPTER 6

RIGHTS AND WORK

The Universal Declaration of Human Rights states that 'Everyone has the right to work, to free choice of employment, to just and favourable conditions of work and to protection against unemployment' (UN 1948: Article 23[1]). In practice, however, no right to work exists in British law. The availability and choice of employment are subject to market forces and, although macroeconomic and local development policies may aim to create jobs, employment for all is not and never has been guaranteed. Rights *at* work are not social rights, but primarily civil or contractual rights. Contracts of employment are subject to legislative regulation and limited protection exists, for example, against unfair dismissal, but there is no protection against unemployment. To the extent that social security provision exists for the protection of people during unemployment, the rights afforded by such provision are clearly tied to a *duty* rather than a right to work.

It was observed in Chapter 5 that rights to social security are generally predicated on assumptions about people's duties to maintain themselves. This is implicit not only in British social legislation, but in the UN declaration itself, which also asserts: 'Everyone who works has the right to just and favourable remuneration ensuring for himself and his family an existence worthy of human dignity, and supplemented, if necessary, by other means of social protection' (*ibid.*: Article 23[3]). While the right to work has not been translated into British social policy, the assumptions of this last-mentioned clause have been:

- The existence of individuals and families is assumed normally to be ensured through remuneration obtained by 'work'.
- 'Work' is synonymous with employment. It does not encompass such activities as caring for children and invalids, domestic labour or voluntary effort expended in the interests of the community. However important these activities may be to the maintenance of 'human dignity', they need not and do not attract 'just and favourable remuneration'.
- Where remuneration from employment is insufficient some form of 'social protection' may be afforded. Economic rights may therefore be supplemented, though they will not be supplanted, by social rights.

This chapter will examine the relationship in Britain between 'work' (narrowly defined as employment) and 'rights' (where these are specifically defined in social legislation). The chapter focuses first, on the protections which employees have at work and second, on the rights, penalties and duties to which unemployed people are subject. Attention then turns to two forms of social protection: first, the 'in work' benefits available to low-paid employees; and second, the benefits available to employees and others prevented from working by 'incapacity'. Finally, the chapter will consider the position of part-time employees, students and people on job training schemes.

Employment protection

Policies for social protection in employment have been the subject of contradictory pressures in the 1980s and 1990s. On the one hand, the EC (now the EU) has been concerned to promote a 'social dimension' to the process of European economic integration and development (Commission of the European Communities 1993). To this end the Charter of Fundamental Social Rights of 1989 and the Social Protocol to the 1992 Maastricht Treaty (to which Britain is not a signatory) have sought to build on earlier measures under the Treaty of Rome relating to freedom of movement, health and safety at work and the equal treatment of men and women. The measures belatedly bring a limited degree of enforceability to certain of the principles contained in Council of Europe's largely declaratory Social Charter of 1961. The outcome has been a programme of reforms for the harmonisation of certain employment protection measures, and some more general proposals for enhanced protection for socially excluded groups. On the other hand, the British government has been seeking to curtail social protection for employees, claiming that the costs of such protection make British industry uncompetitive. For example, certain European reforms relating to maximum working hours and the extension of part-time workers' rights have been resisted by Britain. None the less, other reforms extending maternity rights have been imposed as a result of European directives and, at the time of writing, the government is contemplating a limited extension of part-time workers' rights as a result of a House of Lords ruling that, in so far as women predominate among part-time employees, current employment law is indirectly discriminatory and contrary to European law. At the same time, existing domestic employment protection provisions, such as the minimum wage provisions guaranteed by Wages Councils, have recently been abolished (with the sole exception of the Agricultural Wages Board). Employment protection is a complex area of law (for a straighforward guide to employees' rights see, for example, WMLPU 1993) and what follows is but the briefest résumé.

The rights of workers, before they were ever enshrined in statute, were articulated and defended by trade unions, and the right to form and to join trade unions is one of the 'universal' rights declared by the UN (1948: Article 23[1]). The position under British law is that nobody may legally be refused work, dismissed or victimised for being or for *not* being a member of a trade union. The government during the 1980s and 1990s has sought to erode the power of trade unions (see Johnson 1990: 30–1) and trade union membership has declined (Bassett 1989). In spite of this the services of a trade union are often an effective means of enforcing individual rights in employment.

Many workers are currently excluded from some or all statutory rights, including 'part-time' workers (those working fewer than 8 or 16 hours per week, depending on the entitlement in question), 'self-employed' workers (though the distinction between the status of an employee and an independent contractor is fraught with difficulty) and people over pensionable age (who are subject to the expectation that they may retire – see Chapter 5). Most workers' rights, even statutory rights, arise because they are implied or imposed within a contract of employment (whether it be written or unwritten). With few exceptions, legislation does not regulate such matters as hours of work, rates of pay, holiday entitlements and grievance/disciplinary procedures, though employers are required within a specified period of time to provide full-time workers with a written statement of their main terms and conditions of employment. Protected employees are therefore entitled to be informed, both of their contractual rights, and of their rights in matters which may be governed by statutory regulation, including sick pay and pension arrangements and the length of notice required to terminate their employment. This applies whether or not the provision which the employer makes is more generous than the statutory minima laid down. Disputes over terms of employment may be resolved by the Industrial Tribunal (see Chapter 9). The entitlements of protected employees to information also extend to a right to receive itemised pay slips and, in the event of dismissal, to a written statement of the reasons for dismissal.

The rights of employees to statutory sick pay and statutory maternity pay are discussed later in this chapter. Pregnant women, in addition to maternity pay, are entitled to maternity leave and may reserve the right to return to their jobs. An entitlement (at the time of writing) to up to 18 weeks' maternity leave (with statutory maternity pay) is 'earned' after six months' employment with the same employer, providing earnings exceed the national insurance minimum. The right to return to work after having a baby may be exercised at any time within 29 weeks of the birth, but this right is restricted to women who have been working for two years for the same employer (longer for part-time employees) and is subject to a number of exceptions and to very strict procedures as to the giving of notice.

In addition to maternity rights, women are also to some degree protected by the Equal Pay Act 1970, which imposes on all contracts of employment the condition that the employer shall not provide less favourable pay or conditions on the grounds of sex. However, because labour market practices often result in segregation between women's jobs and men's jobs, it may be difficult to prove that women are being paid less for work that is the same as or that is of equal value to that performed by men. The Sex Discrimination and

Race Relations Acts (of 1975 and 1976 respectively) also provide redress before the Industrial Tribunal should employees be directly or indirectly discriminated against in the course of their employment on the grounds of sex, race, colour, national or ethnic origins. Unlike other employment rights, these extend to all employees, regardless of length of service and apply equally to job applicants. In practice, however, it may once again be difficult to prove that less favourable treatment has resulted from gendered or racial motives, or that the imposition of particular criteria necessarily bear unequally on different sexes or ethnic groups. In the case of disabled people employers may be permitted to discriminate if they can establish a 'justifiable reason'. At the time of writing legislation to protect disabled people from discrimination is planned. The government's proposals (Minister for Disabled People 1995) imply a lesser degree of formal protection for disabled people than that which applies under sex and race discrimination law, but the exact form of the legislation which may emerge remains to be seen.

Employment law also provides protection against involuntary unemployment since it defines the circumstances in which employees may be 'fairly' dismissed. The right *not* to be *un*fairly dismissed is heavily qualified. At the time of writing it is only available after two years' full-time service with the same employer. To dismiss unprotected workers employers need have no reason. Otherwise they may rely on one of five possible causes:

1. reasons relating to the employee's capability (because, for example, s/he is no longer fit to do her/his job);
2. because of misconduct;
3. redundancy (because the employee's job has ceased to exist);
4. because of some legal constraint (as would apply, for example, if a driver were disqualified from driving); or
5. for some other substantial reason.

It must additionally be reasonable to dismiss for the reason on which the employer relies and the employer must act reasonably when deciding to dismiss somebody. In practice, the Industrial Tribunal – which considers complaints of unfair dismissal – makes this test of 'reasonableness' a test of the employer's conduct, rather than an objective test of 'fairness'. An employee who is subsequently proved innocent of an alleged offence at work may still be held to have been fairly dismissed, provided her/his employer acted reasonably at the time and genuinely believed the employee to be guilty. Industrial Tribunals have the power to order employers to reinstate or re-engage unfairly dismissed employees; however, it is more usual for employers to be ordered to pay compensation. Similarly, protected employees who are dismissed on the specific ground of redundancy must, in any event, be paid compensation subject to a statutory minimum based on their length of service with the employer concerned. When it is available, compensation may represent a remedy in the legal sense, but it does not of course prevent unemployment.

Jobseeker's allowance

Jobseeker's allowance is a social security benefit (due at the time of writing to be introduced in the course of 1996) for people who are unemployed. The name of the benefit announces its primary purpose: it is a benefit providing social protection to unemployed people only if they are seeking employment. What is more, the rules of the jobseeker's allowance scheme function to penalise people who may have become voluntarily unemployed.

The jobseeker's allowance is in fact two schemes in one (see Unemployment Unit 1994; DE/DSS 1994). It includes a short-term contributory benefit which, prior to 1996, was called unemployment benefit, and a means-tested benefit which is a form of income support. What they have in common is that both are payable subject to the terms of a Jobseeker's Agreement into which claimants are required to enter. The benefits themselves are to be administered by the Social Security Benefits Agency, but Jobseeker's Agreements will be administered by the government's Employment Service: the operations of both agencies are to be integrated and situated in Job Centres. Contributory jobseeker's allowance is payable only for the first six months of a spell of unemployment and on condition that the claimant meets stringent contribution conditions which exclude those who have not recently been in employment. (The requirement is that the claimant must within the preceding two years have actually paid employee's national insurance contributions equivalent to half a year's worth of minimum level contributions, and s/he must have paid or been credited with a year's worth of minimum level contributions in each of the preceding two years.) Though it is not fully means-tested in the way that income support is (in so far as the claimant's savings and the resources of her/his partner, if any, are not taken into account), the contributory allowance is means-tested in respect of any part-time earnings which claimants might obtain and any occupational or private pension which they might have as a result of early retirement. Means-tested jobseeker's allowance is subject to the same means test as income support (see Chapter 5), albeit with a rule which permits the partners of claimants to work up to 24 hours per week – rather than 16 hours per week – without disqualifying the claimant (though the partner's earnings are still taken into account). Both forms of the allowance are subject, after three months, to special earnings disregard rules which allow claimants to 'roll up' a proportion of deducted part-time earnings above the standard disregard level and to have these deductions repaid (subject to a maximum) as a lump sum 'back to work bonus' when the claimant leaves benefit for full-time employment.

The rates (or 'applicable amounts') for the means-tested allowance are the same as income support and the rates of the contributory allowance are aligned with those of a single person's personal allowance for income support purposes (so that young people are paid less than older people). Claimants who qualify for the contributory allowance but who have dependants (assuming their partner, if any, is not working full-time and they do not have significant income from other sources) will also have to claim means-tested jobseeker's allowance. After six months' unemployment, all claimants are entitled to the means-tested allowance only.

Claimants of jobseeker's allowance are required to register ('sign on') with the Employment Service and to declare not only that they are unemployed, but that they are actively seeking work. They must declare their willingness to take full-time employment (defined for these purposes as up to 40 hours per week, although claimants may be expected to accept employment for fewer hours per week if it is offered). Since unemployment benefit was first introduced in 1911 it had always been subject to a condition that its recipients should be available for work, and at various times additional conditions were imposed requiring that claimants should be 'genuinely' or 'actively' seeking work, with provision for benefit to be withdrawn if claimants should fail without reasonable excuse to take up a job offer or a place on a government retraining scheme. The same rules were applied to unemployed people who claimed social assistance benefits. The latest device, the Jobseeker's Agreement, requires the claimant to agree as a condition of entitlement to a programme of activities in order to find or return to work. Only during an initial 'permitted period' (currently 13 weeks) are claimants allowed to seek employment in their former occupation, after which they must agree to look more widely for work. Allowances are withdrawn if agreements are not 'honoured'. Explicit obligations are defined and enforced for each claimant and the terms of Jobseeker's Agreements are periodically reviewed. Employment Service 'advisers' have the power to make Jobseeker's Directions requiring claimants, for example, to attend workshops or courses in jobseeking skills or to improve their acceptability to employers in other ways. Claimants who fail to meet the 'labour market conditions' for benefit (by not proving they are available for and actively seeking work and/or by failing to complete and sign a Jobseeker's Agreement) receive no benefit. Claimants who flout Jobseeker's Directions are disqualified from benefit for a fixed period. The explicit intention is that it should be possible for 'benefit to be stopped where the unemployed person's behaviour is such that it actively militates against finding work' (DE/DSS 1994: para. 4.13).

Not only are the claimants of jobseeker's allowance coerced into 'jobseeking' on terms imposed by the Employment Service, they may also be penalised depending on the circumstances in which they come to be on benefit. Rules of this nature have applied since unemployment benefit was first introduced and have functioned as a deterrent to unemployment. The penalties involved take the form of a disqualification from benefit (currently, for up to six months), with provision for hardship payments (a reduced level of benefit) if it can be demonstrated that a member of the claimant's household will suffer hardship as a consequence of the sanction. The sanction applies if a claimant is deemed to have given up her/his previous employment (or a place on a government approved training scheme) without 'just cause', or if she/he has been dismissed from employment (or a training scheme) for misconduct. The effect is to ensure that employees should cling to their jobs, however unsuitable, and to inflict a double punishment on anyone who is sacked from a job (for a fuller discussion, see H. Dean 1991: 104–7).

Jobseeker's allowance is also denied to people who are on strike or who are prevented from working as a result of a trade dispute. The dependants of such people may be eligible to claim income support, although their entitlement is reduced by a set amount on account of assumed income from strike pay (whether or not any strike pay is received). This provision was originally applied to unemployment benefit in order that the government should not be seen to give succour to one side in a trade dispute, though in practice the rules relating to social assistance for dependants were made more stringent in the 1980s and it is difficult to construe the effect as anything other than the punishment of strikers and their families.

The advent of jobseeker's allowance has in many ways made the nature of benefits for unemployed people more transparent. The White Paper which preceded its introduction openly declared that the benefit regime proposed represented an 'important step' in the government's labour market reforms (DE/DSS 1994: para. 1.2) and was noted by some commentators to be 'soaked in the language of labour deregulation and the free market' (CPAG 1994c: 7). Arguably, such benefits have always been extended not so much as a social right as an incentive to remain in, to enter or to re-enter the labour market. The conditions attaching to benefit have implied a certain reciprocity between citizens' rights to benefit and their obligation to work. The introduction of the Jobseeker's Agreement has translated such reciprocity from a general principle to an explicit requirement. It has turned social rights and obligations sanctioned by general rules into individual rights and obligations sanctioned by an individual agreement.

'In work' benefits

One of the fundamental assumptions of the Beveridgian social security system had been that, subject to the availability of universal health care and family allowances, wages from employment would always be sufficient to ensure against poverty. Whether or not such an assumption was ever justified, it has been completely invalidated by employment market trends which have seen the emergence on a substantial scale of 'atypical' forms of work, especially part-time employment, temporary/casual employment and intermittent self-employment (Blackwell 1994) and, since the 1970s, growing wage inequality with downward pressure on wage levels at the bottom of the earnings distribution (Goodman and Webb 1994): Those classes of employee who tend to be excluded from employment protection measures (see above) are those most likely to be in receipt of wages which are insufficient for subsistence. The persistence of low-paying forms of employment together with the expansion of 'atypical' employment patterns have necessitated (and have to an extent been facilitated by) the introduction since the 1970s of means-tested 'in work' benefits.

A precedent for such benefits had been established, albeit briefly, in the eighteenth century by the Speenhamland system of poor relief (see George 1973), though for a century and a half the idea that the state should intervene to subsidise low wages had been shunned by governments of all political persuasions. The eventual reintroduction by a Conservative government of a benefit by which to top up the wages of working families was justified as a preferable alternative to any extension of universal family benefits. The benefit, originally called family income supplement, was revised in 1988 to become family credit and promoted, again by a Conservative government, as a benefit which – unlike universal child benefit – was 'targeted' on those working families in greatest need.

Family credit is payable to lone parents or (usually) the woman in a couple with dependent children, where the lone parent or either member of the couple is in full-time employment (defined as employment for more than 16 hours per week). It is not therefore available to part-time employees, who may only claim income support (if they are lone parents) or jobseeker's allowance (where they are one of a couple and if they can establish their availability for employment of 24 hours or more per week). The calculation of family credit is a 'taper' calculation. It is a more complex form of 'needs minus means' calculation than the income support calculation described in Chapter 5:

- needs are determined with reference first, to a set 'applicable amount' (which is the *same* for all families, but is set at the level of the personal allowance for an adult couple on income support); and second, to a *maximum* family credit level, determined with reference to a scale of allowances for one adult and for each child in the family (the level of these allowances being rather less than the level of personal allowances for income

support purposes, though there is an additional allowance if the claimant or her partner works more than 30 hours per week);
- means (taking into account both income and capital) are determined in the same way as for income support purposes, but with some differences as to income disregards;
- the maximum family credit is payable if a claimant has less than the permitted amount of savings/capital and her income is less than the 'applicable amount'; but
- if the claimant's income exceeds the 'applicable amount', the maximum family credit will be reduced by a proportion (currently 70 per cent) of that 'excess', so that the benefit 'tapers' off as a claimant's income increases (and as her need for the benefit reduces). A schematic representation of the calculation is set out in Figure 6.1; for a fuller explanation see, for example, Webster *et al.* (1994).

Family credit is an especially significant benefit for lone parents; first, because the cost (subject to a modest maximum) of certain forms of child care may be counted as an earnings disregard; second, because income from child support (i.e. maintenance from an 'absent parent') is also subject to a small disregard. These disregards do not apply to income support and the object of these concessions to lone parents is to encourage them to come off income support and enter employment. However, family credit is not a widely understood benefit. Uncertainty about entitlement is compounded by the precariousness of the jobs which are likely to be available (McLaughlin *et al.* 1989). The evidence also suggests that the actual availability of suitable child care arrangements is more likely than awareness of family credit entitlement to encourage lone parents to enter or return to employment (Marsh and McKay 1993).

The other means-tested in-work social security benefit is disability working allowance. Introduced in 1993, the benefit is modelled on family credit but is available to disabled people – whether or not they have dependent children – who are in full-time work. To qualify it is necessary that the claimant should have a physical or mental disability which puts her/him at a disadvantage in getting a job and that s/he had previously been receiving incapacity benefit (see below) or a disability benefit (see Chapter 5). As with family credit, entitlement is determined using a taper

| If **NEEDS** (applicable amount) | > (is greater than) | **MEANS** (income) subject to 'disregards' and to disqualification if capital exceeds a ceiling | then | **ENTITLEMENT** (benefit payable) | = (equals) | MAXIMUM (maximum credit/allowance/benefit) |
| If **NEEDS** (applicable amount) | < (is less than) | **MEANS** (income) subject to 'disregards' and to disqualification if capital exceeds a ceiling | then | **ENTITLEMENT** (benefit payable) | = (equals) | MAXIMUM − ([NEEDS − MEANS] × n%) (maximum credit/allowance/benefit minus a proportion of 'excess' income) |

Figure 6.1 'Taper' means test calculation.

calculation. The only significant differences are that, for disability working allowance: the amount of saving/capital a claimant may have before becoming ineligible for benefit is higher; there is a lower level 'applicable amount' for single claimants (unless they are also lone parents); but, if the claimant is one of a couple, both partners' needs are recognised in the calculation of the maximum disability working allowance (and at a slightly more generous level than for family credit). Like family credit, disability working allowance has not proved especially effective as a means of encouraging disabled people into full-time employment (Rowlingson and Berthoud 1994) and the availability of accessible and practicable forms of employment is likely to be a more important factor than the incentive afforded by a complex means-tested benefit in allowing disabled people into the labour market.

At the time of writing, the government is considering the introduction of an in-work benefit similar to family credit for people who neither have children nor are disabled.

Incapacity

This section will consider the various forms of protection which are provided for people on the basis that they are incapable of work through illness. As such, these benefits are distinguishable from disability benefits since they depend explicitly on a test of a claimant's capacity in relation to employment. It is possible for people to qualify both for a disability benefit – for example, disability living allowance – and for a benefit because of incapacity for work. The legislation recognises two forms of incapacity: short-term (incapacity lasting less than a year) and long-term. For short-term incapacity different provisions apply during the initial period of incapacity (currently, the first 28 weeks) and the remaining part of the first year of incapacity. Additionally, there are four different mechanisms for providing benefits: benefits which employers are required to pay; a contributory benefit called incapacity benefit; a non-contributory, non-means-tested benefit called severe disablement allowance; and income support, which may be paid in addition to or in lieu of any of the other benefits (see Chapter 5). The section will discuss: first, the incapacity for work test; second, statutory employer benefits; third, incapacity benefit; and finally, severe disablement allowance.

The incapacity for work test was remodelled and made more restrictive in 1995 (see CPAG 1994a, 1994b). It consists in fact of two tests, an 'own work' test and an 'all work' test. The 'own work' test is applied during the initial period of sickness, provided the claimant has a recognised occupation (at which s/he has worked during not less than eight of the preceding 12 weeks). The test requires that the claimant must be incapable 'by reason of some specific disease or mental disablement' of carrying on such work as might reasonably be expected in the course of her/his usual job and, for most purposes, a certificate to this effect from the claimant's own doctor will be accepted as sufficient evidence. After the initial period, or if the claimant has no usual occupation, the 'all work' test applies. This requires that a claimant's medical condition be measured against a range of functional capacities, namely: walking; standing; sitting; climbing stairs; rising from sitting; bending and kneeling; manual dexterity; lifting and carrying; reaching; speech; hearing; vision; continence; fits; mental health. The severity of a person's 'impairment' is assessed against each criterion according to a scale and, if her/his total score exceeds a set threshold, s/he is adjudged incapable of work. Claimants must declare the extent of their impairment using a questionnaire and be prepared to submit to medical examination by a Social Security Benefits Agency doctor. The test excludes consideration of non-medical factors, such as the claimant's age, education, training or suitability for the jobs of which s/he might functionally be capable, or whether such jobs in reality exist. During long-term incapacity, the extent of incapacity may be periodically reviewed and benefits may at any time be withdrawn if claimants are considered to be capable of work.

People in employment – unless they are over pensionable age or earn less than the national insurance minimum contributions level – are entitled to statutory sick pay. Statutory sick pay has effectively replaced national insurance sickness benefit and is both administered and financed by employers. Statutory sick pay is payable only for the initial period (currently, 28 weeks) of sickness, after which an employee would normally claim incapacity benefit. There are no contribution conditions attaching to statutory sick pay and, subject to the general rules of the scheme, claims procedures and payment arrangements are essentially a private matter between employers and their employees. Claims may be made after four days' sickness absence, and most employers require some form of self-certification for absences of up to a week and medical certificates thereafter. Statutory sick pay is currently payable at a fixed rate, currently equivalent to about 90 per cent of the level of a single person's basic retirement pension. None the less, it counts as wages and is taxable.

Although it is not a benefit for incapacity, statutory maternity pay is a benefit modelled closely on statutory sick pay and, like statutory sick pay, it has substantially replaced an earlier short-term national insurance benefit (maternity allowance) and is now administered and financed by employers. Pregnancy does not necessarily imply incapacity for work, but it is treated for social security purposes in a similar way. Statutory maternity pay is payable during the period of maternity leave to which employees are at present statutorily entitled (currently, 18 weeks – see above). For the first six weeks of that period, statutory maternity pay is payable at 90 per cent of the claimant's normal earnings and, for the remaining 12 weeks, at the same level as statutory sick pay. Although responsibility for administering statutory sick pay and statutory maternity pay rests with employers, the schemes are closely regulated, to the extent that disputes over entitlement may be referred by employees to a Social Security Appeal Tribunal (see Chapter 8).

The burden of protection for employees during initial periods of sickness absence is effectively therefore borne by employers, rather than the state. The initial period coincides in length with the period to which the less rigorous 'own work' test of incapacity relates. Employees who remain absent from work through sickness after that period, in order to claim state incapacity benefit, must meet the relevant contribution conditions and the 'all work' test of incapacity. Claimants who are not currently in employment, provided they meet the contribution conditions, may be able to claim incapacity benefit on the basis of the 'own work' test for the initial period (28 weeks), after which they too must submit to the 'all work' test. The contribution conditions for incapacity benefit are broadly similar to those for jobseeker's allowance, though somewhat less strict (in so far as the paid contributions which are required may include self-employed contributions and may have been paid in any previous year).

Incapacity benefit is payable at three levels: the lower short-term rate, which is currently set at a level equivalent to around three-quarters of a single person's basic state retirement pension and applies during the initial period of sickness; the higher short-term rate is set at the same level as statutory sick pay and is payable after the initial period until the end of the first year of incapacity (i.e. currently, for the 24 weeks after the first 28 weeks of sickness); the long-term rate, payable only after a year of incapacity, is currently set at a level just beneath that of the state retirement pension. As with retirement pension, additions for dependants may be claimed with long-term incapacity benefit, and for people who become incapable of work below a certain age (currently 35 or 45) there are small age additions which can in fact bring the level of incapacity benefit just above that of the basic retirement pension. However, unlike retirement pension, earnings-related additions are no longer payable with long-term incapacity benefit. Once entitlement to incapacity benefit has been established it will remain in payment so long as the claimant is adjudged to remain incapable of work or until the claimant receives a retirement pension. After the initial period of incapacity, incapacity benefit is taxable. The present incapacity benefit scheme was introduced in 1995 and people who became incapable of work prior to its introduction may under transitional arrangements be entitled to benefits under the rules of the schemes which it replaced.

People who cannot meet the contribution conditions attaching to incapacity benefit may, after an initial period of incapacity (currently, 28 weeks or, more precisely in this instance, 196 consecutive days), be eligible to receive severe disablement allowance. This benefit was originally called non-contributory invalidity pension and, when it was introduced in 1975, it was explicitly intended to address the needs of people whose incapacity for *employment* had prevented them from establishing a contribution record. Subsequently, it was extended to include married women who were incapable of 'normal household duties'. Criticism of the discriminatory nature of the 'normal household duties' test led eventually in 1984 to the introduction of severe disablement allowance scheme (see Ogus and Barendt 1988: 144–5). The scheme now represents a hybrid which combines an incapacity and a disability test. Severe disablement allowance may be claimed by people aged between 16 and pensionable age provided they satisfy the 'all work' incapacity test. Transitional arrangements have enabled people who received the old non-contributory invalidity pension to continue to receive severe disablement allowance, but more recent claimants, unless they establish their claims before their twentieth birthday, must *additionally* satisfy a disability test based on criteria established under the industrial injuries and war pensions schemes (which have been mentioned in Chapter 5, but which it has not been possible within the scope of this book to elaborate upon). People who have been severely disabled from birth or since childhood are therefore able to claim the benefit with comparative ease, but it is now only really available to people with poor employment records who become severely disabled in circumstances not associated with employment (or war). The benefit is payable at a flat rate, fixed at around 60 per cent of the level of the single person's basic retirement pension, though dependants' additions are payable. Age-related additions are also payable, such that people who become incapable of work at younger ages receive a little more, though even the highest rate of benefit is still only just over 80 per cent of the single person's basic retirement pension. The benefit is not taxable, but unlike other disability benefits (see Chapter 5) it is taken fully into account as income in the calculation of entitlement to income support.

The low level of the various benefits available to people adjudged incapable of work are such that many recipients are also eligible for income support to 'top up' their income to subsistence level. Receipt of any of the benefits described in this section automatically entitles claimants to do so, provided they also meet the other conditions attaching to the receipt of income support.

Part-time work, studying and training

Finally in this chapter, it is important to discuss the position of people who are only partially engaged with the labour market or who may be preparing through education or training to enter or re-enter the labour market.

People who work part-time (currently, fewer than 16 hours per week) may, if their circumstances entitle them, receive income support or means-tested jobseeker's allowance. Reference has already been made to the 'earnings disregards' to which such people are entitled. These are the weekly sums which part-time employees are entitled to earn (net of tax, national insurance and 50 per cent of occupational pension contributions, if any) before their benefit is reduced, or – put another way – it is the amount of money which people are allowed to keep each week before their net earnings are deducted in full from their benefit entitlement. At the time of writing these income support disregards are very small (just £5 per week for single claimants, £5 per week each for couples and £15 per week for lone parents) and no allowance is made against earnings for travel to work costs or other expenses. In the circumstances there is very little incentive for people on income support to seek or retain part-time employment. At the same time, as has already been explained, incentives have been deliberately created in the family credit scheme to encourage claimants (especially lone parents) to move to full-time work. Increases in income support disregards have been recommended (Social Security Advisory Committee 1994) but, as matters stand, the system operates to discourage part-time employment (see P. Hewitt 1993).

As a general rule, students are not entitled to means-tested benefits, but are assumed to be provided for by student grants, student loans or parental contributions. There are exceptions. For social security purposes, a student is anybody in higher education or anybody aged 19 or over in any kind of full-time education. Students who qualify for income support because, for example, they are also lone parents, or pensioners, or are disabled, are able to receive benefit and study at the same time, as may people on funded vocational courses who are in receipt of training allowances (see below). To receive means-tested jobseeker's allowance, however, a student must show that s/he remains available for work, that her/his studies are only part-time (not more than a prescribed number of hours per week) or that s/he is prepared to give up studying if a job becomes available. There are also substantial restrictions on students' eligibility for housing benefit (see Chapter 7). Once again, the government has been urged – by the National Council for Education and Training (see *Guardian* 11.10.1994) – to relax such rules, but as matters stand, the system operates to discourage further or higher education.

The position of people on vocational training schemes is rather different. There is a range of government-funded training schemes for which training allowances are payable in place of benefits, subject (except in the case of Youth Training placements) to a modest additional premium. Recipients of jobseeker's allowance are additionally allowed without loss of benefits to attend other employment or training courses. However, the nature of the training that is encouraged is limited. The non-funded training courses which claimants may attend must (at the time of writing) last no longer than five consecutive weeks, while the quality and purpose of funded training schemes and courses have been the subject of considerable criticism. Responsibility for the various youth and employment training schemes once run by the Manpower Services Commission has been devolved since 1988 to local Training and Enterprise Councils composed of employers' representatives. Pat Ainley points out first, that responsibility for overseeing training policy has thereby been handed back to the very people – employers – whose past failures had originally led to the introduction of state-subsidised training; second, that because the greater part of the TECs' funding is tied to established forms of youth and employment training, the TECs have in any event 'found themselves responsible for lower-level skill training and unemployment programmes rather than able to train for their own firms' higher skill requirements' (1993: 128). While 16 and 17 year olds are supposedly guaranteed a Youth Training place, many TECs are failing to provide them. While a range of schemes is supposed to enable older unemployed people to obtain additional job training (the Training for Work scheme), to obtain job experience in the community (the Community Action scheme), or undertake vocational training using training credits (the Learning for Work scheme), the practices of individual TECs 'are diverging further and further from each other and from any consistent approach to raising the skills of those with fewest qualifications' (Christopher 1992, cited in Ainley 1993: 128). Ainley's prediction is that training schemes 'will be tied yet more closely to social security and unemployment relief, and will become part of a "workfare" programme, offered under whatever guise' (*ibid.*: 129). Whether or not this is borne out, the incentive and the opportunities offered to unemployed people for employment training in pursuance of Jobseeker's Agreements are at best ambiguous.

Conclusion/summary

Claus Offe has argued that 'The owner of labour power first becomes a wage labourer as a citizen of a state' (1984: 99). What this chapter has illustrated is that the conditional nature of individual rights guaranteed by social legislation is calculated to underwrite the citizen's status as a wage labourer. Such rights function to limit rather than defend the security of the citizen and so to ensure her/his complaisance *in* employment and her/his availability *for* employment.

A complex array of protections exists for employees in the course of their employment, though the extent of such protection is often less than in other Western countries; many peripheral and 'atypical' employees are excluded from full protection; many rights, such as those arising under anti-discrimination legislation, are difficult to enforce; and protection against dismissal is in practice limited.

Protection of income during unemployment is now to be provided through jobseeker's allowance, a hybrid benefit with a vestigial contributory element and a predominant means-tested element. The benefit is explicitly conditional, not only on claimants' availability for employment, but their compliance with the terms of individual agreements requiring them actively to seek work. The withholding or withdrawal of jobseeker's allowance is used as a sanction by which to control the behaviour of unemployed people and to deter voluntary unemployment.

The social security system also provides protection through 'in-work' benefits for certain low-paid full-time employees. In-work benefits are means-tested, using a 'taper' calculation, the complex nature of which renders the basis of entitlement less than transparent to most recipients. At the time of writing, in-work benefits are available to families with children and to disabled people only. However, this form of wage subsidy has become an increasingly important feature of policy under Conservative governments because it is thought that it 'targets' help to the poorest working people and families, and that it provides incentives to disadvantaged groups – notably lone parents – to take low-paid employment.

When people are incapable of work through sickness, social protection is provided, in the immediate term, by way of compulsory employer provision and, in the longer term, by a contributory incapacity benefit or a non-contributory severe disablement allowance (though people of limited means are often obliged to 'top up' these benefits with income support). These benefits are distinguishable from disability benefits because they are subject to a 'work test'. The receipt of benefit is conditional on claimants establishing, not illness or disability, but that they are medically incapable of the functions or activities required for employment.

Finally, this chapter has discussed the ways in which the social security system tends to disadvantage people who are employed on a part-time basis or who may wish to study. This is in spite of labour market trends which are creating more part-time jobs at the 'bottom' while demanding higher levels of qualification at the 'top'. Training opportunities are provided for (or even imposed on) unemployed people, though the character of such training may be poorly matched to labour market needs.

Far from providing a right to work, social legislation guarantees neither security in employment, nor security out of employment. Since the 1980s, labour markets have become increasingly polarised between a privileged core of relatively secure and highly skilled workers, to whom social protection may be of marginal relevance, and a vulnerable periphery of insecure low-paid workers, for whom the rights which social legislation affords are contradictory. Social legislation fails to alleviate people's vulnerability within the labour market, while simultaneously compelling people to seek employment.

Recommended additional reading

Current edition of *Employment Law: An advisor's guide to the rights of employees*, published by West Midlands Low Pay Unit (or a similar guide or handbook).

Current edition of the *Unemployment and Training Rights Handbook* published by Unemployment Unit, London.

Current editions of the *National Welfare Benefits Handbook*, and the *Rights Guide to Non Means-Tested Benefits*, published by Child Poverty Action Group, London

Questions for reflection

When we are told there is no such thing as a job for life, what does this imply for the so-called 'right to work'?

To qualify for jobseeker's allowance a citizen must prove s/he is actively seeking and available for work. To qualify for incapacity benefit s/he must prove s/he is medically incapable of work. Where does this leave an unemployed person who can meet neither test?

CHAPTER 7

RIGHTS AND HOUSING

Like nourishment and raiment, shelter is one of the most elemental of human needs. Curiously, food, clothing and housing are recognised in the Universal Declaration of Human Rights quite incidentally: they are numbered among the components of an adequate standard of subsistence (see UN 1948: Article 25). A specific right to a home is nowhere declared. The assumption it would seem is that citizens may secure their homes at will, subject only to the means of payment, and that the primary source of protection lies in civil and not social rights. None the less, where British social legislation does relate to housing, it creates four kinds of rights.

First, there are rights to social benefits and tax concessions to assist with the payment of housing costs. Second, there are protections against exploitation and eviction of residential occupiers. Third, there are protections against unsatisfactory housing conditions. Fourth, there are protections against homelessness. This chapter will consider each type of provision in turn. It will become clear, however, that even the protection afforded to homeless persons falls short of guaranteeing an unconditional right to housing.

Paying for housing

This section will discuss four different ways in which people may be entitled to state assistance with housing costs. The first is housing benefit, a means-tested cash benefit available to tenants with low incomes. The second is council tax benefit, a means-tested benefit closely aligned with housing benefit, which is available to assist people of all forms of housing tenure with the cost of council tax bills. The third is the housing cost element of income support, which may be available to some home-owners. The fourth is a fiscal benefit, namely mortgage interest tax relief, which represents a different kind of subsidy towards the housing costs of home-owners.

The Beveridgian social security system did not make separate provision for housing costs, but had included in national insurance benefits a notional element sufficient to meet average housing costs (Parker 1989). A safety-net was provided to the extent that means-tested national assistance (later supplementary benefit) could take account of actual housing costs. As a result of considerable regional variations in rent levels and rapid housing cost inflation, this arrangement became increasingly unsustainable, partly because it pushed increasing numbers of pensioners and others onto social assistance benefits simply to have their housing costs met, and because this in turn generated considerable inequities as between people outside the labour market with access to social assistance and those in low-paid employment who could receive no benefits. In the 1970s, therefore, during the period in which family income supplement was also introduced (an 'in-work' benefit and the predecessor to family credit – see Chapter 6), rent and rate rebate and rent allowance schemes were instituted. These benefits were the predecessors of housing benefit and council tax benefit. Housing benefit and council tax benefit are social security benefits and are subject to rules laid down by national legislation, but they are administered by local authorities rather than by the Social Security Benefits Agency.

Housing benefit was first introduced in 1982, though its current form was not established until 1988. Housing benefit effectively unified provision for the housing costs of all tenants, whether they be council tenants or private tenants and whether or not they are in receipt of other social security benefits and/or in employment. To do this housing benefit combined the provisions of the rent rebate and rent allowance schemes and the housing cost element of the old supplementary benefit scheme. Other than for claimants who are also in receipt of income support, the means test applied for the purposes of housing benefit is based on a taper calculation (see Figure 6.1 in Chapter 6; and for a full account, for example, Webster *et al.* 1994). The maximum benefit for the purposes of housing benefit is the claimant's 'eligible rent'. Eligible rents do not include mortgage interest repayments, ground rents on long leases or payments under co-ownership and conditional sale arrangements (which may in certain circumstances be met by income support), but they do include payments which are not strictly 'rent', such as licence fees or payments made by a claimant who is not legally a tenant (such as the deserted partner of the original tenant) where payments are necessary for claimants to retain occupation of their present homes. However, the eligible rent will not necessarily be equal to the actual rent payable, since deductions may be made from the actual rent if it includes provision for non-housing costs (such as for meals, heating, laundry or other services), or if the actual rent is deemed excessive (because the accommodation is adjudged unsuitable or too large for the claimant's household, or because the rent charged exceeds either the reasonable market rent or a local limit determined by central government).

Claimants who also receive income support automatically receive maximum housing benefit (i.e. full payment of their eligible rent). Other claimants' entitlement is based on a taper calculation in which:

- needs are determined with reference to the same applicable amounts as apply for the purposes of income support (but with a slight variation in the case of lone parents);
- means are also determined in the same way as for income support, but with some variations in relation to disregards for lone parents and with a higher savings/capital limit (currently twice that for income support);
- the amount of eligible rent that is met is reduced by a proportion of the amount by which the claimant's income exceeds her/his applicable amount;
- the taper that is applied is currently (at 65 per cent) slightly less severe than that applied for the purposes of family credit;
- the amount of benefit payable can also be subject to 'non-dependant deductions' – reductions on account of the contributions which any non-dependent adult members of the claimant's household are assumed to make towards the claimant's housing costs (deductions are related to the income of the non-dependant,

and reduced or no deductions are made for non-dependants who are themselves on low income or are receiving income support).

For local authority tenants, their housing benefit is credited at source to their rent accounts (so reducing the net rent payable), while for private tenants, housing benefit is paid to the claimant, or in certain circumstances, direct to the claimant's landlord.

As with income support, there are restrictions on entitlement for persons from abroad and special rules and restrictions for full-time students. Because the housing benefit means test aggregates the needs and means of families in the same way as income support it also reinforces the same assumptions about family dependence, although it takes these assumptions a step further: first, through the imposition of non-dependant deductions (referred to above); second, through a rule which precludes the payment of housing benefit in circumstances where the claimant is closely related to her/his landlord or landlady. It is explicitly anticipated, on the one hand, that claimants' adult offspring who continue to live in the parental home should contribute to the household costs, but on the other, that people who reside with close relatives should be accommodated without any sort of commercial arrangement between them. Housing benefit also takes the principle of 'selectivity' a stage further than other means-tested benefits in so far as it is possible for benefit authorities to restrict the rents with which they will assist. The imposition of so-called 'rent-stops' may rest on judgements about what kind of accommodation is or is not suitable for a particular person or family and/or on the availability of cheaper alternative accommodation which might be adjudged suitable. Though local authorities have discretion to meet the costs of rents above the 'reasonable' levels determined by rent officers (see below) or the local limits determined by central government, they are penalised for doing so by a loss of central government subsidy. The consequence is that certain types or classes of accommodation may effectively be placed out of bounds as far as people on state benefits and low income are concerned.

The council tax is the successor to the community charge (or poll tax) and local general rates. For an explanation of the basis on which liability to council tax is determined see, for example, M. Ward (1994). As a tax on occupancy it may be regarded as a housing cost and the council tax benefit scheme is closely related to the housing benefit scheme. Entitlement is based on a taper calculation in which the maximum benefit is the full amount of the claimant's council tax liability and the taper (currently at 20 per cent) is gentler than for either family credit or housing benefit. Like housing benefit, council tax benefit may be subject to non-dependant deductions. However, there is an alternative form of rebate, the 'second adult rebate'. This rebate compensates council taxpayers for the effect on their tax liability of the presence within their household of any non-dependent adult whose status does not attract a council tax discount but whose income is such they cannot contribute to the council tax. Second adult rebate is available to taxpayers whose circumstances are such that they would not themselves qualify for means-tested benefits, but where their non-dependants' circumstances are such that they need assistance. The application of non-dependant deductions in both housing benefit and council tax benefit and the provision of second adult council tax rebates all involve the means testing, not of claimants and their immediate families, but of other members of their households. Arguably, housing benefit and council tax benefit embody more elaborate means-testing principles than could be provided by a single social assistance benefit.

However, it is through income support, the main social assistance benefit, that assistance with housing costs not met by housing benefit may still be obtained. As was explained in Chapter 5, the 'applicable amount' used to determine a claimant's and her/his family's needs for the purposes of income support may in certain circumstances include their housing costs. The most commonly included housing cost is mortgage interest repayments (including interest payments on loans and second mortgages previously incurred to meet the cost of essential repairs, improvements or adaptations). The scope of this provision is being progressively curtailed: first, by placing an upper ceiling on the size of the mortgages on which interest repayments may be fully met; second, by imposing an initial period at the beginning of a claim for income support during which reduced or no mortgage interest costs will be met. The precise extent of the assistance which is available will therefore depend on when the claimant's mortgage was taken out. At the time of writing, the government proposes that for mortgages taken out after October 1995, claimants of income support will not be able to receive any assistance in respect of the amount by which that mortgage exceeds £90,000 and will in any event receive no assistance for the first nine months of any claim. For claimants with mortgages taken out earlier, no assistance is to be given for the first two months of any claim and only 50 per cent of the interest payments due will be met for four months after that. Home-owners are expected increasingly to take out private insurance to meet the cost of mortgage repayments in the event of unemployment and sickness. For low-income home-owners who are not eligible for income support because they are in full-time employment there is at the time of writing no form of assistance with mortgage interest repayments (this contrasts curiously with the position of tenants in low-paid employment who may obtain assistance with their rent through housing benefit).

As with housing benefit, income support is subject to non-dependant deductions where provision is being made for housing costs. Similarly, there is provision to restrict the amount of housing costs which are eligible to be met if such costs are adjudged to be 'excessive', because the claimant's accommodation is larger than required for her/him and her/his family and/or because there is cheaper suitable alternative accommodation available in the area in which the claimant lives. Claimants in receipt of income support are also generally prevented from increasing their housing costs: tenants who buy their homes while in receipt of income support may receive assistance with housing costs only to the extent of their eligible rent for housing benefit purposes prior to the purchase; and home-owners who take out additional mortgages or who move house and take out a bigger mortgage while in receipt of income support will receive no additional assistance with housing costs (unless, for example, the loan was required to fund adaptations or the move was to a home specially adapted to meet the needs of a disabled person). To the extent that means-tested benefits guarantee a right to housing, it is a right that is conferred at the expense of a claimant's right to choose.

Finally, this section will briefly mention mortgage interest tax relief. A tax relief functions so as to exempt a citizen from paying tax on a portion of her/his income. In the case of mortgage interest tax relief, it is that portion of income (or a part of it) which is expended on interest repayments. The tax that is forgone represents a 'tax expenditure' (Wilkinson 1986) for the government equivalent to the 'tax saving' for the citizen. In practice, mortgage interest tax relief has, since 1983, been given 'at source', so that home-owners make reduced mortgage repayments and the lending institutions are reimbursed by the government. The value of tax relief, especially to affluent and middle-income owner occupiers, has been considerable and, in the 1980s, the cost of this subsidy spiralled almost out of control, reaching a peak in 1990/91 of £7.7 billion (CSO 1992). However, for mortgages which exceed a set ceiling (£30,000) income tax relief is restricted to the interest payable up to that ceiling. More recently relief has been given at a rate beneath the basic rate of tax. In 1993, the government declared its intention of phasing out mortgage interest tax relief by the year 2000 by reducing the rate of relief by 5 pence in the pound each year (from 20 pence in 1994). For a full account of the rights of home-owners, see Moorhouse and Thomas (1994).

Under certain circumstances, tenants and home-owners are therefore entitled to various kinds of subsidy in relation to their housing costs. These are subsidies to the 'consumption' of housing rather than its 'production' (Ungerson 1994). Such subsidies may indirectly stimulate the supply of housing and, certainly, the right to mortgage interest tax relief helped to fuel the expansion of owner-occupation in the 1980s. Mortgage interest tax relief, however, is now to be more tightly regulated and is scheduled to be phased out. Other forms of consumption subsidy – housing benefit and the housing cost element of income support – are strictly conditional on a means test. These subsidies are 'targeted' selectively to people whose purchasing power in the housing market (whether in the rented or owner-occupier sector) would otherwise be limited or non-existent, but with strict controls intended to temper 'excessive' costs and expectations. By themselves, such subsidies are not best calculated to stimulate supply, still less to guarantee the provision of housing of an acceptable standard.

The regulation of rents and security of tenure

An alternative strategy for ensuring the availability of housing is for legislation to be used to limit the rent levels charged by private landlords and to restrict the circumstances in which people may be evicted from private rented accommodation. This was one of the key strategies pursued in Britain during the earlier part of the twentieth century when renting was the dominant form of housing tenure. At the same time, governments of all political persuasions made a considerable investment in subsidising the provision of low-cost public rented housing by local authorities. By the later part of the century, however, home-ownership had become the dominant form of housing tenure and, in the 1980s, Conservative governments attempted deliberately to 'deregulate' what then remained of the private rented sector on the one hand, and to diminish the public rented sector on the other (see, for example, Johnson 1990). Believing regulation to be the cause rather than a bulwark against the contraction of private rented housing, the government legislated to diminish the controls on private landlords. Distrusting the role played by local government, the government gave the tenants of council housing the right to buy their homes at a discount, while local councils were at the same time subjected to a greater degree of regulation.

As a result there are now three main 'species' of tenancy with varying degrees of legislative protection: protected tenancies, which are private tenancies created prior to 15 January 1989; secure tenancies, which are mainly public sector tenancies; and assured tenancies, which are private tenancies created since 15 January 1989. Additionally, there are several other forms of tenancy which attract lesser degrees of legislative protection. What is outlined below is an incomplete and much simplified account of a highly complex field of law. For a fuller explanation see, for example, Arden and Hunter (1992).

Protected tenancies, where they survive, are those which still enjoy 'traditional' Rent Act protection, specifically under the Rent Act 1977. Protected tenants enjoy the right to have a 'fair rent' determined for their tenancy by the rent officer. Since this right would be valueless if tenants who availed themselves of it could be evicted by their landlords, the legislation also affords security of tenure (see below). Certain tenants with 'restricted contracts' are excluded from full protection, including: tenants with a resident landlord if the tenancy was created since 1974; furnished tenants with a resident landlord if the tenancy was created before 1974; and any tenants who share living accommodation with their landlord. Either tenants or landlords can apply to have a 'fair rent' registered for a letting and, once registered, that rent becomes the maximum rent which may legally be charged. Applications to review the registered rent may be made every two years. The rent officers who determine and register 'fair rents' are independent public officials employed in local offices. In registering 'fair rents' they are required to ignore the effect of market conditions and to assume that no scarcity value attaches to rented accommodation. The number of tenancies over which rent officers have jurisdiction is declining, though under the Housing Act 1988 they were given a new jurisdiction under which they may be called on by local authorities to determine 'reasonable rents' for the purposes of limiting the amount of housing benefit payable on any particular dwelling (see above).

Prior to the 1980s, it was assumed that, because public sector landlords and charitable bodies such as housing associations did not seek to return a profit, it was not necessary for their tenants to have special legislative protection. The Housing Acts of 1980 and 1985, however, introduced the concept of the secure tenancy and gave the tenants of local authorities and of other public bodies and housing associations a form of security of tenure broadly similar to that enjoyed by protected tenants. However, no specific legal mechanism is available to local authority tenants by which to challenge the level of rents, though, because they are elected bodies, local councils remain in principle democratically accountable: a council tenant enjoys political as well as legal rights against her/his landlord. Rents for local authority tenancies remained in theory at the discretion of councils, albeit with a requirement that rents should approximate more closely to the levels charged in the private rented sector. However, the financial regime imposed on councils by the Local Government and Housing Act 1989 restricted their discretion and in effect forced council rents to rise. Housing association tenancies had been and continued to be subject, like protected tenancies, to the 'fair rents' scheme, but housing association tenancies granted since the enactment of the Housing Act 1988 are no longer secure tenancies but assured tenancies, and rents are governed not by the 'fair rents' scheme but by the same rules as for other assured tenancies.

Assured tenancies are the creation of the Housing Act 1988, and – subject to some exceptions – any private or housing association tenancy granted since that legislation came into force is an assured tenancy. Though assured tenants enjoy a broadly similar (if slightly reduced) degree of security of tenure to protected tenants, they are not entitled to a 'fair rent'. Landlords may let premises for whatever rent a tenant will agree to pay and they may stipulate express terms for future rent increases. If terms for the variation of the rent have not been agreed, it is possible for the landlord – and in some circumstances the tenant – to serve notice to vary the terms of the tenancy and for the proposed variation of terms, if it is not agreed, to be referred by either party to the rent assessment committee (a body which began life as a higher appellate tribunal to the rent officer). The rent assessment committee has power to determine and to impose on the parties what it adjudges to be the *market* rent for the property.

Where protected tenancies and assured tenancies are initially granted for a fixed contractual term, on the expiry of that term the tenancies do not cease and, unless the tenancy is renewed by agreement, they become 'statutory' tenancies on the same terms and conditions as the contractual tenancies which preceded them. Landlords under protected, assured and secure tenancies cannot recover possession against their tenants unless they can establish permissible grounds for doing so. Such grounds are specified in the relevant legislation and are of two kinds: discretionary and mandatory. There is some variation between the different species of tenancy, but generally possession may be sought where the tenant is in arrears with her/his rent or is in breach of some express or implied term of the tenancy. In such circumstances the county court *may*, if it is reasonable, grant an order for possession against the tenant. In the case of assured tenancies, the court *must* grant an order for possession if a tenant is more than three months in arrears with her/his rent both at the date the landlord served notice of seeking possession (see below) *and* at the date of hearing. Similarly, in the case of both protected and assured tenancies, the court must grant possession if the landlord is a former owner-occupier of the property in question and it was let to the tenant on the express basis that the landlord would at some time return to occupy the property; or where the tenancy had been an out-of-season holiday or student letting. In the case of secure and assured tenancies, the court must grant possession if the landlord seeks to redevelop or demolish the property, though – only in the case of secure (i.e. public sector) tenancies – the landlord must make suitable alternative accommodation available to the tenant. The court also has a general discretion to grant possession to private landlords under protected and assured tenancies if it can be shown that suitable alternative accommodation is available to the tenant. To recover possession landlords under protected tenancies must first serve a notice to quit to terminate the contractual tenancy and then apply to the county court for an order. Landlords under secure and assured tenancies must first serve a notice of seeking possession, since only the court has power to terminate the tenancy. The court has power to suspend or attach conditions to an order for possession, but once an order is made and becomes effective, it may be enforced by eviction.

On the death of a protected, secure or assured tenant, her/his spouse may succeed to the tenancy or, in certain limited circumstances, another member of the tenant's family may do so, though the provisions for succession are particularly restrictive in the case of assured tenancies. Except in certain circumstances (where, for example, the property is sheltered accommodation or has been specially adapted for disabled occupiers), secure tenants after two years' occupation have a right to buy the property they occupy. No such right extends to protected or assured tenants, although they may in some circumstances have a right of 'first refusal' if the landlord seeks to sell the property.

In addition to the main species of tenancy, there are a number of forms of occupancy which attract a much lesser degree of protection. First, there are 'restricted contracts' referred to above, a term which most usually applies to tenancies granted by resident landlords. The rent tribunal (a body which formerly had an independent existence, but is now coterminous with the rent assessment committee) has jurisdiction to determine 'reasonable' rents for restricted contract tenancies and, for tenancies granted before 1980 (of which very few survive), to defer temporarily the operation of notices to quit and so delay the commencement of any possession proceedings. For tenancies granted since 1980, the county court has power temporarily to suspend a possession order. However, other than the requirement that tenancies must be determined by notice to quit before repossession is sought, tenants under restricted contracts have no security of tenure. Second, there are 'shorthold' tenancies, of which there are two kinds: protected shortholds (which could only be granted between 1980 and 1988) and assured shortholds (which may have been granted since 1988).

Shorthold tenancies are ostensibly the same as either protected tenancies or assured tenancies, but with the fundamental difference that they are originally granted for a fixed term and subject to notice from the landlord that possession may be recovered after the expiry of that term on the special mandatory ground that it is a shorthold tenancy. Though tenancies may continue as statutory tenancies after the expiry of the original fixed term, the tenant remains vulnerable indefinitely to repossession on the shorthold ground. Protected shorthold tenants had the right to a 'fair rent' and assured tenants have the right to apply to a rent assessment committee for a rent to be determined if they can demonstrate that their rent is higher than other rents for assured tenancies. While restricted contract tenants, protected shorthold tenants and assured shorthold tenants all therefore have rights to challenge the level of the rents they pay, their vulnerability in due course to retaliatory possession proceedings makes it unlikely (unless they have other accommodation to which to go) that they will avail themselves of such rights.

There are other forms of residential occupier with limited rights, including: people whose accommodation is 'tied' to their employment; people who are sub-tenants or the tenants of mortgagors; people who are boarders or lodgers; people who are 'licensees' (who may be obliged, for example, to share the occupancy of premises). One unintended effect of the Rent Acts was to spawn various attempts by landlords to devise ways of evading them and, through such ploys as bogus 'non-exclusive occupation agreements', to deny their tenants legal protection. In general, however, virtually all residential occupiers are protected from summary eviction and harassment by the Protection from Eviction Act 1977 the effect of which is to make it necessary or advisable for any landlord to seek an order from the court before evicting a residential occupier. Criminal proceedings may be taken against landlords by or on behalf of tenants and other occupiers who are unlawfully evicted or harassed. Alternatively, affected tenants may seek injunctions and damages by way of civil proceedings for breach of their right to quiet enjoyment. There are, however, a small number of tenancies and licences excluded from such protection by the Housing Act 1988. These excluded categories relate principally to arrangements created since the Act by resident landlords who share a part of their accommodation with their tenants/licensees: the removal of this regulation had been intended to encourage people to let out rooms in their own homes, though it represents a significant breach of the only universal right to be enjoyed by all residential occupiers.

Even trespassers or 'squatters' have some limited protection against violent eviction. The traditional protection against forcible entry was repealed by a more limited form of safeguard under the Criminal Law Act 1977, which made it an offence to use or threaten violence to gain entry to any premises on which a person present is opposed to such entry. The only exception allowed is in the case of an actually displaced residential occupier who may use reasonable force to evict squatters who have taken up residence in his/her home. Characteristically, however, squatting occurs in unoccupied property and it behoves the owners of such property to obtain court orders using special expedited procedures in either the county court or the high court. Additionally, the Criminal Law Act 1977 makes it an offence for a squatter to refuse to leave residential property if requested to do so by a 'protected intending occupier' (being an owner or prospective tenant who wishes to move in), and the Criminal Justice and Public Order Act 1994 has more recently made it a criminal offence for a trespasser to fail to vacate residential property within 24 hours of service of an interim possession order. The implication of this last provision is that, in the case of squatters, possession orders may be enforced, not by civil procedures involving court bailiffs, but by arrest and criminal prosecution.

The class of residential occupier whose rights have not so far been discussed is the owner-occupier. To the extent that home-owners have the greatest degree of security of tenure under civil law, their need for statutory protection is correspondingly less. The rights of freehold owners, provided their property is not mortgaged, can only be interfered with in exceptional circumstances: for example, by compulsory purchase or closing orders made by public authorities or by orders made in the course of matrimonial or bankruptcy proceedings. However, some home-owners are in fact long leaseholders (i.e. they may have purchased a lease, or an unexpired portion of a lease, of more than 21 years' duration) and both long leaseholders and freeholders may well have mortgages on their property. The 'ground' rents which long leaseholders pay are characteristically small and are not subject to regulation. Although most long leases are in fact longer than a natural life span (99 or even 999 years), when they expire they may become statutory protected tenancies or, from 1999, assured tenancies. In practice, however, it is comparatively rare for the term of a long lease to expire without the leaseholder acquiring the freehold. Under the Leasehold Reform Act 1967 long leaseholders of *houses*, provided they have been in residence for more than three years, can compel the freeholder to extend the lease or to sell the freehold to the leasholder. Long leaseholders of *flats* have in certain circumstances a right of first refusal should the freeholders decide to sell their interest. People who buy their homes with mortgages or who borrow against the value of their homes for other purposes consent to a legal charge against the value of their home and, should they default on the terms of their mortgage by failing to make repayments, the lender has the right to repossess the home in order to recover the borrower's debt. As any other residential occupier, an owner-occupier has the right not to be summarily evicted. If a mortgagor falls into arrears with repayments, the lender must first serve a formal notice requiring repayment of all capital and interest due and only thereafter, if the mortgagor does not comply, proceed to court for a possession order. The court has power to suspend possession if suitable terms for the repayment of arrears can be set.

Housing conditions

While the last section considered rights to security of tenure, such rights do not by themselves ensure that the conditions in which people live will be satisfactory. This section will therefore consider first, the rights which tenants (and in some circumstances other occupiers) have to obtain repairs and improvements in their homes, and second, the rights which owner-occupiers (and in some circumstances, tenants) have to financial assistance with essential repairs and improvements.

This book is not concerned to elaborate on the multifarious civil remedies (in contract and tort) which may be available under landlord and tenant law. There are, however, two important legislative provisions on which tenants may rely in this connection. The first is section 11 of the Landlord and Tenant Act 1985, which makes it an implied term or 'covenant' within any periodic or short-term residential tenancy created since 1961 (being the date of the legislation by which the provision first originated) that the landlord is responsible for keeping in repair the structure and exterior of the dwelling concerned and such installations as may be provided for the supply of water, gas, electricity, sanitation and space/water heating. Tenants, conversely, are generally liable for minor internal repairs and decorations. The other provision is section 4 of the Defective Premises Act 1972, which imposes an explicit duty of care on all landlords subject to a repairing obligation such that they may be held liable for any personal injury or damage to property arising from any defect occurring on the premises for which they are responsible.

Of greater concern in the context of this discussion are two legislative frameworks conferring specific powers on local authorities and specific rights of complaint on individuals: the first has arisen under housing legislation and is currently to be found in consolidated form within the Housing Act 1985; the second has arisen under public health legislation and is currently to be found in consolidated form in the Environmental Protection Act 1990. The former is concerned to ensure the fitness of dwellings for habitation; the latter to prevent conditions which may be prejudicial to health.

Under the Housing Act 1985 (as amended), the environmental health departments of local authorities have power in relation to any dwelling that is unfit for human habitation to serve notices or orders on the owners or the persons responsible. Depending on which is the more satisfactory course, such notices may require either that repairs be carried out to make the property fit; or the closure or, in some circumstances, the demolition of the property. Owners may appeal against such requirements to the county court but, if they neither appeal nor comply with the requirements, the local authority has power to carry out works to the property in default and to recover the cost. Occupiers who are displaced as a result of closure or demolition orders are entitled under the Land Compensation Act 1973 to rehousing and to compensation. Additionally, local authorities may serve repairs notices on landlords or managers of properties that are not technically unfit but that are in serious disrepair. Local authorities also have powers to institute group repair (or 'envelope') schemes or to declare renewal or (very exceptionally) clearance areas as a means of dealing with pockets or whole areas of unfit housing. Fitness for habitation is to be judged with reference to structural stability; freedom from serious disrepair and dampness; the adequacy of provision for lighting, heating (and hot water), ventilation, cooking facilities, water supply, drainage and sanitation. Tenants or occupiers may make complaints to their local authorities if their housing conditions are such as to interfere with personal comfort, and local authorities are obliged to act. Failure to act may be challenged by judicial review or, alternatively, by a complaint to a magistrate (under section 606 of the Housing Act 1985), who, if satisfied that a dwelling or dwellings may be unfit for habitation, must require the local authority to make an inspection and report.

Under the Environmental Protection Act 1990 the environmental health departments of local authorities are also responsible for ensuring the abatement of 'statutory nuisances', a term which includes any premises in such a condition as to be prejudicial to health or a nuisance. This additional power enables local authorities to serve an abatement notice on the person by whose act, default or sufferance the statutory nuisance arises (or on the owner of the property concerned) requiring that such repairs or other works as may be necessary be carried out. Such notices may be appealed against in the magistrates' court, but if an abatement notice is neither appealed nor complied with, the local authority may prosecute the person(s) concerned in the magistrates' court, and/or carry out works in default and recover the costs. Individuals who are 'persons aggrieved' by a statutory nuisance may complain to their local authority or may alternatively lay information before a magistrate (under section 82 of the Environmental Protection Act 1990) so as to institute a prosecution against the person(s) responsible for an alleged statutory nuisance. This last-mentioned remedy may be especially useful or necessary for dissatisfied local authority tenants. While the environmental health and housing departments of a local council may be quite separate, a local authority cannot prosecute itself!

The environmental health departments of local authorities have a range of other powers in relation to housing conditions which may be invoked on complaint by a citizen. Such powers relate, for example, to overcrowding, dangerous buildings, fire precautions, drains, sewers and vermin control. Of particular significance are local authorities' powers in relation to houses in multiple occupation. These powers are potentially extensive and can include the operation of registration schemes, the issuing of overcrowding notices, the service and enforcement of works and repairs notices, the making and enforcement of management regulations and, in extreme circumstances, the making of control orders by which the local authority may itself assume management of premises.

Owner-occupiers, of course, are responsible for their own repairs. What is more, tenants are entitled in certain circumstances to carry out repairs to their homes, if their landlord has failed to do so. Secure tenants have the right under the Housing Act 1985 to do this, subject to giving notice to their landlord, and to recover the cost, and other tenants have a right established by case law to effect essential repairs and to set off the cost against future rent. Protected tenants and secure tenants (but not assured tenants) also have the right to carry out improvements to their homes, subject to their landlords' permission (though such permission may not be unreasonably withheld). An 'improvement' in this sense (for example, the provision of a bathroom where none existed before) is more than a repair and, if the tenant has improved a property, the rent which the landlord subsequently recovers may not reflect the value of that improvement.

It is possible for owner-occupiers, landlords or tenants to obtain grants towards the cost of repairs and/or improvements. Such grants are administered by local authorities under powers currently conferred by the Local Government and Housing Act 1989. Some such grants are specifically intended to assist landlords with renovations to remedy unfitness in premises served with repairs notices under the Housing Act 1985 and/or to carry out repairs or improvements to the common parts of inhabited buildings or to houses in multiple occupation. Discretionary grants are also available towards the cost of converting property so as to provide residential accommodation to let. The amount of grant which is given is a proportion of the cost of the works to be done, calculated on the basis of the likely return which landlords might expect on their investment, and subject to conditions as to the standard of the works to be carried out and the future use of the premises.

The grants which individual owner-occupiers and (less usually) tenants may claim are of two sorts: renovation grants and disabled facilities grants. The former are mandatory if the premises concerned are adjudged to be unfit for human habitation and if the works of renovation for which a grant is sought represent the most satisfactory means of making the premises fit: renovation grants for owner-occupiers are also mandatory if a repairs notice under the Housing Act 1985 has been served (see above). Disabled facilities grants are mandatory provided they will help meet the cost of works which are necessary, appropriate and practicable for the purposes of specifically facilitating the occupation of premises by a disabled person. Grants for other sorts of works – for example, home insulation – may also be available to owner-occupiers and tenants on a discretionary basis. Grants for owner-occupiers and tenants are means-tested and the maximum grant (the estimated cost of the eligible works) is reduced having regard to the level of the applicants' income and savings.

Homelessness and the rationing of public housing

Housing and public health legislation therefore provide some measure of protection against overcrowded and insanitary housing conditions. This is similarly reflected in a duty laid on local housing authorities (currently, by section 22 of the Housing Act 1985) by which they are required, in the allocation of public housing stock, to give 'reasonable preference' to people living in such conditions, to those with large families, to those living in otherwise unsatisfactory conditions and to those to whom authorities may owe a statutory duty. In practice, however, local authorities are not legally required to have any housing stock at all. Even where they have statutory duties to rehouse people – as under the Land Compensation Act 1973 (see above) or Part III of the Housing Act 1985 (see below) – they may achieve this by way of arrangements with third parties, such as housing associations or even private landlords. Since local authorities were first empowered to provide public housing, access to such housing has always been rationed. Characteristically, rationing has been by way of waiting lists and schemes by which to prioritise the claims and needs of prospective tenants. Local authorities are obliged to publish the details of their allocations policies, but the determination of criteria for allocation remains largely at their discretion. The purpose of council housing – as to whether it is to meet the general needs of the population or the special needs of the poorest – has always been a source of political controversy (Short 1982). Since the 1980s, however, the status of public or 'social' sector housing has unequivocally been reduced to that of a residual housing tenure (Clapham *et al.* 1990). In many parts of the country, the principal route by which to enter public sector housing is the 'emergency' route under the homeless persons provisions of Part III of the Housing Act 1985 (Niner 1989).

Access to public housing has never been acknowledged as a universal right, even for homeless people. State policy for the relief of homelessness has always been either deterrent or selective. In the fifteenth century homelessness, or 'vagrancy', could be subject to such violent punishments as whipping and branding. Under the Poor Laws it could result in an enforced return to the parish of one's birth and quite possibly incarceration in a bridewell or workhouse. The Beveridgian welfare state may have put an end to the workhouse, but the relief of homelessness was a social service reserved primarily for people who were aged or infirm and for 'persons in need of care and attention' (which term primarily referred to homeless women and children for whom only temporary shelter might be arranged). The current homeless persons legislation was originally enacted in 1977 and, for the first time, placed a clear duty on local housing authorities to provide permanent not temporary accommodation to certain classes of homeless person. It may be seen, however, first, that the right to housing which this provides is strictly conditional, and second, that the government intends at the time of writing significantly to dilute that right.

Legislative provision for the protection of homeless persons is now to be found in consolidated form in Part III of the Housing Act 1985 (for a fuller explanation see, for example, Arden and Hunter 1992). The definition which the legislation gives to homelessness is ostensibly widely drawn. A person is homeless if s/he has no accommodation which s/he, together with her/his family, has a legal right to occupy. The definition extends to include people who, though they have accommodation, may be at risk of violence from some other person residing there, or if the condition of the property is so bad that they might not reasonably be expected to continue to reside there. In practice, local authorities and the courts (see Chapter 8) have often interpreted this definition narrowly. People living in great insecurity whose sole right to accommodation may be the law which protects them from eviction without a court order (see above) may be held not to be homeless unless and until such an order has been made. Additionally, it may be held reasonable for people living in appalling physical conditions to continue living there if the conditions prevailing in the area of the local authority concerned are generally so poor that other people can be shown to be living in conditions which are worse or at least equally bad.

People who establish that they are homeless must additionally surmount two further hurdles if they are to obtain housing. First, they must establish that they are in 'priority need'. This condition perpetuates the selective nature of the state relief of homelessness. Excepting provision for those made homeless by fire, flood or natural disaster, only certain categories of person may receive substantive assistance (other than advice). Only households with dependent children (or households which consist of or include a pregnant woman) and households consisting of or which include someone who is 'vulnerable' by reason of old age, disability, learning difficulty, mental health problems or 'other special reason' will otherwise qualify. Second, people must establish that they did not become homeless intentionally. This provision enables local authorities to probe into the backgrounds of homeless people to establish the chain of causation resulting in their present circumstances and the degree of culpability which may attach to their present or indeed their past conduct.

A homeless person surmounting these hurdles is entitled to be rehoused by or through arrangements made by a local authority. The right remains conditional, on at least three further factors. First, if the homeless person has a local connection with another local authority area, s/he may be referred for assistance to that authority. Second, permanent accommodation need not be made available immediately and may be offered only after the homeless person and her/his family has undergone a stay in some form of temporary accommodation, such as a bed and breakfast hotel. Third, homeless persons rehoused in this manner, though they are entitled to accommodation that is suitable, are unlikely to be given much if any choice as to the nature of the accommodation they are offered. It should also be noted that assistance under the homeless persons provisions of the Housing Act 1985, like social assistance, expressly qualifies as 'recourse to public funds' for the purposes of immigration law (see Chapter 5) and it is a right which is not in practice exercisable by people whose immigration status is not secure.

At the time of writing the government has expressed itself to be committed to new legislation which will again reduce the rights of homeless people (see *Guardian* 19.7.1994; Burns 1994). It is proposed that local authorities will no longer have to provide permanent rehousing, but temporary housing for a limited period (of 'at least a year'); that local authorities with housing stock will be required to operate a single 'streamlined' waiting list system giving no automatic priority to people adjudged statutorily homeless; that the onus of proof should be changed so that applicants will be obliged to prove they are not intentionally homeless (rather than local authorities having to prove that they are).

Conclusion/summary

Inevitably, perhaps, within a democratic-welfare-capitalist state housing remains highly commodified (see Chapter 1 and, for example, Ball 1983). Dwellings and land, even when their use is regulated or they are owned by the state, are leased or rented out, bought or sold as commodities in the marketplace. To the extent that it is possible for social legislation to create rights in relation to housing, it is constrained by the nature of property relations and the character of real estate as a particular kind of commodity. This chapter has reflected on four rather different kinds of legislative intervention.

First, social legislation may be used to guarantee the position of citizens in the housing market by underwriting their capacity to pay for housing. The most privileged form of housing tenure, owner-occupation, has in the past benefited from a universal fiscal subsidy. In contrast, less privileged forms of housing tenure, the private and public rented sectors, are assisted by a selective form of social security subsidy. With the ascendancy of owner-occupation at the close of the twentieth century, the indiscriminate subsidy to personal housing costs which had been provided through mortgage tax relief is to be curtailed. For people remaining in the residual rented housing sectors, and for those owner-occupiers who find themselves on social assistance, the selectivity of means-tested benefits encroaches to the point that it may even take account of the quality and size of a person's home in relation to her/his needs and the composition of her/his household. The principal framework of social rights is therefore one which supports only those at the margins of the market. It is a framework which requires a considerable degree of surveillance of individual citizens' housing arrangements.

Second, social legislation may be used to achieve stability in the housing market. In the past tenants in the private rented sector were given certain rights with regard to rent levels and security of tenure. This process, however, became increasingly complex over time and increasingly marginal as the public rented sector and, more particularly, owner-occupation became more dominant forms of housing tenure. Latterly, Conservative governments have rejected any form of rent regulation which might hold rents beneath their 'natural' market level. This chapter has discussed the different regulatory regimes which apply to private sector tenants (under both pre- and post-1980s legislation), to public sector tenants, and to other forms of residential tenure, some of which are subject to minimal or no legal protection. The nearest thing to a universal right to be achieved under modern social legislation is the right of a residential occupier (including owner-occupying mortgagors) not to be evicted without a court first making an order for repossession. It is a right which fetters the power of market forces, albeit in many circumstances only to a minimal degree, and it is a right which has been eroded by more recent legislation.

Third, social legislation may be used to guarantee certain standards of production; that is to say, to ensure that housing is provided to a standard that is habitable and reasonably conducive to public health. This chapter has discussed the rights of redress which tenants have against landlords in respect of disrepair; the powers which local authorities may exercise to compel repairs and improvements to unsatisfactory housing; and the rights which people have to grants towards the cost of repairs and improvements. It may be noted, however, that landlord and tenant law is primarily a matter of civil not social rights; that the citizen's right to invoke the protective powers of local authorities under housing and public health legislation are subject to the willingness and capacity of local authorities to respond; and that the right to financial assistance with essential repairs and improvements is not universal but selective, being conditional on a means test.

Finally, social legislation may be used to guarantee citizens access to housing. Legislation relating to the direct provision of public housing has been largely permissive, however. Local housing authorities have never been able unconditionally to guarantee access to housing. The nearest thing to a right to housing is a right afforded only to certain categories of homeless persons and is conditional on their past behaviour. The government has proposed that even this right should be eroded.

Citizens do enjoy certain rights in relation to housing, but they are complex and qualified rights. Where social legislation protects or creates such rights, it does so by and large selectively. In housing, as with 'work', though social rights may ameliorate the impact of market forces, it is the latter which generally take precedence.

Recommended additional reading

Current editions of the *Guide to Housing Benefit and Council Tax Benefit*, published by Shelter Housing Aid Centre/Institute of Housing, London, and the *Rights Guide for Home Owners*, published by Child Poverty Action Group, London.

Current edition of Arden, A. and Hunter, C., *Manual of Housing Law*, published by Sweet and Maxwell, London (or a similar guide or handbook).

For a simpler kind of explanation, readers may wish to turn to Shelter's *Housing Rights Guides*, nos 1–13, Shelter Housing Aid, London.

Questions for reflection

In a property-owning democracy, how far is it appropriate statutorily to guarantee a person's right to a home?

Housing and public health legislation confers extensive powers on local authorities with regard to the maintenance of housing standards. How effectively do these powers translate into enforceable rights for the citizen?

PART III

CHAPTER 8

SOCIAL WELFARE AND
THE COURTS

In democratic-welfare-capitalist societies, the courts are the ultimate guardians of citizens' legal rights rather than their welfare rights. The judiciary and the courts represent a limb of the state apparatus which, in theory at least, is kept constitutionally distinct from both the legislature (parliament) and the executive (the government). The courts, however, do enter the sphere of social rights for two principal reasons. The courts have responsibility first, for being the final arbiters of how social legislation should be interpreted and second, for ensuring the 'legality' of the executive's administrative actions. The court systems of modern welfare states have generally developed as part of a process by which state power has grown and become centralised. In place of the local *ad hoc* assemblies of medieval times, at which disputes were resolved in accordance with local custom and by the grace of the sovereign's local representative, uniform and centrally regulated institutions have emerged for the dispensation of justice. The precise manner in which this has occurred has differed between countries and, in this chapter, what will be discussed is the role of the courts in Britain (or more specifically, in England and Wales). Most particularly, the chapter will be concerned with the influence exercised by the English judiciary over social rights.

However, there is an important preliminary point to be made about what distinguishes the basic tenets of English law (which have been adopted in other Anglo-Saxon countries such as the USA, Canada, Australia and New Zealand) from that of Roman or 'Continental' law (characteristic of other Western European nations). In Chapter 3, I drew on the work of Mann (1987) to distinguish historically between the 'constitutionalist' regimes of the Anglo-Saxon world and the 'absolutist' regimes of Western Europe, a distinction which was then linked to the development of more restrictive/liberal welfare regimes in the former nations and more expansive/corporatist welfare regimes in the latter. A discussion of the part played by different kinds of legal system falls beyond the scope of this book, although the issue deserves one or two speculative remarks.

The English revolutionary settlement of 1688 was to result in the constitutional separation of the crown from the functional limbs of the state apparatus, the supposed sovereignty of parliament, the accountability of the executive and the independence of the courts. This represented a necessary precondition for the early development of industrial capitalism in Britain. However, the classical sociologist Max Weber remained puzzled by the inherent irrationality of English law, compared with its Continental counterpart. For Weber, the adherence of English law to adversarial procedures and a common law tradition (rather than inquisitorial procedures and codification) was inconsistent with the degree of predictability required to underpin the economic calculus of free market capitalism (see, for example, Hunt 1978: ch. 6). The adversarial procedure which characterises English law is descended from the ancient practice of trial by combat. Though combat now takes place by way of formalised verbal argument, the judge is not required to enter the contest between the disputing parties, merely to enforce the rules of combat and determine who has won. It is a procedure which, without substantial safeguards (including the use of juries in certain criminal trials), will tend inevitably to disadvantage weaker parties at the expense of the powerful. Adversarial procedure constrains the nature of judicial intervention in procedural matters. On the other hand, the common law tradition affords great flexibility to judges in matters of legal interpretation and gives them power in effect to create law. The common law is so called because it imposed itself in place of a variety of local customs: it is none the less a form of law not determined by any code or statute, but built up over time by judicial custom. Judges are required to make decisions, not by following any central logical precepts, but on the basis of precedents established in earlier judgments. The effect of this, as Rheinstein (the editor of the English language edition of

Weber's *On Law and Economy in Society*) has said is that it enables the courts:

> to hide behind a screen of verbal formulae of apparent logically formal rationality, those considerations of substantive rationality, that is, of social policy, by which the decision has been actually motivated but which judges are reluctant to reveal to the public and, often enough, to themselves. (quoted in Hunt 1978: 124)

The distinctiveness of Anglo-Saxon welfare regimes may in part relate to the fact that in Anglo-Saxon jurisdictions the courts have lacked procedural power to protect the weak, while simultaneously possessing the legal power to advance a very particular social policy agenda. This is a contention to which the final section of this chapter will return. First, however, it is intended to outline the structure and powers of the court system in England and Wales, to discuss its accessibility to the ordinary citizen, and to consider examples of the ways in which the courts have intervened in matters relating to social security and housing provision.

The court system

In origin the powers of the English courts are those delegated by the crown, although the removal in 1701 of the monarch's direct control over the hiring and firing of judges assured the degree of independence supposedly necessary to guarantee the 'rule of law'. The complex structure of the modern court system was largely established in the nineteenth century and is strictly hierarchical. The significance of the hierarchy is twofold. First, lower courts are bound by the precedents decided in higher courts. Second, appeals against decisions in lower courts are heard in the higher courts. At the pinnacle of the system sits the judicial committee of the House of Lords, providing a surviving if symbolic link between the courts and parliament. Beneath the House of Lords comes the Court of Appeal (with separate civil and criminal divisions), followed by the High Court (with four main specialist divisions). The lower courts of the system include the county courts (which have a civil jurisdiction), the crown courts (which have a criminal jurisdiction), and at the bottom of the hierarchy are the magistrates' courts (which have a mixture of jurisdictions and are presided over, not by judges, but by stipendiary or lay magistrates). Much more recently, English law has also been affected by the jurisdiction of the European Court of Justice (responsible for the interpretation and enforcement of the legislation and directives of the EU) and the European Court of Human Rights (responsible for the interpretation and enforcement of the Council of Europe's Convention for the Protection of Human Rights and Fundamental Freedoms). For a fuller account readers are referred to one of the many textbooks on the English legal system (e.g. Bailey and Gunn 1991).

Of interest here are the circumstances in which the courts are drawn into the arena of social rights. There are two principal ways in which this can occur. First, the specific jurisdiction conferred on the courts (generally the lower courts) by legislation may directly or incidentally incorporate functions relating to social welfare provision. Second, the inherent prerogative or supervisory jurisdiction of the higher courts may enable them to intervene to review the decisions or actions of welfare administrators.

Specific jurisdictions may be imposed by legislation, but in the field of social welfare there has been a strong tendency to create specialised administrative tribunals to deal with justiciable issues where these arise. The role of tribunals and their supposed advantages over the courts will be considered in Chapter 9. Opposition to the idea that courts should meddle in matters of social administration can be traced back to Edwin Chadwick, one of the architects of the 1834 Poor Law. Chadwick was concerned that courts hearing individual pleas out of context would not take account of those 'large classes of cases and general and often remote effects, which cannot be brought to the knowledge of judges' (cited in Cranston 1985: 287). Soon after the turn of the twentieth century, Dicey (1915) and other legal writers were voicing concerns that the courts should be brought in to supervise the burgeoning state apparatus and subject it to the rule of law. The incursion of the courts into the everyday administration of the welfare state has none the less been resisted by politicians as diverse as Winston Churchill and Aneurin Bevan. In 1911, Churchill, then a Liberal Home Secretary, expressed doubts about the capacity of the judiciary to handle public policy matters of concern to working-class people, since 'where class issues are involved, it is impossible to pretend that the courts command the same degree of general confidence [as in ordinary criminal and civil matters]' (cited in Cranston 1985: 288). In 1946, Bevan as Labour's Minister of Health was equally explicit that social policy reforms should as far as possible be insulated from 'judicial sabotage' (*ibid.*: 288–9). Where they have been afforded a specific jurisdiction, as occurred with the county courts under the Workmen's Compensation Act 1897, the courts have not always coped well. The inability of the county courts to deal with an unforeseen flood of disputed compensation claims under that Act was a factor which contributed to the view that specialist tribunals would provide a more suitable forum for handling the claims of working people (Abel-Smith and Stevens 1967). Not only were alternative adjudicative arrangements devised under the National Insurance Act 1911 (namely the Court of Referees – see Chapter 9), but the workmen's compensation scheme was in time removed from the courts with the introduction of the industrial injuries scheme under the National Insurance Act 1946. At about the same time, the rent control functions of the county courts were entrusted to new tribunals and later, in the 1970s, the creation of the Industrial Tribunal also removed from the civil courts the bulk of litigation relating to the interpretation and enforcement of employment protection provisions and the law governing individual contracts of employment.

However, the ordinary courts cannot avoid the affairs of poor and working-class people in such areas as landlord and tenant law, which has been a concern of social policy (see Chapter 7). County courts are routinely concerned with claims by both private and public sector landlords against their tenants for possession, but may also entertain claims by tenants against their landlords for disrepair, unlawful eviction or other breaches of covenant. The magistrates court also has jurisdiction in respect of such specific legislation as the Protection from Eviction Act 1977 (which defines the criminal offences of harassment and illegal eviction) and the Environmental Protection Act 1990 (being the current enactment to provide remedies against the landlords of property which is prejudicial to health).

Prior to the Child Support Act 1991 (see Chapter 5) the lower courts also had a role in securing income maintenance for children, a jurisdiction they continue for the time being to exercise in relation to cases in which the need for maintenance first arose before 1993 and the parent with care is not receiving social assistance. More generally, the protection of children in need represents an entire area of welfare law not touched on in this book but in which the courts have developed and continue to exercise a central, specialised role.

It remains the case, however, that social legislation has by and large entrusted the lower courts with only an indirect role in relation to the exercise of social rights. A far more influential role is that which has been seized by the higher courts in reviewing the decisions of lower courts or tribunals or the administrative actions of central and local government. It is the higher courts which have the power to determine how social legislation will be interpreted. The power arises either when a decision of a lower judicial forum is appealed against (if provision for such an appeal exists) or, alternatively, on an application for judicial review. Judicial review is the legal remedy by which judges may ensure that the powers exercised by public authorities are kept within legal bounds. Relatively speaking, it is a remedy of growing importance. The number of applications for leave to apply for judicial review multiplied almost fourfold during the 1980s (from 533 in 1981 to 2,129 in 1990 – see Lewis and Birkinshaw 1993: 201).

When a higher court is required to rule on an appeal from a lower judicial forum the substantive decision-making powers normally remain with the judicial forum below and it is only points of law which the higher court determines. In the case of judicial review, however, the court has powers to intervene at its own discretion. The powers derive primarily from the ancient prerogatives of the crown (the powers of *certiorari*, *prohibitio* and *mandamus*), but are informed by the more recent legal doctrine of *ultra vires*. The powers of ministers, civil servants, administrative tribunals and local government are all defined by statute. Actions which exceed or lie beyond such definition, which are wholly unreasonable or which breach the rules of natural justice may be deemed *ultra vires* and therefore invalid (for a fuller discussion see, for example, Turpin 1990: 414–8). Therefore, though the courts have complete discretion *not* to intervene, should they elect to do so they potentially wield considerable power over the implementation of social policy. Such power can only be invoked in the course of proceedings actually before the court and two important limitations which therefore apply are the doctrine of 'ripeness' and the doctrine of *locus standi*. The doctrine of 'ripeness' requires that an individual litigant should have exhausted all other appeals and remedies before bringing issues before the court: complaints must therefore first have been referred to and considered by every other competent authority before they are finally 'ripe' for intervention by the court. The doctrine of *locus standi* requires that only those individuals having a direct and material interest in a matter may bring it before the court: individuals or groups with wider social or political concerns are not generally recognised as having standing before the court, though some concessions have recently been made by the courts in the case of specialised pressure groups (see below). To these constraints must be added the sheer complexity and expense of litigation. In the circumstances, the significant powers of the higher courts and of the even remoter European Courts are invoked comparatively infrequently.

Access to the courts

This leads directly to the question of the accessibility of the court system. The individual's right of access to the courts and to the advice, assistance and advocacy which this might require is itself an issue. Is this a legal right, a social right, or as the National Consumer Council (1977) have claimed, a 'fourth right of citizenship'?

The technical character of welfare rights and social legislation and the rarefied nature of the court system are such that the capacity to seek relief in the courts is for most citizens dependent on the availability of expert help. At the most basic level the rule of law requires that all should have equal access to redress: mechanisms to ensure this are part and parcel of our legal rights. To the extent that poor or disadvantaged people may have particular kinds of legal problems it may be argued that they are or ought to be entitled to receive publicly provided legal services (see, for example, Royal Commission on Legal Services 1979). At another level, the meeting of legal needs, like the meeting of health needs, is fundamentally necessary to our capacity to function as full citizens: access to legal aid is therefore a social right. There is, however, a further sense in which all our rights of citizenship require that we should have information about our entitlements and, if needed, assistance to pursue our remedies. If this access is not guaranteed the citizen's access to goods, services and benefits and the effective implementation of protective legislation is jeopardised.

In this last, more general sense, the right to advice, assistance and advocacy is one which extends beyond the question of access to lawyers and the courts. In spite of this, the courts remain the ultimate guardians of legal rights and, historically, it is lawyers who have exercised a virtual monopoly of expertise over the provision of aid in respect of access to the courts. It is necessary therefore to consider the development of public legal services, both as a development in social policy, but also as a factor influencing or inhibiting the role of the courts in relation to social rights. The fact that the development of legal services was not seen as an integral part of the development of the welfare state cannot be unrelated to the attempts already described to shut the courts out from matters of social policy.

Prior to the Legal Aid and Advice Act 1949 such limited concessionary provision as had been made available to poor people by the legal profession had been essentially charitable in nature. Provision dating from the fifteenth century relating to the prosecution of civil proceedings and the more recent 'dock brief' system for the defence of criminal proceedings allowed persons without means to have counsel assigned from among any willing to take on their cases free of charge (Zander 1978). The introduction in 1949 of a publicly funded legal aid scheme was based on a report commissioned by the war-time coalition government (the Rushcliffe Report 1944) and implemented by the reforming post-war Labour government. In such circumstances, it might be supposed that the scheme would have followed the Beveridgian principle of universal provision. It did not. There was to be no national legal service. Though public funding was to be made available it was to be channelled through a privately organised and self-regulating legal profession and based on a strict means test. Marshall looked on the introduction of legal aid as an attempt 'to remove the barriers between *civil* rights and their remedies' [emphasis added] (1950: 29). The fact that financial eligibility would be determined by the National Assistance Board (currently this is done by the DSS) established a link with the Poor Law which Marshall foresaw might make legal aid 'unsavoury to many of those entitled to avail themselves of it' (*ibid.*: 30). He also foresaw difficulties in 'combining in one system the two principles of social justice and market price' (*ibid.*: 29): the market would still largely determine the charges levied by lawyers in the course of litigation and the combination of high fees and a strict means test would act to the disadvantage of litigants with modest means, a complaint which others have repeated since and which more recent retrenchment of the legal aid system has done nothing to quell (see Hansen 1993).

The scheme introduced in 1949 was restricted to civil proceedings. A legal advice scheme provided for within the legislation was not implemented until 1959 (though this was subsequently revamped under the Legal Advice and Assistance Act 1972) and a formal system of criminal legal aid was not effective until 1967. Legal aid is not available for all types of court proceedings and civil legal aid is subject not only to a means test, but also to a merits test administered by the Legal Aid Board, which took over responsibility for legal aid administration from the Law Society in 1988. The merits test applies both to the legal merits (does the applicant have a good case in law?) and the wider merits of an applicant's case (would a solicitor advise a paying client of modest but sufficient means to run the risk of the litigation contemplated?). Intended to prevent the abuse of public funds, these additional hurdles place poorer citizens with uncertain or unusual cases, or cases involving small rewards but important principles, at a disadvantage compared with more affluent litigants. At the time of writing, the Lord Chancellor has mooted proposals for far-reaching changes to the legal aid scheme. The system proposed would involve budget-limited block funding for selected franchise-holding legal service providers, including advice agencies. The explicit purpose is to curtail public expenditure on legal aid and the propsals have been opposed by consumer groups and the legal profession alike: the President of the Law Society has expressed the fear that implementation would lead to a 'rationing of justice' (*Guardian* 12.1.1995). Ironically, however, the proposals, if implemented, will focus state legal aid more narrowly into areas such as housing, welfare benefits, debt, immigration and employment which it did not necessarily reach before (see *Guardian*, 3.5.1995).

The right to legal aid is therefore a qualified right. Cranston (1985: 89) has suggested that it is as a consequence of the charitable origins of legal aid that the right to it has been so slow to develop. It is significant that the other ways in which attempts have been made to advance the achievement of the 'fourth right of citizenship' should have involved new forms of charitable endeavour. Charitable status is the common thread which has underpinned the development both of the advice and law centres' movements and of the major pressure groups which comprise the 'poverty lobby'.

The 1960s and 1970s in Britain witnessed the birth of a radical new enthusiasm for 'rights'. This was fuelled to an extent by the civil rights movement in the USA, by the popularisation of new ideas about community action (exemplified in the works of Alinsky 1969 and Friere 1972) and the pioneering approach of American neighbourhood law firms first sponsored under the Economic Opportunity Act 1964.

New proactively oriented grant-aided advice centres sprang up in inner city areas as part of a wider growth in community development initiatives. The British law centre movement was founded, funded primarily by grants from local and/or central government and with a mission to use the law to tackle the structural causes of poor people's disadvantage (see Cooper 1983). A new breed of national charities, including Child Poverty Action Group, Shelter, Disablement Income Group, National Council for One Parent Families, emerged not with a traditional emphasis on fundraising and voluntary service, but with a view to campaigning on policy issues and for the rights of disadvantaged groups (Whiteley and Winyard 1983). The independence of the new advice centres and law centres (most of which were registered as charities) and of the charitable national pressure groups enabled them to take up or support individual test cases in the area of welfare rights. The 'test case strategy' (see Prosser 1983) became a major weapon in the armoury of welfare lawyers and the poverty lobby. The cases of individual social security claimants, homeless people and council tenants were taken before the higher courts with a view to establishing more general points of principle by which to clarify or develop the law or to force changes in policy. Recently, the courts have begun to acknowledge that national bodies such as CPAG should in certain circumstances be recognised as having the *locus standi* required to bring cases on behalf of the groups they represent (see *R v. Secretary of State for Social Services ex parte Child Poverty Action Group* [1989] 1 All E.R. 1047).

The 'success' of test case strategies is open to question. The outcome of test cases was not always that which was desired. What is more, if the legal precedent established by a test case was unwelcome to the government, the end-result could be legislation to frustrate or overrule the test case outcome. The significance of these test cases was that, for good or ill, they brought to the higher courts a range of social policy issues which would not have got there by other means.

The courts and social security

This was particularly so in the case of the social security system. Not only had the administration of social security been effectively insulated from the interference of the courts, but the courts had been largely insulated from all acquaintance with social security. Excepting rare applications for judicial review brought usually with trade union backing against the rulings of Medical Appeal Tribunals, Industrial Injuries or National Insurance Commissioners (Ogus and Barendt 1988: 586), it was not until the 1970s that the courts were to any extent troubled with matters relating to social security. What is more, largely as a result of a restructuring in 1980 of supplementary benefit (the main social assistance benefit at that time) and the introduction of a right of appeal in supplementary benefit cases to Social Security Commissioners (see Chapter 9), the number of such cases reaching the courts was to decline again in the 1980s. Of the intervening period Prosser has concluded:

> the decisions of the courts were generally depressing and marred by ignorance of social welfare matters, and by an approach which did not rely on consistent legal principles, but rather made results seem something of a lottery. There was no attempt to develop an understanding of the system or to develop principles to give it a proper legal structure. An aversion to decisions which might work in favour of claimants was always a possible response. (1983: 42)

Decisions tended to fall into one of two categories: those by which the courts sought to avoid involvement and to leave matters to the 'common sense' of tribunals and administrators; and those in which the courts felt obliged to displace policy-directed decision-making with the individualistic logic of liberal jurisprudence. What determined the approach in any particular instance it is difficult to say with certainty, but the clearest examples of the former approach related to cases involving students and young unemployed people (*R* v. *Preston SBAT ex parte Moore*, *R* v. *Sheffield SBAT ex parte Shine* [1975] 1 W.L.R. 624 and *R* v. *South West London SBAT ex parte Holland and Szczelkun* (1978) SB 109), while perhaps the clearest example of the latter related to a case involving a person with disabilities (*R* v. *South West London SBAT ex parte Wyatt* [1978] 1 W.L.R. 240). Arguably, the courts were prepared to give closer attention to 'deserving' than to the 'undeserving' poor. In *Shine* the court went so far as to say that, because the supplementary benefit scheme was supposed to be administered with as little technicality as possible, the court should hesitate to interfere with a tribunal's decision, 'even though it may be erroneous in point of law'. *Wyatt* in contrast was one of several cases in which the court applied the principle of administrative law, which requires that a discretion must be exercised with regard to the merits of an individual case and not fettered by the adoption of a rigid policy.

On the one hand, the courts demonstrated 'judicial ignorance salted with a large dose of judicial bias against the poor' (deSmith, quoted in Prosser 1983: 32), but on the other they were capable, when so minded, of undermining the restrictive policies of benefit administrators. Where decisions in favour of claimants were made this generally resulted in hasty legislative changes to nullify the effect. Eventually, a wholesale reform of the supplementary benefit scheme translated administrative policy into statute and a mass of detailed regulations (Walker 1993), the implementation of which would be less vulnerable to judicial criticism. The flexibility which the discretionary nature of the old scheme permitted had undoubtedly been capriciously exercised but, by a no less capricious string of judgments, the courts unwittingly helped put pressure on the government to have parliament squeeze nearly all elements of discretion out of the scheme, so setting the scene for the introduction of even greater rigidity at a later stage (see Chapter 6).

Since 1980 a right of appeal in respect of decisions affecting all social security benefits has lain from the Social Security Commissioners directly to the Court of Appeal, though the volume of litigation has been small and the Court of Appeal has remained by and large content to bow to the expertise of the Commissioners. Above the Court of Appeal, the House of Lords has proved itself 'unwilling to probe deeply into the subtleties of social security law' (Ogus and Barendt 1988: 587).

A more direct influence on British social security policy has been the European Court of Justice. There have been two instances in which rulings of the ECJ have forced Britain to make legislative changes. Both have arisen as a result of EU equal treatment directives (see Baldwin-Edwards and Gough 1991). The first was in 1985 when a case was successfully brought against the British government claiming that the British invalid care allowance scheme discriminated unlawfully against married women since it excluded them from benefit on the assumption that they would in any event have been available to care for a disabled spouse in a way which men would not. As a result invalid care allowance was subsequently extended to working-age married women. The second instance relates to ECJ judgments which initially indirectly compelled Britain to amend the state regulation of occupational pension schemes so as to ensure that men and women retiring or being made redundant at any given age shall receive parity of treatment; and which more recently resulted in the equalisation of the state pension age for men and women (by raising the age for women to 65).

The courts and housing policy

In the field of housing policy, involving as it does matters of property, the courts have had a rather more substantial role. As was observed in Chapter 7, such social legislation as has created rights in relation to housing has taken a variety of forms. In some instances, legislation has necessarily impinged on the rights of property-owners and landlords. This has applied first, in the case of public health and regulatory planning legislation by which local authorities may require the improvement or even the wholesale clearance of property; and second, in the case of legislation which creates rights for tenants against their landlords in respect of security of tenure, rent levels and repairs. Both kinds of legislation have generated conflicts to be resolved in the courts. There are other instances in which social legislation has imposed duties on public authorities with regard to the provision of housing; duties which individuals have attempted to enforce through the courts.

A thorough exposition of the history of judicial intervention in such matters is beyond the scope of this book. I shall, none the less, briefly illustrate that the overall tendency in judicial decision-making has been to side with property-owners against local authorities and tenants, but with the local authorities against, for example, the 'undeserving homeless'. This is not to say that there have not been some important judicial rulings whose effects have served to advance social rights, but that the net impact of the courts' role has inclined towards the restraint rather than the development of housing policy.

Since the nineteenth century social legislation has entrusted to local authorities an expanding array of powers by which to compel property-owners to provide sanitation, by which compulsorily to acquire property for slum clearance, and by which to regulate the use and development of property. The response of the courts has been to insist on the most rigorous observance of procedural safeguards, enjoining local authorities 'to keep strictly within [their] powers, and not to be guided by any fancied view of the spirit of the Act which confers them' (from *Tinkler* v. *Wandsworth District Board of Works* [1858] 44 E.R. 989). During the nineteenth century, a tide of informed opinion in favour of improved sanitary conditions resulted in some softening of judicial attitudes, but it is striking that when local authorities were challenged in the courts for failing to provide or maintain sewers, the courts then became reluctant to intervene, fearing the policy and cost implications should they compel the authorities to undertake large-scale schemes of public works (Cranston 1985). Similarly, during the first part of the twentieth century the courts' insistence on rigid compliance with procedure seriously inhibited the slum clearance policies of successive governments and some commentators of the day accused the courts of deliberately frustrating the purposes of social legislation (Jennings 1936). With the outbreak of the Second World War and the exigencies of the defence of the realm the judiciary became more sympathetic to the need for government intervention in relation to the control and requisition of property.

The 1960s witnessed a 'revival of judicial activism' (Cranston 1985: 148) when once again the courts began to assert themselves by supporting challenges to local authority and ministerial decisions in housing and planning matters. Such support was selective, however. Of these more recent cases, Griffiths has observed:

courts do pay the closest attention to arguments advanced on behalf of [large private property] owners, and require local authorities and ministers to behave with meticulous propriety in dealing with them. Whereas the individual owner-occupier or tenant tends to find himself more often dismissed with homilies about the public interest, with reference to his immigrant status, or with Ciceronian precepts of doubtful relevance. (1981: 137)

In matters of landlord and tenant law judges have displayed a tendency to resist statutory regulation in an area which was once the preserve of common law. It has been suggested in the past that much of the complexity which has beset social legislation in landlord and tenant matters stemmed in fact from parliamentary manoeuvres to close judicially created loopholes (Cranston 1985: 150). Equally, the confused state of judicially created case law relating, for example, to the interpretation of non-exclusive occupation agreements (see Chapter 7 above) has stemmed from past attempts by judges to stretch distinctions in common law so as to permit the evasion of such protective legislation as the Rent Acts. In fairness, the House of Lords has sought (in *Street* v. *Mountford* [1985] A.C. 809) decisively to counter the effects of earlier Court of Appeal rulings, but this did not prevent a great many landlords from exploiting dubious forms of 'licence' agreement, nor it seems has it entirely removed uncertainty (see Arden and Hunter 1992: 30–1). The tenor of many judicial pronouncements has been such as to construe social legislation not as an aid but as an obstacle to the attempts of the 'owner of housing accommodation to provide it at a profit for those in great need of it' (from *Somma* v. *Hazelhurst* [1978] 1 W.L.R. 1014). Judicial rulings have sometimes sought to soften the impact on landlords by placing countervailing obstacles in the way of their tenants. Where legislation has imposed repairing obligations on landlords (such as may apply under section 8 or 11 of the Housing Act 1985, provisions which date back to 1909 and 1961 respectively) the courts have sought in various ways to restrict the liabilities of landlords by, for example, placing duties on tenants as to the 'unequivocal' notification of disrepair.

Though the courts have tended to require strict procedural observance on the part of local authorities and tenants, quite different standards have been applied, for example, in the case of property-owners seeking to evict squatters. The 'rights' of squatters have been progressively diminished since the resurgence of squatting during the homelessness crisis of the 1960s and 1970s. The response of the courts was to hold that 'if homelessness were once admitted as a defence to trespass, no one's house would be safe' (from *Southwark LBC* v. *Williams* [1971] 1 Ch. 734). New Supreme Court and county court rules were introduced to provide a speedy procedure for the eviction of squatters, albeit with safeguards to protect the interests of occupiers. However, having created rules for property-owners to follow, in a series of controversial cases, the courts proceeded to excuse owners who had not fully complied with the rules. In one such case, where owners had taken only minimal steps to determine the identity of the occupants they sought to evict, the judge waived the irregularity since too rigorous an application of the rule requiring such steps to be taken could turn proceedings

> into something of a lottery, a forensic game of snakes and ladders, since the plaintiff could never know until he came to court whether the court might not, prompted by the ingenuity of counsel, find some further step which was reasonably practicable which had not been taken . . . (from *Burston Finance* v. *Wilkins and persons unknown, The Times*, 17.6.1975)

This, ironically, describes the predicament facing many a disadvantaged or unrepresented litigant and seems out of place when applied to a finance company enjoying the full benefits of legal representation. Griffiths (1981: 142) cites it as an instance in which rules are judicially manipulated to favour one side in a dispute. More fundamentally, it demonstrates how 'robust' judges can be when they choose, and how 'frail' can be the rights of the undeserving homeless, even when they can secure the services of an ingenious advocate.

Even when they do not resort to squatting, homeless persons have not always been treated favourably by the courts. The major piece of social legislation to afford rights to homeless people has been the Housing (Homeless Persons) Act 1977 (since incorporated as Part III of the Housing Act 1985). When called on to interpret this legislation the courts have done so by and large restrictively so as to limit the effect of challenges brought by homeless persons against local authorities. In particular, the courts have sought to make such challenges difficult by insisting that they may only be brought by judicial review (i.e. in the High Court), for which leave may be granted only reluctantly (see *Cocks* v. *Thanet DC* [1982]

A.C. 286 and *R* v. *Hillingdon LBC. ex parte Puhlhofer* [1986] A.C. 484). Given the ambivalent relationship between the courts and local authorities it is not surprising that there should have been occasions on which the courts have sided with homeless applicants against local authority housing departments, particularly when housing officials have sought to bend the meaning of 'homelessness' and 'available accommodation' (see *R* v. *Ealing LBC ex parte Sidhu* [1982] 80 L.G.R. 534 and *R* v. *Hillingdon LBC ex parte Islam* [1983] 1 A.C. 688). None the less, in cases involving allegations of 'intentional homelessness', the judiciary has adopted an important role in legitimating the scrutiny to which homeless people are subjected by local authorities and the strict discipline imposed on people threatened with homelessness. Housing officials have been permitted to search out chains of cause and effect leading back into a homeless person's past (*Dyson* v. *Kerrier DC* [1980] 1 W.L.R. 1205) and to exercise sanctions against people who do not observe the rules by which access to social housing is rationed (*Din* v. *Wandsworth LBC* [1983] 1 A.C. 653). In the case of *Din*, the House of Lords held that a family who ignored advice from the local authority and voluntarily vacated accommodation from which they would shortly have been evicted had thereby forfeited the right to assistance because, in the judges' view, the apparent object of the legislation was not to meet housing need in any absolute sense, but

> to lay down conditions for retaining priority and thereby discourage persons from so acting as to increase the already heavy burden on housing authorities. The method was to postpone the claims of those who so acted and to give their places in the queue to those who did not. (*ibid.*)

That any fundamental right to shelter is not supported by the British judiciary is most graphically illustrated by a ruling in a dispute concerning a family from Bangladesh in which one Law Lord called into question, in an *obiter* remark, whether it was ever intended that homeless persons legislation should apply to 'immigrants' (legal, it seems, or otherwise) (*R* v. *London Borough of Newham ex parte London Borough of Tower Hamlets* [1990] 22 H.L.R. 29).

Social policy and the judiciary

Such a record as the courts have had in defending social rights can only be described as poor. To what extent, however, is the judiciary influenced by social policy considerations or by its own perceptions of social policy? Dicey's (1885) classical nineteenth-century legal theory – which still represents the orthodoxy of the legal establishment (see Harden and Lewis 1986) – would reject the very idea that judges might be beholden to policy, rather than to the law. The guarantee which has supposedly underpinned the British (or English) constitution since the late seventeenth century is 'the rule of law' or, more precisely, 'government under the law'. It is a twofold guarantee to ensure the protection of the people from any exercise by government of arbitrary power: first, that sovereignty should reside in a representative parliament; second, that the role of the courts should be the preservation of the common law. By this means, governments must in theory account to parliament for the policies they pursue and to the courts for the legality of their actions. Until as recently as 1992 (see *Pepper* v. *Hart* [1992] 3 W.L.R. 1032) the judges remained so aloof from the business of policy-making that if, when applying the law, the meaning of the words of a statute was not literally clear, they would not permit themelves to seek clarification from the record of the relevant parliamentary debate, preferring instead to divine the intentions of parliament from the context of the legislation.

In practice, as some constitutional authorities have long realised (for example, Wade 1939) and many textbooks on government and politics will argue (for example, Kingdom 1991), government under the law has become a fiction. As Harden and Lewis have put it, the precept simply fails to recognise how, beginning in the nineteenth century, 'the trappings of modern democracy were superimposed on an existing constitutional structure, and a modern administration similarly grafted on to pre-existing patterns of government' (1986: 27). The form of modern party politics and the sheer complexity of modern government are such that, in most circumstances, a prime minister and the cabinet with an electoral mandate can so control the policy-making agenda and the processes of administration as to wield almost absolute power. The checks and balances to be provided by parliament on the one hand and the courts on the other are of strictly limited effect. As has been explained already, much of the machinery of the welfare state has been generated with decision-making powers which are far beyond any routine scrutiny or intimate knowledge on the part of either parliament or, still less, the courts.

In fact the problem for all democratic-welfare-capitalist societies is that of how an independent judiciary, operating within an autonomous law paradigm, may develop a constructive role in matters of social policy. The German social systems theorist, Niklas Luhmann has argued that

> law, particularly in its conceptual structures, has not yet adapted to the exigencies of a highly differentiated society. Legal doctrine is still bound to the classical model of law as a body of rules enforceable through adjudication. The legal order lacks a conceptual apparatus adequate for the planning and social policy requirements that arise in the interrelations among specialised social subsystems. (quoted in Harden and Lewis 1986: 34)

The problem is especially acute for English law, which has remained 'stuck in a constitutional time warp' (*ibid.*). Recalling Marshall's schematised account of the development of citizenship (which I considered in Chapter 1), the greatest advances in the development of civil or legal rights based in common law may be said to have occurred following the 'glorious revolution' and in the course of the eighteenth century. Political rights were not properly developed until the nineteenth century and social rights did not appear until the twentieth century. The argument of constitutionalists and systems theorists is that the development of legal rights in relation to matters in the public sphere of policy and administration have lagged behind the development of legal rights in relation to matters in the private sphere of property and contract. Prevailing legal doctrine and the judges themselves are not equipped with any of the principles which might be appropriate to a role in the oversight of social policy.

Where the judges have had the opportunity to review the substance of policy they have for the most part, according to Harden and Lewis, 'treated the idea of policy in the most crude fashion' (1986: 207). They have failed to make the most fundamental distinctions, for example, between the values which inform policy, the specific objectives to be served by a policy, and the measures required to implement that policy. As a result, it must be conceded, the judges have on occasions invited the conclusion that they are motivated by political prejudice. Harden and Lewis' argument is that, if the courts are to have a role in the application of legal principles to the making of social policy, the entire field of administrative law must first be 'considerably developed in a procedural direction' (*ibid.*: 208).

A rather different view is taken by J. A. G. Griffiths (1991). His argument is that the English judiciary is most certainly influenced by a very particular perception of what constitutes 'the public interest'. The supposed neutrality of the judiciary is not only put into question by the outcome of certain celebrated 'political' cases, but has never been anything more than a myth. Often characterised as a Marxist, Griffiths none the less distinguishes himself from the more instrumentalist of the neo-Marxist theorists (see Chapter 4) who look on the judiciary as conspirators and agents of a ruling class. His assertion is that there is an inherent contradiction between the judiciary's position as upholder of law and order and its role as protector of the individual against a powerful executive. It is as a result of that contradiction that judges are compelled to function politically. Griffiths' thesis is

> that judges in the United Kingdom cannot be politically neutral because they are placed in positions where they are required to make political choices which are sometimes presented to them, and often presented by them, as determinations of where the public interest lies; that their interpretation of what is in the public interest and therefore politically desirable is determined by the kind of people they are and the position they hold in our society; that this position is a part of established authority and so is necessarily conservative and illiberal. From all this flows the view of the public interest which is shown in judicial attitudes such as tenderness towards private property and dislike of trade unions, strong adherence to the main-tenance of order, distaste for minority opinions, demonstrations and protests, indifference to the promotion of race relations, support of governmental secrecy, concern for the preservation of the moral and social behaviour to which it is accustomed . . . (1991: 319)

The social background of judges (predominantly white, male and upper or upper-middle class), their education (predominantly independent school and Oxford or Cambridge University), their training (based conventionally on a long and successful career as a barrister) and the method of their appointment (effected on the advice or recommendation of the Lord Chancellor) inclines them towards 'a strikingly homogeneous collection of attitudes beliefs and principles, which to them represents the public interest' (*ibid.*: 275). Recent attempts have been made to broaden the social spectrum from which judges are drawn, but this by itself does little to blunt Griffiths' underlying point which is that senior judges in particular are part of a small establishment elite, which represents authority within, he claims, an essentially and increasingly authoritarian society. Historically, their role has been to defend property rights and the stability of the existing order. To the extent that they are also charged with the defence of the individual against the power of the state, it is only exceptionally and in quite particular circumstances that they have been prepared to challenge the authority of the government of the day. As Lewis and Birkinshaw have remarked, the English judiciary have proved on occasion 'to be more executive minded than the executive' (1993: 208), but to Griffiths this comes as no surprise.

In drawing attention to the deeply conservative nature of the judges, Griffiths does not imply that the judiciary as an institution is in any way passive. On the contrary, judicial creativity is essential to the political function of the courts in the maintenance of social order. In charting the application of such creativity in a number of controversial cases – especially in the spheres of industrial relations, public order, property rights and 'race' and immigration – Griffiths bolsters his case that, while the neutrality of the courts is a myth, their power is real. In an ideal society, Griffiths concedes, he does not know what the attitudes of judges would be, or whether indeed they would be needed (1981: 241). He does not address the question of whether the creative power of the judiciary could be harnessed to advance social rights.

In part at least, this is the question which Lewis and Birkinshaw (1993) have sought to tackle. The starting point, they suggest, is to resolve the fundamental 'intellectual problem' (*ibid.*: 201) of the distinctions drawn between private law and public law. Subject to this, the judges should be allowed to do what they do best, which is creatively to settle points of law. While the everyday administration of justice in areas relating to social policy might safely be left to specialist tribunals and ombudspersons, the job of the higher courts would lie in 'determining the law and setting the broad matrix within which administrative justice operates and in which rights provide security' (*ibid.*: 202). This would require that a number of failings should be addressed, including:

- That a better basic test should be provided by which to review the exercise of discretionary power. The current test – based on *Associated Provincial Picture House* v. *Wednesbury Corporation* [1948] 1 K.B. 223 – holds that the courts should only intervene if the decision under challenge is so unreasonable that no reasonable authority having regard to the relevant considerations could have arrived at it. This tautology is so open and indiscriminate as, arguably, to be no test at all.
- That provision should be made to allow the higher courts to examine and investigate all relevant facts in their exposition of the law. The convention by which the higher courts must decide the law on the basis only of such evidence as is disclosed or admitted in the papers set before them is unsatisfactory.
- The rules of *locus standi* (see above) by which the courts may restrict who might legitimately challenge an administrative decision should be broadened and consistently applied.
- Assistance should be provided to enable litigants to bring appropriate cases before the higher courts.
- The entire procedure relating to judicial review should be codified so as to render it transparent.

Conclusion/summary

In addressing the role of the courts in relation to social welfare this chapter has raised a number of questions concerning the relationship between legal rights and social rights.

First of all, the position of the courts within the English constitutional system and the distinctive nature of the common law tradition are such that the courts are not best suited to protecting the welfare of the individual citizen, although they do potentially possess considerable power either to create or frustrate social policy. In practice, the courts have been distanced from matters of social policy. The marginal nature of their role has been the result first, of deliberate decisions on the part of policy-makers; second, of a reluctance on the part of the judiciary to take up the causes of poor and homeless people; and third, because of a failure to develop consistent legal principles appropriate to the concerns of public policy rather than private disputes.

Because welfare rights find expression in legal form, the legal enforceability of social legislation is important. However, rights to legal advice and assistance have not been developed on the same footing as other social rights and this limits access by citizens to the courts. At the same time, the administration of welfare has been developed largely beyond the gaze of the courts and with its own mechanisms of adjudication and redress, to which the next chapter of this book will shortly turn.

The courts have none the less proved themselves capable of exercising checks on the standards of discretionary decision-making and of balancing the exercise of administrative power. In the process, unfortunately, they have also proved themselves capable of inconsistency if not outright mendacity. In particular, the courts too often have been reluctant to challenge administrative authority on social security matters, but keen to do so in housing matters whenever property interests are at stake. It may be argued that this is an inherent feature of a system in which judges act politically to defend the existing social order. Alternatively, it may be argued that there is a role for the courts in overseeing the exercise of social rights, although to make this possible the system would have to become more sophisticated, disciplined and accessible.

Be that as it may, the fact remains that while civil or legal rights are in theory protected by the courts and political rights may in theory find expression through the electoral system, social rights do not have a distinctive institutional forum. Even if the courts were afforded and would accept a less ambiguous role in relation to social welfare, social rights would remain strategically dependent on political processes for their formation and development, on administrative processes for their implementation, and only incidentally on legal processes for their regulation and defence.

Recommended additional reading

Griffith, J. (1991) *The Politics of the Judiciary*, 4th edition, Fontana, London, Chapter 1 and Part III. Readers without any prior legal background might also do well to have a look at any conventional textbook on the English legal system.

Lewis, N. and Birkinshaw, P. (1993) *When Citizens Complain: Reforming justice and administration*, Open University Press, Buckingham, Chapters 1, 2 and especially 10.

Prosser, T. (1983) *Test Cases for the Poor: Legal techniques in the politics of social welfare*, a pamphlet published by Child Poverty Action Group, London (which retains contemporary relevance in spite of its age).

Questions for reflection

Are social rights justiciable? Do they really lend themselves to enforcement through the courts?

In so far as social welfare cannot, or perhaps should not, be insulated from judicial intervention, what changes might be necessary to the British legal system, the courts and the judiciary?

CHAPTER 9

ADMINISTRATIVE REDRESS

Chapter 8 has demonstrated that social rights are not the same as legal rights and are not easily enforced through the courts. The realisation of social rights involves processes of policy-making and administration. This chapter examines a range of administrative mechanisms by which social rights are or potentially might be protected or advanced. By convention the institutions in question are distinguished from such 'legal' or 'judicial' bodies as the courts, though in practice they include, on the one hand, tribunals which exhibit a more than 'quasi-judicial' character and, on the other, review and complaints procedures which are constituted as direct extensions of an administrative process.

The main institutions with which this chapter will deal are 'administrative' tribunals and ombudspersons. The former are concerned to review on appeal the substantive merits of determinations by welfare administrators or to resolve disputes to which specialised legislative provisions apply. The latter are concerned to investigate complaints of 'maladministration' within the machinery of the welfare state. Additionally, however, I shall examine a number of other mechanisms for reviewing decisions or dealing with grievances in respect of the exercise of social rights and, in this context, will consider again the significance of the *Citizen's Charter* (already discussed in Chapter 1). It will emerge that distinctions between these different kinds of institutional mechanism are not always straightforward. In discussing the differences and similarities involved, the chapter reflects on the extent to which any of these mechanisms of redress can themselves play a part in informing future social policy, rather than merely enforcing existing policy.

Tribunals

In Britain there are more than sixty kinds of tribunal, disposing of over a million cases each year and costing at least £75 million a year to run (Partington 1993). A substantial proportion of these have been created by social legislation or have implications for aspects of welfare rights. These include:

- tribunals created to review the decisions of welfare administrators, such as the Social Security Appeal Tribunal, the Medical Appeal Tribunal, the Disability Appeal Tribunal, the Social Security Commissioners, and the Child Support Tribunal and Child Support Commissioners;
- tribunals created to review the exercise of a wide range of officially exercised powers, including the Immigration Adjudicator and the Immigration Appeals Tribunal, the Mental Health Review Tribunal, the Service Committees of Family Health Service Authorities, local authority Education Appeals Committees, the Registered Homes Tribunal, the Lands Tribunal, and the Valuation and Community Charge Tribunal;
- tribunals created to apply the provisions of social legislation to relationships between landlords and tenants (the Rent Assessment Committee) and between employers and employees (the Industrial Tribunal and its appellate authority, the Employment Appeal Tribunal);
- statutory appellate institutions which fall within the ambit of the Council on Tribunals (see below), but which are not called tribunals, such as the Pensions Ombudsman (who resolves complaints relating to private pension schemes but whose determinations, unlike those of classical ombudspersons, are final and binding);
- a number of bodies not falling within the ambit of the Council on Tribunals and which may not be fully 'independent', but which have been created by social legislation, including Housing Benefit Review Boards, local authority Children's Complaints Panels and Community Care Complaints Panels.

A summary of the numbers of appeals or cases received by the particular tribunals relevant to the specific areas of rights discussed in preceding chapters is set out in Table 9.1.

The development of tribunals

Although bodies such as the Commissioners of Income Tax had existed before the twentieth century and although many tribunals, such as the Civil Aviation Authority and the Betting Levy Appeal Tribunal, have nothing to do with social policy, the development of the modern welfare state has represented the biggest single factor in the emergence of administrative tribunals (Wraith and Hutchinson 1973). As has been discussed in Chapter 8, policy-makers have been reluctant to involve the ordinary courts in matters of social policy, and a significant innovation was achieved in 1911 with the creation of the Court of Referees: a three-member independent tribunal established to deal with disputes arising under the unemployment benefit provisions of the National Insurance Act 1911. The tribunals so created consisted of a legally qualified chairperson together with two lay people – one a trade union

Table 9.1 Number of cases submitted to selected tribunals in 1992

Social Security		
Social Security Appeal Tribunals		169,836
Disability Appeal Tribunals		7,007
Medical Appeal Tribunals	(England and Wales)	17,124
	(Scotland)	1,818
Employment		
Industrial Tribunals	Unfair dismissal cases	37,703
	Equal pay cases	643
	'Race' discrimination cases	1,463
	Sex discrimination cases	4,640
	Other cases	22,576
	Total	67,025
Housing		
Rent Assessment Committees		21,699
Rent Tribunals		160

Source:
Council on Tribunals Annual Report, House of Commons, Session 1992–93, HC78, HMSO.

nominee, the other an employer's representative. Such an arrangement was proffered, in part at least, as a concession with which to offset the possibility of working-class resistance to the idea of compulsory National Insurance contributions (see H. Dean 1991: ch. 5). A similar political motive was evident in the creation in 1934 of a rather different tribunal, the Unemployment Appeal Tribunal, whose existence ministers hoped might deflect popular resentment against a deeply unpopular form of means test (Lynes 1975). The Unemployment Appeal Tribunal was intended to be more administrative in nature than the Court of Referees: it was not chaired by lawyers and one of its members was a direct nominee of the Unemployment Assistance Board, whose decisions the Tribunal was supposed 'independently' to review. The Court of Referees eventually evolved to become the National Insurance Local Tribunal and dealt with appeals relating to insurance-based social security benefits, while the Unemployment Assistance Tribunal became the National Assistance Tribunal (later the Supplementary Benefits Appeal Tribunal) and dealt with appeals relating to national means-tested benefits. The two different kinds of tribunal were merged in 1984 to become the Social Security Appeal Tribunal.

It has been observed that 'once an administrative tribunal is set up, it appears to give such satisfaction that it is never replaced by the ordinary courts' (Street 1975: 10). Certainly, policy-makers, especially after the Second World War, began to see tribunals as a satisfactory way of handling disputes in almost every area of public administration. They similarly began to see the use of public enquiries as a way of legitimating discretionary decision-making in planning and other controversial matters. However, public concern that politicians and officials might be relying too much on tribunals and enquiries led to the commissioning in 1955 of the Franks Committee. The resulting Franks Report (1957) endorsed the role of tribunals, but made clear that they were to be regarded as 'the machinery provided by parliament for adjudication rather than as part of the machinery of administration'. In making this emphasis, Franks also expressed the advantages of tribunals over courts, namely their greater 'cheapness, accessibility, freedom from technicality, expedition and expert knowledge' (1957: para. 38). In its recommendations, the Report laid down three fundamental principles for tribunals: 'openness, fairness and impartiality' (*ibid.*:

para. 41). The recommmendations led to the creation of the Council on Tribunals, a statutory consultative body with responsibility for overseeing the work of tribunals within its ambit and for advising on rules and standards of procedure.

The Franks Report marked not only the acceptance of tribunals as adjudicative forums, but the beginning of a process by which tribunals have become increasingly 'judicialised' (H. Dean 1991: ch. 5). The norm that has been established is closer to the example set by the old Courts of Referees than by the former Unemployment Assistance Tribunal. Tribunals are almost invariably chaired by qualified lawyers, other 'wing' members are selected for their independence of any relevant administrative authority and will characteristically have some appropriately specialised expertise or experience, and the jurisdiction of tribunals is always closely tied to the application of the law and not departmental policy. Tribunals specialise in areas of law which are policy-relevant and may therefore be more 'policy-conscious' than the judiciary, but the idea that tribunals administer policy while only the courts administer law is, according to Abel-Smith and Stevens, a myth: 'Properly understood, tribunals are a more modern form of court' (1968: 228).

The ideal implied by the Franks principles is that tribunals provide a form of justice that is more informal and accessible but no less rigorous than other courts. This raises two questions: first, does this render tribunals a more appropriate forum for the realisation of social rights? Second, are such principles realised in practice? Social rights are creatures of a regulated society. This means that they may reflect collective rather than individual objectives on the one hand, but that they are subject, on the other, to rules and criteria which can become highly complex and controversial when applied to individual cases.

Informal justice?

Reference has been made in Chapter 4 to the distinction drawn by Titmuss (1971) between the strictly 'proportional' justice of a welfare system based on adjudicated entitlements and the more 'creative', responsive or individualised justice which could be exercised by expert administrators. Titmuss did not object to safeguards to prevent the abuse of power by administrators, but the direction in which tribunals have developed in pursuit of the Franks ideal is at odds with the distinctively Fabian notion of social rights which he espoused. For Titmuss welfare rights should reflect a balance struck between individual needs and collective priorities: they were the product of administration and not law. Lewis and Birkinshaw (1993) have interpreted the thrust of commentaries by Mashaw (1983) and Tweedie (1986) as making a related if slightly different point, namely that tribunals can hamper efficient government. Large numbers of social security or school admissions appeals, for example,

> may be good for individual justice but they may have the consequence of promoting individualistic values to get a larger share of what is being provided at public expense. They encourage selfishness. The consequence may be an overall reduction in what is being provided collectively, a diminution in efficiency and no means to ensure that the same problems are not repeated. (Lewis and Birkinshaw 1993: 90)

In this respect, the effect of tribunals is indeed no different from those of the courts. A judicial approach, even when adopted by a specialist tribunal, can as easily undermine social rights as advance them, a point to which I shall return in Chapter 10.

Though no less judicial in their approach to decision-making, tribunals are less formal than courts if only in matters of procedure. Because some tribunals sit in a variety of local venues, they may also be more physically accessible. This is entirely consistent with a wider trend towards what has been called 'legal informalism', a trend which critics suggest may serve to depoliticise or neutralise conflict by channelling and defusing protest against private capital and the state (Abel 1982; and see my discussion of neo-Marxist critiques of social rights in Chapter 4). Evidence suggests, however, that 'informalism' is of limited effect, though this does not necessarily mean that tribunals are ineffective in enhancing social control.

Research commissioned by the Lord Chancellor's Office into the effectiveness of legal representation at tribunal hearings (Genn and Genn 1989) has demonstrated that the varying degrees of informality which tribunals exhibit (as to seating arrangements, forms of address, order of proceedings, rules of evidence, etc.) may be quite superficial. The study included Social Security Appeal

Tribunals, Immigration Appeals, Industrial Tribunals and Mental Health Review Tribunals. In every case, the complexity of the law which such tribunals have to apply proved such as to necessitate the injection of a considerable degree of technicality and formality into the conduct of hearings. Genn and Genn point to a fundamental conflict between the requirements of openness, fairness and impartiality on the one hand, and the desire for cheapness, expedition, informality and freedom from technicality on the other. Franks, they suggest, 'like a bad parent, established conflicting standards of behaviour and left those who might aspire to the standards to resolve any conflicts for themselves' (1989: 112). Of the tribunal chairs and adjudicators they interviewed, many

> who had taken Franks' various exhortations to their hearts, felt unhappy about the situation. . . . When describing their adjudicative function and their method of reaching decisions, the process adopted and described . . . was a traditional legal model. . . . [T]he technicality of this process presents problems not only for tribunals but also for appellants and applicants since it is they who must provide the tribunal with much of the material necessary to this process. . . . [W]here the demands of justice require consistency in decision making, it is arguable that informality and freedom from technicality are limited to such matters as the atmosphere of proceedings and tribunal documentation. (*ibid.*: 112–14)

The 'traditional' legal model which the tribunals adopt is of course the model of the English legal system and, though some tribunals claim, for example, to adopt an inquisitorial rather than an adversarial style, this is not necessarily reflected in the perceptions of the participants. Tribunals like the Industrial Tribunal, because they resolve disputes between employees and employers, are explicitly adversarial. Other tribunals resolve disputes between citizens and state administrators and some of these explicitly emphasise their inquisitorial nature. This is precisely the sense in which some Social Security Appeal Tribunal chairpersons would claim 'informality':

> SSATs are less serious than other tribunals. Here we have an investigatory approach. We get to the bone of it and ask questions. You need to get the facts out of appellants. (quoted in Genn and Genn 1989: 160)

There is perhaps a danger that instead of tribunals presiding over

an unequal adversarial contest between a trained departmental
Presenting Officer and an unrepresented social security claimant
there will be substituted an accusatorial inquisition by the tribunal
itself (cf. Ganz 1974). However, Genn and Genn's (1989)
observations found that tribunal hearings can tend to be more
adversarial in nature than might be claimed. Interviews with
appellants' representatives revealed that most of them believed the
tribunals to be quite incapable of a genuinely inquisitorial function.
This author's own research on Social Security Appeal Tribunals
(see H. Dean 1991: ch. 6) confirms that there is an unresolved
tension between the adversarial tradition and the inquisitorial
aspirations of the tribunals. A pattern was observed in the way in
which tribunal chairpersons orchestrated the proceedings. If
appellants were represented, if they came with arguments prepared
or if they displayed any degree of aggression or belligerence, then
the chairperson was likely to manage the appellant (or her/his
representative) by subjecting her/him to the rules of adversarial
procedure. If, however, the appellant was unrepresented, or if s/he
diplayed passivity or deference, then the chairperson was likely to
manage the appellant by subjecting her/him to an inquisitorial
procedure. It is suggested that the tribunal appellant, as the
instigator of the appeal process, 'is constituted and subjected as an
object of that process' (*ibid.*: 159). The tribunal is not 'informal'
but adapts its formal nature so as to accommodate the appellant
and her/his appeal on the terms and within the bounds which the
law allows and for which the tribunal is equipped. This may involve
some quite subtle processes through which the protests or demands
of social security claimants may be contained, redefined or
assimilated. To this extent, in the process of upholding social
legislation, tribunals also function to protect the policy-making
processes and administrative systems from effective challenge, in
much the same way as the judiciary have been observed to do.

The future of tribunals

If tribunals therefore offer little or no advantage over the ordinary
courts by way of informality, what of their supposed advantages in
terms of expertise, cheapness and speed?

The diversity of tribunals makes it difficult to generalise, though the common experience of tribunal chairpersons and adjudicators in Genn and Genn's study (1989) was that all tribunal jurisdictions tend over time to become increasingly technical as bodies of case law develop. On the one hand, this risks stretching the expertise of the tribunals beyond the limits of sustainability:

> Even a qualified chairman, if he is a part-time chairman, comes here maybe twice a month or only once a month for a few hours and then he goes away for the next four weeks and forgets all about his insurance law. He has other things to occupy his mind. (Social Security Appeal Tribunal chairperson, quoted in Genn and Genn 1989: 116)

On the other hand, the tribunals' very expertise generates a self-justifying ratchet effect. The cleverer they make themselves, the more indispensable tribunals will become.

Once tribunals are looked on as permanent substitutes for the courts in the adjudication of specialised types of dispute, fears must then be raised that the quality of the justice they dispense may be compromised in the interests of the cheapness of operation. The procedural criteria advocated by the Council on Tribunals represent a standard of 'judicial purity' which may be inappropriate to the roles fulfilled by some tribunals (see Lewis and Birkinshaw 1993: 92). There are other tribunals, especially in the sphere of welfare rights, before which appellants or applicants may be subject to all the disadvantages of appearing before a court, but with none of the advantages which might flow, for example, from guaranteed legal representation. From appellants' or applicants' point of view, tribunals may be cheap because no fees are charged on the issue of proceedings and, generally, unsuccessful litigants cannot be held liable for costs (an exception arises in the case of those Industrial Tribunal applications which are deemed 'frivolous or vexatious'). None the less, if an appellant or applicant requires representation, at the time of writing no legal aid is available for the purpose (except in the case of the Employment Appeal Tribunal, the Lands Tribunal, the Commons Commissioners and limited assistance for Mental Health Review Tribunals) (see Hansen 1993). Unless an appellant or applicant has access to an advice agency, law centre or trade union able to represent free of charge, the cost of representation may be prohibitive. From the government's point of view, the cheapness of the tribunal system lies partly in the use which is made of tribunal members, chairpersons and adjudicators who in some cases may be part-time or even unpaid, but more particularly because of the absence of legal aid. In spite of continued protestations by some tribunal chairpersons that legal representation before tribunals is undesirable, Genn and Genn's research (1989) has demonstrated beyond doubt that representation directly influences the outcome of tribunal hearings. The government none the less resists pressure from a wide spectrum of advisory and professional bodies for a universal extension of legal aid (see Harlow and Rawlings 1984: 184-7; Bailey and Gunn 1991: 745) and it would seem unlikely that recent proposals for the reform of legal aid (see Chapter 8) will ensure anything approaching a right to legal representation before tribunals.

As for speed, the evidence is that tribunals are hardly better than other courts in combating delay. Genn and Genn found that, in 1986/7 the average delay between the lodging of an appeal or application and its final hearing (if the case was not settled or withdrawn) ranged from a relatively modest 107 days in the case of Industrial Tribunals, to a staggering 339 days in the case of appeals to Immigration Adjudicators (1989: ch. 5). Significantly, where appellants or applicants sought advice on the preparation of their cases or did obtain representation, this tended to increase the delay. Speed in adjudication, it might be inferred, may be achieved at the expense of adequate preparation. If tribunals are to pursue the same standards of 'judicial purity' as the courts, this may ultimately dictate an erosion of such supposed advantages as cheapness and speed.

Because of this, perhaps, there has been a trend since the 1980s away from the creation of tribunals in the classic mould and in favour of one-person adjudicators, such as the Pensions Ombudsman (see above; also Lewis and Birkinshaw 1993: 100), and internal review procedures. This trend emerged in 1982 when the housing benefit scheme was first introduced (see Chapter 7). Challenges to determinations of entitlement to housing benefit have been made subject to a two-stage internal review procedure: the first stage involves a re-examination by local authority officers; the second a review by a Housing Benefit Review Panel composed of elected members of the local authority concerned. The Review Panels, although a form of tribunal, do not have any independent element and research into their functioning (Eardley and Sainsbury 1991) has recommended that their role would be better entrusted to the Social Security Appeal Tribunal. However, not only has the government declined to add to the Social Security Appeal Tribunal's jurisdiction, it has even removed elements of that jurisdiction. The social fund, which was established in 1988, replaced certain provisions of the former supplementary benefits scheme which had been subject to a right of appeal to the Social Security Appeal Tribunal. A more limited right was provided for claimants wishing to challenge decisions by Social Fund Officers. This is once again a two-stage internal review: the first stage involves re-examination by local Social Fund Officers; the second a review by regionally-based Social Fund Inspectors, subject only to monitoring by a Social Fund Commissioner appointed by the Secretary of State. These less judicial forums of redress will be discussed later in this chapter, but the point to be noted is that they represent an alternative to independently constituted tribunals and a model to which policy-makers may increasingly turn.

Ombudspersons

The other alternative to tribunals is that of ombudspersons. The 'Ombudsman' concept has its origins in Scandinavia and dates back some two centuries (see, for example, Stacey 1978). The Scandinavian countries and the welfare states which they have developed differ in several respects from Britain (see Chapter 3). In particular, their traditions of government were and remain less dependent on the concentration of administrative power which characterises the Westminster model. The distinctive idea of an independent and universally accessible citizen's champion has spread around the world and been adapted to provide mechanisms of redress within a variety of quite different jurisdictions. Britain's interest in the idea dates from the publication of the Whyatt Report (JUSTICE 1961) and the example of New Zealand, which established a Parliamentary Commissioner (or ombudsperson) in 1962.

Three main statutory schemes were subsequently established: the Parliamentary Commissioner for Administration; the Commissioners for Local Administration or local ombudspersons (consisting of a body of commissioners for England and Wales and a separate commissioner for Scotland); and the Health Service Commissioner. There is a separate Commissioner for Complaints for Northern Ireland. There are also a number of private schemes – for example, the Insurance Ombudsman – and some local authorities have established a voluntary ombudsperson (or complaints executive officer) scheme as part of their internal complaints procedures, but these non-statutory schemes will not be considered here.

Classical ombudspersons enjoy independent investigatory powers and, in theory, may 'dig where the courts and tribunals cannot trespass' (Lewis and Birkinshaw 1993: 78). While the proceedings of courts and tribunals are primarily adversarial, those of an ombudsperson are truly inquisitorial. In the Nordic tradition, ombudspersons are allowed to point up systemic weaknesses in policy and administration and to propose improvements. In establishing ombudsperson schemes elsewhere governments have sought to impose a distinction between the role reserved for courts and tribunals and that to be conferred on the ombudsperson; the former's responsibility is to review administrative decisions on their merits in law; the latter's is for finding defective administration. In the event, there may be a 'substantial degree of overlap between the two systems' (JUSTICE–All Souls 1988: para. 5.27). When it comes to securing the citizen's social rights, it will matter little whether the remedy is 'legal' or 'administrative' if indeed the outcomes are similar. It has already been argued that the effectiveness of legal remedies is inherently limited – including such remedies as are dispensed by 'administrative' tribunals. Is administrative redress through ombudspersons any more effective?

The statutory ombudsperson schemes introduced in Britain are significantly compromised versions of the Nordic ideal. As Lewis and Birkinshaw have put it, the Parliamentary Commissioner Act 1967, which established the Parliamentary Commissioner for Administration (PCA), 'can be seen as a weak concession to the reformists to avoid a broader examination of administrative justice', though they add: 'a weak ombudsperson system is more significant in a country like Britain where other safeguards are meagre compared to the record of other advanced democracies' (1993: 112).

The PCA is empowered to investigate complaints where personal injustice is alleged to have been suffered by an individual as a result of 'maladministration' on the part of a central government department (see, for example, Harlow and Rawlings 1984: ch. 7 or Turpin 1990: 471–6). The jurisdiction of the PCA has been extended to include the government's newly created executive agencies, such as the Social Security Benefits Agency, and some quangos, though it does not extend to advisory bodies, nationalised industries and commercial quangos. Complaints against health authorities and NHS Trusts are also excluded, but are dealt with separately by the Health Service Commissioner (see below). The power of the PCA, when compared with that of ombudspersons in several other countries, is fettered in two ways: first, by the way the PCA has been made an adjunct to parliament; and second, by the restrictive notion of 'maladministration'.

Citizens cannot complain directly to the PCA, but must first complain to their Member of Parliament who may, at her/his discretion, refer the complaint for investigation by the PCA. This 'sifting mechanism' is defended on the basis that 'In effect, every individual MP is himself an Ombudsman and deals in his elected capacity with many complaints without having to seek recourse to the PCA' (Select Committee on the PCA 1987–8: para. 9). The PCA is thus portrayed as a way of assisting MPs who may lack the time and resources to pursue enquiries on behalf of their constituents. The inability of citizens to approach the PCA directly is widely perceived as a 'weakness' (Stacey 1978: 170), not least because there is massive variation in the frequency with which different MPs refer complaints.

The small numbers of complaints accepted for investigation by the PCA (see Table 9.2) are subjected to what has been described as a '"Rolls Royce" standard' of investigation (Lewis and Birkinshaw 1993: 115). Whether such high standards would be maintained in the event of more widespread use is an open question. Reports on individual investigations are made to the sponsoring MP and the department or agency investigated. Where maladministration leading to injustice is found to have occurred, the PCA may recommend a remedy, including *ex gratia* compensation to the person aggrieved and/or changes in administrative procedures. Where such recommendations are not acted on, the PCA may lay special reports before parliament. The PCA also makes more general periodical reports to parliament and is supported in her/his work by the Select Committee on the PCA.

Table 9.2　Complaints referred annually to the Parliamentary
Commissioner for Administration, 1967–1992 (five-year intervals)

Year	Number of complaints referred	Number of complaints investigated (and as a percentage of complaints referred)	Number of complaints upheld (and as a percentage of complaints investigated)
1967	1,069	188 (18%)	19 (10%)
1972	573	261 (46%)	79 (30%)
1977	901	312 (35%)	111 (36%)
1982	838	202 (24%)	67 (33%)
1987	677	145 (21%)	63 (43%)
1992	945	265 (28%)	143 (54%)
			[and 103 (39%) 'partially upheld']

Source:
Compiled from memoranda of evidence by the Parliamentary Commissioner and
by the National Consumer Council submitted to the Select Committee on the
Parliamentary Commissioner for Administration, *Minutes of Evidence*, House of
Commons, Session 1993–94, HC33–II, HMSO, pp. 2 and 242.

There is no legal sanction by which government departments or
agencies may be compelled to respond in compliance with the
PCA's findings. Ultimately, the only sanction is beyond the control
of the PCA and lies within the vagaries of the political process.

The other related weakness of Britain's PCA is that her/his brief
has been restricted so as to exclude matters of policy (which are for
parliament) and law (which are for courts and tribunals) and to
concentrate on 'maladministration'. Maladministration has no
statutory definition and the only definition to be offered during the
passage of the Parliamentary Commissioner Act came from
Richard Crossman, who cited the examples of 'bias, neglect,
inattention, delay, incompetence, ineptitude, perversity, turpi-
tude, arbitrariness' (*Hansard*, vol. 734, col. 51, 18 October 1966).
Any such failings might seriously obstruct the exercise of social
rights, though it remains a curiously narrow catalogue;

> The concern of the PCA was not with the technical correctness of
> the decision, but with the administrative quality of the decision. He
> rarely comments on the 'bad rule' and is not prepared to condemn a
> decision purely on the basis that it was 'wrong'. (Lewis and
> Birkinshaw 1993: 115)

In 1974 the ombudsperson concept was extended from central to
local government with the creation of the Local Commission for
Administration for England and Wales, followed in 1975 by the

Local Commissioner for Administration for Scotland. The local commissioners' terms of reference were modelled directly on those of the PCA. They were restricted to investigating allegations of personal injustice occasioned by maladministration on the part of local authorities and, initially, such complaints could only be referred by elected members of the local authorities concerned. Since 1988, however, citizens have been able to complain directly to local commissioners. Local commissioners have gone much further than the PCA in publicising their existence and promoting their function (dealing in the year to March 1990 with 8,733 complaints – *ibid.*: 123). They have also been quite imaginative in their approach by, for example, investigating group complaints, in one instance by parents aggrieved by their local authority's schools admission procedures, and in another by a group of local advice agencies who advanced a complaint based on their clients' shared experiences of their local authority's homeless persons unit. Local commissioners have been able, for example, to draw attention to deficient administrative standards and practices in local authority Housing Benefit Offices. Though local commissioners have arguably done rather more than the PCA to interpret their brief, they have also experienced more difficulty in enforcing their recommendations.

Local commissioners report the findings of their investigations directly to the local authorities concerned and, if they have found that an injustice arising from maladministration has occurred, the local authority must respond to the report within three months. Should the local commissioner be dissatisfied with any response, s/he must make a further report with recommendations and, if this is not acted on by the local authority, that authority may be directed to publish a statement giving details of the local commissioner's findings and recommendations and its reasons (if any) for failing to comply. Though local authorities do by and large comply with local commissioner recommendations, such compliance is not assured and may sometimes be only partial or tokenistic. As with the PCA, there are no legal sanctions to ensure compliance.

Finally, the PCA also acts under a separately created jurisdiction as the Health Service Commissioner (HSC), a responsibility conferred in 1973. The role of the HSC is especially confusing since it coexists with that of the Service Committees of the Family Health Service Authorities (who may hear complaints against family practitioners and dentists) and the statutory Hospital Complaints Procedure established in 1988. Additionally, the HSC is expressly prevented from investigating actions taken in consequence of the exercise of clinical judgement, which are subject to a clinical complaints procedure established in 1981.

British ombudspersons do not enjoy the more freeranging powers available to ombudspersons in other countries, such as the Scandinavian countries, but also to varying degrees in New Zealand, Australia, Canada, France and Austria. They cannot conduct investigations without first receiving an explicit complaint, they are prevented from investigating complaints where a complainant has alternative means of redress, and they must not investigate matters encroaching on organisational, personnel or contractual matters. What is more, the peculiarly British notion of 'maladministration' has had several implications. First, it tends to assume the applicability of narrow but generic principles of administration and therefore to preclude a broad and informed view in specialist policy areas: for example, research in the early 1970s of PCA complaint investigations in cases involving supplementary benefit administration suggested that the PCA did not properly appreciate the nature of the then prevailing social assistance policy (Partington 1975). Second, a preoccupation with administration without regard to the purposes of social policy may provoke defensive blame-avoidance behaviour on the part of welfare administrators, so stunting initiative and flexibility in service provision (see discussion in Harlow and Rawlings 1984: 219–26). Third, the term has come to be so restrictively interpreted as to preclude any challenge to policy: for example, in 1981 the HSC found that delays in hospital accident departments, even if 'unacceptable', did not amount to maladministration if they were due to 'resource problems beyond the control of the Department' (*ibid.*: 226).

In its boldest form the office of ombudsperson can extend beyond that of 'citizen's defender or protector into a citizen's advocate, thereby crossing the administrative realm of government into more publicly controversial ground' (Caiden 1988: 7). The role of British ombudspersons is in contrast far more constrained and indeed ambiguous. Even allowing for constraints on their effectiveness, it is difficult to ascertain whether their function is to remedy individual injustices or to promote good administration.

Internal reviews and complaints procedures

The interests of good administration are not necessarily consonant with the demands of individual justice, nor with the cause of social rights. Good administration primarily benefits organisational or 'business' needs and, only secondarily, the needs of citizens or 'customers'. It has been remarked already that internal review mechanisms appear to be replacing tribunals as a form of redress within the welfare state. At the same time, the doctrine of new public management and the consumerist discourse of the *Citizen's Charter* are bringing to the welfare state new approaches and a new emphasis on complaints procedures (see Chapter 1).

Once again, the distinctions which may be drawn between different mechanisms of redress are not hard and fast. Some internal review mechanisms exhibit some of the hallmarks of a 'tribunal-like' adjudicative approach. The social fund internal review procedure, as a result of systematic intervention by the Social Fund Commissioner, has achieved standards of procedural fairness and efficiency which even critics of the social fund and its discretionary nature have acknowledged to be 'impressive' (Lewis and Birkinshaw 1993: 96). In some local authorities, Housing Benefit Review Boards operate with close regard to standards of judicial propriety, although approaches vary considerably from authority to authority (Eardley and Sainsbury 1991). There are further inconsistencies between local authorities in their handling of housing benefit reviews simply because there are no commonly held criteria by which to distinguish between ordinary 'enquiries' about housing benefit determinations on the one hand, and formal requests (or 'appeals') for internal review. Research has shown that substantial variations in the numbers of reviews conducted by different local authorities in fact result from different conceptions of what constitutes an appeal against a determination (*ibid.*).

In spite of this, local authorities have been required to establish further statutory complaints procedures under the Children Act 1989 and under the community care provisions of the NHS and Community Care Act 1990. The first procedure is for children aggrieved by matters relating to their care, the second is for service users and carers aggrieved by matters relating to services or, for example, the discretionary needs assessments and associated assessment of means which local authorities conduct (Gordon

1993). Both these procedures require authorities to establish a Review Panel though, unlike the Housing Benefit Review Boards, there is a requirement that the panels should be independently chaired, so conferring one of the characteristics of an administrative tribunal. Practice and interpretation, however, varies between authorities. It is rare that a lawyer is sought to preside as an independent person and quite common for senior council officers as well as local councillors to be allowed to sit on such panels (Dean and Hartley 1995). The model for the new statutory complaints procedures is a three-stage procedure (rather than the two-stage procedure favoured for more adjudicative forms of 'internal review') and is outlined in government guidance (DH 1991):

1. an informal problem-solving stage, at which attempts will be made to mediate and resolve the complaint;
2. a formal 'registration' stage, at which an unresolved complaint is formally recorded and investigated by specially designated staff who may make recommendations for the resolution of the complaint;
3. a review stage, at which unresolved complaints are referred to the Review Panel.

The author's own research on the application of this procedure suggests that the pattern observed by Eardley and Sainsbury (1991) in relation to Housing Benefit Review Panels is being repeated in the case of complaints about community care assessments. There are considerable variations in the numbers of complaints being recorded by different local authorities and this would seem to stem from inconsistency in the definition of what constitutes a 'complaint' requiring investigation or review, rather than perhaps a mere 'representation' which does not (Dean and Hartley 1995).

As education authorities, in addition to pre-existing appeals arrangements relating to school admissions arrangements (which fall within the purview of the Council on Tribunals), local authorities have also acquired new obligations for the operation of complaints procedures in respect of the assessment of special education needs, and in respect of the application of the National Curriculum.

In addition to this burgeoning array of statutory procedures, many authorities operate voluntary complaints precedures, sometimes on an authority-wide basis. To this extent, local authorities have ostensibly been following advice from the Commission for Local Administration (1978 and 1992), who provide guidelines on setting up complaints procedures and who emphasise the efficacy of complaints monitoring as a means to detect trends which may require changes in policy or procedure. Similarly, the Audit Commission has pressed local authorities to establish 'robust monitoring systems' which should operate 'both reactively, by monitoring complaints, and proactively, by public opinion surveys' (1989: 19). Research by Seneviratne (1991, cited in Lewis and Birkinshaw 1993: ch. 8) suggested that local authorities had a 'long way to go' in realising such objectives and, although most authorities were monitoring complaints, comparatively few had been analysing them. None the less, the Commission for Local Administration (1992) has reported at least a willingness among local authorities to study complaints as a means of informing service development.

Similar principles have been urged on health authorities. Under the statutory hospital complaints procedure introduced in 1988, District Health Authorities were required to designate complaints officers and have been required by guidelines to monitor complaints activity. Some DHAs and NHS Trusts have established complaints committees which analyse complaints with a view to improving their systems and procedures.

Procedures involving the review of administrative decisions begin therefore to shade into procedures for recording complaints. There is a fudging of the purposes of the procedures and of the values which underpin them. As Gray and Jenkins (1993) have put it, when commenting in more general terms on the impact of new public management on the welfare state:

> A stress on honesty, fairness and equity leads to a different administrative structure than one on speed of response and cost minimization. It is therefore essential to determine what values administrative structures are attempting to serve. (p. 22)

When local government and the health authorities are required to separate their 'enabling' or 'purchasing' roles from their 'provider' roles and when NHS Trusts and government executive agencies are required to function as 'businesses', citizens who were once 'clients' of local and central government are reconstituted as 'customers'. The *Citizen's Charter* initiative has resulted in the setting of a variety of targets for the provision of public services, but the benchmarks which those targets address relate to the quality or performance of the service providers and not the rights of the 'customer' as a citizen. The *Citizen's Charter* approach to complaints, redress and standard setting in the public sector is predicated on the values of market competition. According to the defenders of the *Charter*, it is competition or the fear of it, and not judicial or administrative authority, which will make providers take complaints seriously (Pirie 1991). Welfare providers are concerned to manage the quality of services to customers and they attend to complaints as means towards a business end, or so as to thwart the threat of competition. As 'customers' the views of citizens may be taken into account, but this is not the same as a political right to participate in the policy process. As 'customers' citizens have a right to complain, but this is a right founded on a notional contract: it has the form of a civil right not a social right.

Conclusion/summary

This chapter has discussed the part which administrative redress can play in securing social rights. In doing so, the chapter has considered a variety of mechanisms.

First, there are 'administrative' tribunals, which tend in fact to be more judicial than administrative. Tribunals have power to review administrative decisions made in pursuance of social legislation. They therefore adjudicate the substantive merits of individual cases, but they are procedurally bound by the terms of such policies as have been incorporated into law. To the extent that they can exercise discretion so as to give effect to social rights, it is discretion within very narrow bounds. Tribunals therefore function to uphold existing social legislation, subject to all its limitations.

Second, there are ombudspersons, who in theory have the freedom to intervene should the effects of social legislation prove unjust. In practice, however, the powers of British ombudspersons are fettered so that they are more administrative than political. Ombudspersons can act so as to ensure good practice in the administration of welfare services, but their terms of reference are such that they cannot remedy injustices which arise through bad policy, rather than bad administration.

Third, there are internal review and complaints procedures. Certain of these procedures appear to have been devised to shield policy-driven discretionary decision-making from the rigours of tribunal scrutiny. On the other hand, such procedures may also exhibit a quality monitoring function. Complaints can help to inform the development of social policy, but the objectives of existing complaints procedures focus narrowly on the needs of administration (or 'business') and not the needs and rights of citizens.

The social rights of citizenship are necessarily tied to administrative processes and mechanisms for administrative redress are therefore important. However, just as the courts cannot guarantee social rights, neither can administrative forms of justice. Mechanisms of administrative redress may be more or less effective in securing procedural justice, good administration and even 'business-like' efficiency in the implementation of social rights, but they do not protect or advance social rights in any wider sense: they do not ensure social justice. It is to this wider notion of social justice that the next chapter will turn.

Recommended additional reading

Dean, H. (1991) *Social Security and Social Control*, Routledge, London, Chapters 5 and 6.

Lewis, N. and Birkinshaw, P. (1993) *When Citizens Complain: Reforming justice and administration*, Open University Press, Buckingham, Chapters 3–8 (though readers without any prior legal background might also do well to have a look at a standard recent textbook on administrative law).

Questions for reflection

Administrative tribunals represent a means of enforcing social rights, but whose interests do they serve?

What's the point of complaining? Is a review or complaints procedure a mechanism for individual redress or for service monitoring? Can it effectively be both?

PART IV

CHAPTER 10

SOCIAL JUSTICE:
A QUESTION OF RIGHTS?

The object of this book has been to provide an overview of both theory and practice; to consider both the form of welfare rights and the substance of social legislation. This final chapter will consider relationships between theory and practice; in particular, it will question the extent to which the ideal of social justice is realisable through procedural rights to welfare. I shall review recent contributions to the debate about the nature of social rights and social justice, after which I shall discuss the problems of rights-based strategies and the importance of social rights in relation to other kinds of rights. Finally, the chapter will provide some speculative remarks about the prospects for developing social rights in ways which might transcend the bounds of democratic-welfare-capitalism. First, however, I shall retrace the main arguments of the preceding chapters.

One of the fundamental premisses of this book has been that rights are ideological. The distinction has been drawn between civil rights (the legal framework on which capitalism depends), political rights (on which 'liberal' democracy is founded) and social rights (which found expression in the creation of the welfare state). T. H. Marshall has argued that such rights developed as reflections of competing values, but that the existence and continuing equilibrium between these three kinds of rights is functionally necessary to the survival of 'modern' capitalism. Social rights are ambiguous, however. Social rights are bestowed in legal form, but as a consequence of processes which are political. It is also possible that the goods and services to which social rights allow access, though

215

to varying degrees detached from the processes of the market economy, may none the less assume the form of quasi-commodities.

On the premiss that poverty is inimical to full citizenship, the supposed function of social rights is to guarantee the satisfaction of human need. The problem is that definitions of poverty and human need are contested and that the relevance of social rights to citizenship is not clear. The relief of poverty may be a necessary condition for the achievement of human emancipation, but the prescription of rights (and obligations) may militate against the achievement of a form of citizenship from which nobody may be excluded. Certainly, there is no universal formula for human liberation. The organisation of human welfare differs around the globe and there is little evidence that any one form of social rights will attain ascendancy. What is clear is that social rights in Western-style welfare states are ineluctably associated as much with controlling human behaviour as with meeting human need. It may be argued that not only do social rights coexist uneasily with other kinds of rights, they also have the propensity to be exploitative, disciplinary and/or divisive.

Though Britain is by no means a typical case, this book has considered the manner in which rights to subsistence, to work and to housing are currently guaranteed. In so far as the highly complex British social security system guarantees the subsistence needs of its citizens, it does so selectively, treating different social groups in different ways; it functions so as to enforce particular patterns of family dependency and social exclusion. British social legislation does not guarantee a right to work; it provides limited protection to employees and subsidies to support the incomes of some low-paid employees; it imposes stringent conditions on those who are unemployed or who are incapable of work. Similarly, British social legislation does not guarantee a right to a home; it provides increasingly selective subsidies to enable people to meet housing costs and a diminishing level of control over excessive housing costs; it gives powers to local government to remedy deficient housing stock, but only a limited duty to secure accommodation for homeless persons.

To be of value rights must be enforceable. Within liberal democracies, this means they must be legally enforceable. The British courts have shown themselves to be capable both of advancing and obstructing the exercise of social rights; of tempering or colluding with the administrative power of the welfare state. By and large, however, the enforceability of social rights has been entrusted to administrative forms of redress: to tribunals, ombudspersons and complaints procedures. Such remedies have shown themselves capable of providing for citizens a strictly technical or procedural form of justice, but also of catering to the needs of welfare administrators and providers.

This leaves unanswered a number of questions. Can social rights be constituted as a meaningful and necessary component of citizenship? Can social rights provide more dependable guarantees of human welfare than is currently the case in Britain? Can social rights be made properly enforceable?

The existence of social rights

Raymond Plant has answered the first of these questions in the affirmative. He argues that social rights (and 'economic' rights, by which he refers to rights to income and to work, which I and other commentators encompass within the term social rights) 'are not in fact categorically different from civil and political rights' (Plant 1992: 17). In response to neo-liberal critiques (which I have discussed in Chapter 4), Plant asserts that positive social rights cannot be dismissed as mere desires, interests or claims, unless one is prepared similarly to dismiss the 'negative' rights associated with civil and political freedoms. Social rights may make claim to the allocation of scarce resources, but this is no different from such rights as the right to physical security, the enforcement of which may entail the allocation of considerable resources on the apparatuses of law and order. Social rights are invariably predicated on contestable conceptions of need, but this is no different from such rights as the right to privacy, the definition of which is no less problematic and no less susceptible to changing social expectations and technological contexts. It is difficult to achieve consensus about the extent of social rights, but this is no different from other kinds of rights, which depend on achieving a measure of political consensus as to what is just. The defenders of 'negative' freedoms insist that free markets cannot be blamed for unjust outcomes provided such markets have been constituted with just intentions, but Plant argues that the injustices which demonstrably flow from the free play of market forces, though they may not be intended, are foreseeable. Measures to ensure social justice are therefore as logically and morally necessary as any civil or political freedoms.

The essence of Plant's argument is 'that the freedoms and immunities which are guaranteed [by] civil and political rights remain wholly abstract if people do not have the social and economic resources to be independent citizens' (*ibid.*: 21). Our liberties and our abilities are in no way categorically different. We cannot be free to do that which we are not able to do. The freedom to own one's home is not a freedom if one cannot afford and is not enabled to pay the mortgage. The freedom to compete for a high paid job is not a freedom if one does not have the necessary ability – whether in terms of training or, for example, access to child care. The 'progress' of industrial capitalism has been based on an expansion in the range of some people's abilities and this has been associated with a necessary growth in certain constraints on human conduct in the organisation of productive processes: the expanding range of human abilities has none the less increased rather than diminished the scope of human freedoms. After all, 'what makes freedom valuable to us is what we are able to do with it' (*ibid.*: 25). Abilities underwritten by social rights are no less constitutive of citizenship than freedom underwritten by civil and political rights.

Having argued that social rights are equal in status to civil and political rights, and that they are indispensable, Plant broaches a question to which I shall later return, namely the enforceability of social rights. He acknowledges that because social rights do involve rights to scarce resources, this often involves rationing and the exercise of administrative or professional power. Here he links the concept of social rights with the emerging notion of citizen empowerment and the idea that it is through rights that citizens may enforce their claims against welfare administrators and professionals. In a publication by the influential left-of-centre Institute for Public Policy Research, Anna Coote (1992), has taken Plant's argument as the basis on which to endorse two complementary strategies, one proposed by Lewis and Seneviratne (1992), the other by Galligan (1992). The first is for the enactment of a British Social Charter, based substantially on the Council of Europe's much neglected Social Charter of 1961 (and subsequent elaborations). This would specify substantive rights and provide a framework within which to interpret and develop social legislation, but it would not be directly enforceable by individuals. Rather it would provide a 'supportive environment' for the implementation of the second strategy, the promotion of procedural rights to welfare, based on consistent principles of fairness in relation to all welfare services: that is to say, people should be heard before decisions are made concerning them; decision-makers should be free from bias; people should be treated with equality and consistency; discretion should be structured; reasons should be given for all decisions; provision should be made for complaints and appeals. Coote would seem, however, to be diluting the force of Plant's argument.

First, although Coote supports the entrenchment under British law of a Bill of Rights relating to civil and political rights, she agrees with Lewis and Seneviratne that their proposed Social Charter should not be entrenched (that is to say, it should be an ordinary Act of Parliament rather than a constitutional measure which could not subsequently be revoked or overridden). The explanation for the distinction she draws between civil and political rights on the one hand and social rights on the other is as follows:

> if all individuals in a society were comfortably housed and enjoyed reasonable standards of health care, education and social insurance, but had no civil rights, that society would offer them no constitutional means of winning the rights they lacked. By contrast, a society in which individuals enjoyed the right to vote, and freedoms of speech, assembly, movement and so forth, would hold out the possibility of winning social rights through the democratic process. Civil rights can thus be seen as a means of achieving social rights. Social rights may be necessary for the just enforcement of existing civil rights (since abilities make liberties worthwhile), but on their own they cannot be a means of achieving civil rights. And indeed, without civil rights, social rights are almost certainly unenforceable and therefore meaningless. (Coote 1992: 8)

Coote is right to point out that social rights are dependent for their enforceability on civil rights and for their development on political rights, but it is surely neither necessary nor consistent to accept that social rights ought therefore to remain subordinate to civil and political rights.

Second, Coote's acquiescence to the continued subordination of social rights to civil rights is confirmed by the pragmatism with which she justifies a concentration on procedural as opposed to substantive rights. Procedural rights to welfare she concedes are a 'hybrid' (*ibid.*: 9) between civil and social rights. This she sees as a virtue, since principles of fairness translated from the civil to the social sphere should occasion no alarm because of their familiarity. Courts and tribunals, she suggests, will be more inclined to intervene in matters of procedural detail rather than to challenge governments on sensitive matters of substantive policy. Improvements to procedural rights, what is more, will make less in the way of immediate resource demands than a significant expansion of substantive social rights. Even the confessed champions of social rights can be equivocal about asserting them on an equal footing with civil and political rights.

Achieving social justice

Proposals for substantive reforms in welfare rights and social legislation may be found in the final report of the Commission on Social Justice (CSJ 1994). It is significant that such proposals should be formulated in the language of social justice, not social rights. The language of rights, it seems, is to be reserved for the debate of technical and procedural matters, while the grander rhetoric of justice is applied in discussion of substantive reform. Raz has suggested that, philosophically speaking, 'Rights are intermediate conclusions in arguments from ultimate values to duties' (1984: 208). If this is so, then social rights are merely the medium through which the values of social justice are translated into specified duties for governments. Certainly, so far as the Commission on Social Justice was concerned, its primary preoccupation was with policies, not rights.

The Commission was established in 1992 by the late John Smith, then leader of the British Labour Party. Though broadly left of centre, the Commission was independent and its membership included academics and other experts. The Commission undertook a thoroughgoing examination of the welfare state and reported in 1994 with proposed reforms in education and labour market policies, as well as in social security and other social policy areas.

The Commission has taken a guarded step towards defining the elusive concept of social justice. Social justice is characterised in terms of the equal worth of all citizens, and the ability of all citizens to meet their basic needs: the achievement of social justice is held to depend on opportunities and life chances for all, and the reduction or elimination of unjustified inequalities (CSJ 1994: 17–8; 1993). In fairness, any definition of social justice is bound to leave certain questions open, but two quite essential questions would seem to have been left unresolved by the Commission. First, if all citizens are to have 'equal worth', by whom, by what criteria or processes are those inequalities which will be permitted to exist be adjudged *not* to be 'unjustified'? Second, if the level of the ability which citizens should have must be sufficient only to meet their 'basic' needs, does this imply a restriction on the level at which opportunities and life chances will be guaranteed? Put more simply, when it comes to translating these rhetorical demands for justice into substantive rights, how will citizens be able to assert a right to equal worth, and just how basic are the needs which citizens will be enabled as of right to meet? Answers to such questions must be sought in the wider context of the Commission's proposals.

The key to the Commission's approach is disclosed in the title of their report: 'Social justice: a strategy for national renewal'. The Commission argues that the proper response to the economic, social and political revolutions to which Britain has been subject in the last decades of the twentieth century is neither the 'deregulator strategy' of the New Right nor the 'leveller strategy' of the Old Left, but an 'investor strategy' by which to combine the 'ethics of community with the dynamics of a market economy' (CSJ 1994: 95). The moral commitment to social justice is clearly to be confined within the parameters of a particular nation-state and the limitations of a market economy. The concept of national renewal implies what Offe (1992) would call a 'productivist' design for social policy. It is assumed that social justice is to be achieved and enhanced in concert with processes of nationally based capitalist production and economic growth. The Commission speaks of transforming the welfare state 'from a safety net to a springboard' (CSJ 1994: 20), but while addressing the framework within which opportunities, incentives and choices may be created – for women as well as for men – across the life-cycle, what is advocated in the way of enforceable social rights is comparatively modest.

So far as the social security system is concerned, the centrepiece of the Commission's proposals is a 'new' social insurance scheme, in which membership would be extended to those citizens who are currently excluded (see Chapter 5), including, for example, part-time employees and people whose social participation is based on the discharge of family responsibilities. So far as rights at work are concerned, the Commission proposes the introduction of a national minimum wage, and rights to combat discrimination and promote 'family friendly employment'. While seeking new ways to promote investment in affordable housing, the Commission proposes no new rights to housing. The Commission rejects more radical reforms by which the social security and tax systems might be integrated, such as selectivist forms of negative income tax or universalist forms of basic income/social dividend/citizen's income. The declared emphasis is on a welfare state that is active not passive and which – borrowing a phrase from Bill Clinton's presidential campaign in the USA – gives people 'a hand up, not just a hand-out' (CSJ 1994: 224). The clear implication is that social justice is unavoidably dependent on and subordinate to the imperative of economic productivity.

The struggle for social rights

Must we accept that social justice is subordinated in this way and that social rights are subordinate to civil and political rights? In Chapter 8 we observed that, while civil rights are enforceable in the courts and political rights are enforceable through the electoral process, social rights have no distinctive institutional forum, only a sphere of administrative activity. While Raymond Plant has argued (see above) that the concept and the discourse of social rights may empower the citizen within the administrative sphere, how empowering can this be? If social justice is constrained, might there also be strategies of popular justice by which social rights may be declared and fought for?

Rights strategies have been a significant feature of certain kinds of campaign against poverty (see, for example, Alcock 1993: ch. 15). In the USA in the 1960s, President Johnson's 'War on Poverty' sought the empowerment of impoverished communities through the introduction of community action and legal services programs, organised through an Office of Economic Opportunity. The first OEO Director referred to legal services as the 'heavy artillery' in the war against poverty: poverty was thought to result as much from people's failure to exercise their rights as from any deficiency in those rights. In Britain in the 1970s, the Home Office sponsored Community Development Projects in twelve inner city areas, generating a variety of self-help initiatives and welfare rights services. As has been seen in Chapter 8, the 1970s also witnessed the emergence of the British law centre movement, a major expansion of the Citizen's Advice Bureaux and other independent advice centres, and attempts by national charities like Child Poverty Action Group to employ new forms of 'test case strategy'.

A debate about the uses of law in the struggle for rights has continued among 'radical' or 'critical' lawyers (see Travers 1994). While some critical legal scholars maintain that law is necessarily subordinate to a dominant power in society, others are prepared to argue about the possibilities of counter-hegemonic rights strategies (Hunt 1990) and of law as a mode of resistance to law itself (Fitzpatrick 1992). However, the relationship between critical legal theory and progressive legal practice has been said to be 'at best problematical and at worst non-existent. . . . Most practising lawyers are too busy getting on with their work to notice, let alone worry about, the relationship between their activities and legal theory' (Economides and Hansen 1992).

In spite of this, rights strategies founded in progressive legal practice or in advice and community work clearly can succeed in securing social security benefits for people who are entitled to them, in curbing bad employment practices and in improving local housing conditions. However, the improvements they can bring to the living conditions of poor people are marginal. This is first, because such strategies cannot improve the levels at which social security benefits are set, and they cannot create new jobs or homes. Second, the advantages obtained even from ground breaking test cases may be short-lived given the capacity of the legislature to nullify each victory (Prosser 1983). Third, when resources are rationed, those who exercise their 'rights' successfully may do so at the expense of others: for example, successful social fund applicants may, by using up the local office budget, deprive other applicants of assistance; local authority tenants who successfully exercise their rights under the Environmental Protection Act to obtain improvements to their homes may, by using up the local authority's Housing Investment Programme allocation, prevent their neighbours from having essential works carried out (see, for example, Reidy 1980). In this way, the exercise of rights may even be inimical to social justice.

Reference was made in Chapter 4 to neo-Marxist critiques of rights strategies. Writers like Bankowski and Mungham dismiss as 'a waste of time' any attempt at social or political change through the pursuit of rights and legal remedies. Even they, however, concede that there are occasions 'when people are caught up in the coils of the law, when they have to fight on the stage provided by it' (1976: 112). This admits at least the possibility that social rights might be advanced through the pursuit, not of 'bourgeois' justice, but of popular justice. Drawing on the experiences of campaigns fought in the Rio squatter settlements, de Sousa Santos (1979) argues for a strategy which subverts or enlarges litigation and adjudicative processes so as to encompass 'real' social issues, not narrow 'legal' definitions. Such a possibility is not without precedent in Britain. In the 1970s, more radical welfare rights activists and claimants' unions often adopted a 'carnival style' approach to tribunal appeals which, as Hilary Rose describes, insinuated a 'slice of real life' to the artificiality of the proceedings:

> The bumpy spring-broken mattress, the worn out sheets, the children and their too small vests are brought to the appeal as evidence to challenge the social security decisions. The individuated humiliation of the home visit is turned into an offensive weapon to expose and ridicule the meanness of the social security system. The representative becomes compere and produces exhibit after exhibit while the witnesses – whose role is audience as well as evidence givers – switch mood from laughter, to anger, to pain as the charade is played out. . . . As when the silent speak, these sorts of appeals enter into the mythology as occasions when 'we showed them'. (Rose 1982: 151)

Such tactics were undoubtedly memorable, but by themselves they were seldom effective. Twelve years' experience as an advice worker taught this writer that what counts for most people when they are 'caught up in the coils of law' is to win real rather than merely moral victories.

Foucault has questioned whether any form of popular justice is achievable through the medium of even the most accountable form of adjudicative apparatus. A court, tribunal or adjudicator – even a lay arbitrator – represents a 'third element' who must necessarily claim independence from rather than allegiance to the parties; who must adhere to some ideal of justice that is not 'popular' but claims absolute or universal validity over the people; who has the power to enforce decisions and must therefore remain alien to the people (1980: ch. 1). Popular justice is not social justice. It is by nature anarchic. An anarchic rights strategy is one which self-consciously exploits rights without accepting the authority of those who administer them. Harking back again to the claimants' union movement of the 1970s, Jordan (1973) has identified within it two quite different approaches. Drawing on the distinction made by E. P. Thompson (1968) between the English and the Irish working-class traditions, he observed that unions in the English tradition were organised as mutual aid societies, while those in the Irish tradition pursued a 'claims maximisation' approach. The former collectively cultivated allotments to grow vegetables, organised the bulk puchasing of food, and conducted relations with the social security authorities in an orderly and reponsible manner. The latter ruthlessly wrung from the social security system every advantage obtainable for their members, adopting a combative and abrasive relationship with the authorities. The claims maximisation approach owes it coherence, like that of immigrant Irish workers in nineteenth-century England, to a rejection of Puritan values, a contempt for authority, but an acute knowledge of legal procedure. Elements of the approach are also adopted by those welfare rights activists who see their task as that of manipulating the welfare state to maximum advantage while minimising its controlling effects.

Claimants unions, like the Welfare Rights Organisations which had preceded them in the USA (Piven and Cloward 1977), proved to be transient organisations and have failed to sustain themselves as an integral movement. Their activities remained outside the mainstream of the democratic political process, and their grassroots leaders were often co-opted into more conventional forms of pressure group activity. Claimants' unions and welfare rights organisations never in themselves became a vehicle for political mobilisation to secure social rights. Piven and Cloward have concluded that a rights strategy focusing on individual 'grievance work' is of limited organisational value and they echo a view expressed by Schiengold (1974) that recourse to litigation and individual rights can only be one tactic in any plan for a broad mobilisation for change. Schiengold himself has dismissed as a 'myth' (1974: 5) the very idea that the definition and realisation of social rights can be achieved through the pursuit of enforcement action.

This is not necessarily to say that such action is without its own significance. There is a case for 'rights without illusions' (Hunt 1990: 326); for exploiting a discourse of rights as a tactic within a *political* strategy. Such a strategy would seek to broaden a discourse based on individualised or 'legal' rights so as to encompass collective or 'social' rights. This must contend, however, with a 'blocking' tendency which arises precisely because of the association within dominant hegemonic discourse between 'liberty' and 'rights' (*ibid.*: 315); an assumption, in other words, that rights cannot be 'social' in a collective sense, but are protections which must function within the limits of individually guaranteed civil and political freedoms. This returns us to Marshall's basic premiss regarding the inter-dependency of social, civil and political rights.

Poverty and 'nautonomy'

A new and sophisticated alternative to Marshall's concept of citizenship is to be found in the work of David Held (1994). Marshall's view of citizenship was founded in a certain state-market essentialism (see Hindess 1987). He regarded the different elements to the rights of citizenship as representing necessary antidotes to the mutual antagonism between the state on the one hand and the market on the other, and to the excesses and diswelfares which each was inherently capable of generating. Held's analysis, in contrast, hinges on relations of power and the various sites of power in society.

While the state and the market are each sources of power (which are differently understood within competing theoretical traditions), they do not by themselves encompass 'the range of conditions necessary for the possibility of a common structure of action' (Held 1994: 51). The basis for the 'common structure of action', which Held equates with citizenship, is that of 'equal autonomy'; what a democratic community requires is 'a framework which is, in principle, equally constraining and enabling for all its members' (*ibid.*: 48). What Held calls 'nautonomy' (i.e. the negation of autonomy) occurs when relations of power in society are such as systematically to generate asymmetries of life chances. Such asymmetries in life chances may correlate with geography, class, gender or 'race'. Deprivation and ill-health, for example, are to be found clustered

> among countries of the South, among non-whites, among the poor and working classes and among women. These correlations and clusters are not, however, restricted to countries of the South, and can be found widely in the North as well. The patterns of social closure and opportunity among men and women, working, middle and upper classes, blacks and whites and various ethnic communities profoundly affect their well-being across all categories of health in both Europe and the United States. (*ibid.*: 52–3)

Held relates his notion of autonomy to Townsend's (1979; 1987) and Doyal and Gough's (1991) ideas about the necessary preconditions for 'social participation' and 'human action and interaction' respectively (see discussion in Chapter 2 above). The concept of nautonomy, therefore, is closely related to notions of poverty and deprivation, though its focus is on asymmetries of power.

While Marshall spoke of three kinds of rights, Held differentiates seven sites of power and seven related categories of rights. Held's sites of power are the body, welfare, culture, civic associations, the economy, regulatory and legal institutions, and organised violence and coercive relations. In relation to each site of power there are conditions which must be fulfilled in order to have autonomy: physical and psychological well-being, the means of subsistence, security of personhood and cultural identity, the ability to participate in the economy, in community life, in political processes and to act without becoming vulnerable to physical force or violence. Rather like Marshall, Held asserts:

> Bundles of rights which are pertinent to each of the spheres of power must be regarded as integral to the democratic process. If any one of these bundles is absent, the democratic process will be one-sided, incomplete and distorted. If any one of these categories of rights and obligations is missing or unenforced, people's equal interest in the principle of autonomy will not be fully protected. (*ibid.*: 54)

Held's categories of rights can loosely be equated with Marshall's categories (see Table 10.1). Clearly, Held introduces a greater

Table 10.1 Categories of rights

Held's 'Sites of power'	Held's corresponding categories of rights	Marshall's categories of rights
Body	Health (right to physical and emotional well-being, including control over fertility)	Social
Welfare	Social (right to social security, childcare and education provision)	
Economy	Economic (right to guaranteed minimum income – and to work)	
Coercive relations and organised violence	Pacific (right to due process, physical security, peaceful coexistence)	Civil
Culture	Cultural (freedom of thought and expression)	
Civic associations	Civil (freedom of association)	
Regulatory and legal institutions	Political (right to vote and to participation in debate/electoral politics, etc.)	Political

degree of specificity, but the difference between the two taxono-
mies goes deeper than this. In the concept of nautonomy we have
a sense of the vulnerability of the citizen to the power of others in
society: not only the vulnerability of the working class to the
capitalist class or the vulnerability of the individual to the state, but
the vulnerability of women to patriarchy, of ethnic communities to
racism, and of the citizens of poor countries to the interests of rich
countries.

What we might call welfare rights or social rights are not all of a
piece. They relate to various dimensions of power over human lives.
The rights to subsistence, 'work' and housing on which this book
has perhaps quite arbitrarily focused articulate with a host of
vulnerabilities: vulnerabilities which may, for example, arise in the
context of asymmetries of power within families; the exclusivity of
labour markets; the commodified nature of essential resources. The
exercise of a right under a specific piece of social legislation may
provide or fail to provide relief or protection in relation to several
sites of power. A right to social assistance may protect a citizen from

starvation, but it may do this at the expense of her/his right to autonomy from a partner, and it will not necessarily enable her/him to participate fully in social life.

In Chapter 2 I discussed various definitions of poverty. George and Howards have suggested that it is possible to define poverty 'in a composite manner' (1991: 10) using a continuum of definitions ranging from starvation criteria, through subsistence criteria and social coping criteria, to social participation criteria. They argue that

> Defined in this way, we can meaningfully argue that poverty in Britain and the US has declined in terms of starvation and in terms of subsistence but less so in terms of social coping and it may not have declined at all in terms of social participation. Similarly, when comparing the situation in say Britain and India, we can avoid making such non-convincing statements that poverty is about equally prevalent in the two countries. We can begin to compare like with like, as far as this is possible, in both historical terms and in contemporary comparative terms. (*ibid.*)

This is an approach to poverty that equates with Held's concept of nautonomy to the extent that it is multilayered and recognises a range of qualitatively different requirements for human autonomy. The most basic requirement for human survival is the means to avoid starvation. Beyond this is a requirement for day-to-day subsistence; for an adequate diet, clothing, housing, fuel and for the necessities of daily life. However, for people to cope with the exigencies of an acceptable social existence the quantity and the quality of what they require is greater than the bare necessities for physical efficiency. Finally, for people to flourish, rather than merely cope, they must additionally be enabled to participate in the society of which they are a part. This account of poverty, unlike Held's account of nautonomy, implies a hierarchy of requirements for human emancipation. Clearly the requirements are interdependent in the sense that a guarantee of civil and political freedom will not by itself assure the capacity of a starving citizen to achieve full participation, but there is a logical order of priority. There is a sense in which the social rights of citizenship – the right to health and welfare – must precede the civil and political freedom associated with participation. The fullest or most generous definition of poverty demands social rights of citizenship which themselves begin to encompass the conditions for such freedom. It is from the full realisation of social rights that the freedom to participate springs.

This implies that social rights ought not to be subordinated to civil and political rights, and social justice ought not to be subordinated to economic productivity. Some socialist social policy commentators have argued, on the contrary, that democratic social planning should take precedence over capitalist economic objectives (see, for example, Walker 1984). Held seeks to transcend the grand narratives of liberalism and socialism in order to achieve an *a priori* definition of rights, but the guarantor of rights in the First World – for the time being – is the capitalist state. Resistance to nautonomy still requires a means of harnessing, superseding or resisting the capitalist state.

Social rights and the state

It is the productivist imperative of democratic-welfare-capitalism which makes social rights secondary. What is more, state welfare provision is often regarded by citizens as 'second best' to market, family and other arrangements, or else the state is regarded, not as the guarantor of social rights, but as an adversary (for a fuller discussion, see Dean and Taylor-Gooby 1992). What this final section will tentatively explore is first, the potential for some alternative scenarios to that of democratic-welfare-capitalism and second, some suggestions for how future struggles for social rights might be conducted.

Claus Offe has lately argued that notions of social justice within capitalist welfare states are delimited by what he calls the 'possibility space' of social policies (1992: 64). Notions of what is an adequate level of welfare provision and of what constitutes a legitimate policy intervention have in the past been constrained by a 'productivist syndrome'; a set of assumptions 'centred on the notion that production and productivity are both individually and collectively desirable' (*ibid.*: 67). Such assumptions situated the welfare state in the context of various certainties about the nature of family interdependence, full employment and the dividends to be reaped from continual economic growth. Since the 1970s and 1980s, however, the reliability of these assumptions has been called into question. Changing patterns of family formation, the restructuring of labour markets and a new sense of vulnerability both to global limitations and the power of transnational economic processes have generated new insecurities. Offe dismisses the solutions of economic liberals (curtailing the welfare state and seeking security in the market), conservatives (the use of state power to coerce citizens into dependency on families and employers), social democrats (the expansion of the welfare state and its productivist premises – as per the Commission on Social Justice described above). Offe himself, as has already been mentioned in Chapter 4, advocates the introduction of basic income, a solution he attributes to the 'post-industrial Left', though it is in fact an idea which, in diverse guises, has enjoyed support from several points across the political spectrum (see Parker 1989).

Basic income would be available on a universal basis to every member of society. Entitlement would depend, not on occupational status or past employment record, but on citizenship. Unlike many other proponents, Offe makes clear that basic income should be only one element in an alternative 'non-productivist' policy package. Crucial to this eco-socialist version of the basic income project would be the expansion of the possibility space of social policy so as to admit a concept of social justice which would emancipate society 'from the dictatorial imperatives of economic growth' (*ibid.*: 74). What this might entail is not abundantly clear, but it would involve, for example, co-operative forms of non-wage labour outside formal employment (see also Offe and Heinze 1992).

Quite different responses to the insecurities of late modernity and different approaches to social justice are to be found in religious thinking. I shall here briefly mention the Christian liberation theology to come out of Latin America, and potential innovations attributable to the insights of Islamic thought.

Latin American liberation theology is founded on a synthesis of Catholic doctrine and Marxism. It argues that 'Faith reveals to us the deep meaning of the history which we fashion with our own hands: it teaches us that every human act which is oriented toward the construction of a more just society has value in terms of communion with God' (Gutierrez 1973: 238). Liberation theology emancipates the believer from productivist logic. Rodes puts it thus:

we have been assured at one time or another that the security of property depends on a limited franchise, that the sanctity of the family depends on denying women the vote, that if we free the slaves they will all starve. It is in the same spirit that we are told today that we cannot have prosperity without air pollution, or that we cannot compete with Japan unless we adopt technologies that preclude full employment. The theology of liberation frees us from analysis of this kind. There is a legal maxim *fiat justitia ruat coelum*, let justice be done though the skies fall. Liberation theology teaches us to apply that maxim in the realm of social justice. (1986: 65)

While embracing a class doctrine, liberation theology does not believe oppressed and oppressor classes to be irreconcilable, but on the contrary it seeks the conversion of *all* the people, oppressed and oppressor alike. Liberation lies in the consciousness of the injustices experienced by oppressed people and in redemption from the hegemonic views of the oppressors (cf. Friere 1972). This is what is meant by the 'preferential option for the poor'; the option of deciding against the interests of the international capitalist class and in favour of expanded social rights and redistribution, of a people's economics based on low technology/high employment solutions.

Mention was made in Chapter 3 of ancient Islamic traditions, such as *Zakat*, a form of social assistance that is not organised through the state, but that rests on religious duty. The Islamic state is not a secular state and the muslim perception of individual, community and state does not straightforwardly equate with concepts of citizenship in the Judaeo-Christian tradition. Significantly, the receipt of *Zakat*, unlike social assistance, attracts no shame or stigma. What is more, Islamic politics and jurisprudence are distinctively pragmatic and are capable of responding to changing global circumstances and insecurities. For example, the Q'ran's prohibition on usury, or interest, has not prevented the development of muslim business practices in which enterprises are financed, not by loans at interest, but by risk-sharing schemes (Beedham 1994). While radical democrats and eco-socialists in the West seek ways of revitalising civil society, muslims would seem already to be exploring the potential for risk-sharing without the state. Geopolitical tensions and 'cultural racism' (Modood 1994) notwithstanding, there could be scope for some rapprochement between, on the one hand, debates in the West about altruism and secular citizenship, and on the other, certain distinctively muslim notions of 'virtue', 'tolerance' and 'rights'.

These suggestions may strike some readers as speculative and remote. For people who are poor, the struggle for social rights is more immediate. In Britain, none the less, people who are poor are marginalised from the basic mechanisms and established institutions of the democratic process (Miliband 1974) and even from the debates and campaigns of the professional 'poverty lobby' (Lister and Beresford 1991). Though unemployed people, for example, were able to mobilise in the 1930s, with the development of the machinery of the welfare state they are now 'prisoners of the Beveridge dream' (Bagguley 1994). Certain kinds of social rights attract comparatively little public support. Public opinion consistently favours spending on health and education (rights which nearly all citizens enjoy) far above spending on social security and public housing ('welfare' rights which are reserved for 'the poor') (Lipsey 1994). Welfare rights are not necessarily regarded in the same way as other rights: people may wish state provision to be available, but only as a last resort; the state may not be valued as a guarantor of social rights so much as feared as an alien and forbidding apparatus (Dean and Taylor-Gooby 1992). Welfare rights, as this book has demonstrated, are highly technical. They are, by and large, defined and administered by experts. Even when experts join cause with people who are poor by setting up advice and law centres, their ministrations are received as a charitable or professional service, not as a gesture of solidarity. There is no popular movement for welfare rights in Britain.

If a popular mobilising strategy for welfare rights were to be envisaged in such circumstances, perhaps the closest precedent has been provided by the workers' offices which were operated by the trade union *Kartells* or associations in Germany in the 1894–1906 period. These have been researched and are described by Udo Reifner (1982). The workers' offices differed from present-day advice and law centres in two fundamental respects: first, in the nature of the relationship between 'counsellors' and 'clients'; second, in the scope of their activities. Workers' offices were both staffed and used by trade union members: the staff were democratically elected to office from among the membership of associated trade unions, and entitlement to receive advice and assistance was similarly restricted to union members and their families. The workers' offices offered individual advice and representation, whether people were in employment or not, and in connection with employment, welfare and consumer matters alike. In attending to the full range of their members' needs, the workers' offices not only dealt with individual cases, they also monitored working, housing and social conditions, the work of the courts and the factory inspectors, and they used their findings:

1. As a rhetorical resource in collective struggle.
2. To evaluate individual legal advice.
3. As evidence and argumentation in litigation and extrajudicial settlements.
4. To enlighten union members about the causes of individual misfortune.
5. To develop collective means to counteract the strategies of capital.
6. To assess the effects of the struggle for social progress. (*ibid.*: 94)

The authority of the workers' offices derived from the then considerable power of the trade unions, and their tactics relied as much on the use of such weapons as strikes and boycotts as on legal remedies. As the trade unions became less powerful and less democratic, the workers' offices were in time superseded by or absorbed into more conventional forms of legal service provision. The economic, social and political conditions which pertained in Germany at the turn of the twentieth century bear few comparisons with those in Britain as it approaches the twenty-first century, save that both periods represent a time of global transition and uncertainty. Without seeking in any way to romanticise them, workers' offices provided a glimpse of an integrative strategy for social rights which concerted the efforts and interests of experts and non-experts, of employees and non-employees, of earners and consumers; which integrated the pursuit of social rights with that of other rights; which combined the enforcement of rights with the struggle for the development of rights. It had the makings of an effective strategy against nautonomy but, significantly, it depended on the development of a source of collective power that was independent of both capital and the state.

Conclusion/summary

In so far as all rights are socially or ideologically constructed it may none the less be argued that rights to welfare represent claims which are no less valid or fundamental than claims to civil or political freedoms. In spite of this, rights created by social legislation are seen to be peculiarly problematic. The procedural form of social rights under what Marshall has termed democratic-welfare-capitalism remains subordinate to civil and political rights. The substantive objectives of social legislation may be expressed in the grander language of social justice, but the rights to which such legislation gives effect are constrained by the contradictory nature of democratic-welfare-capitalism itself. Even the expansive review of the welfare state conducted by the Commission on Social Justice has recommended a political strategy which explicitly acknowledges capitalism's economic imperatives and the limits these place on the development of social rights.

This chapter has therefore turned to the idea that substantive social justice, or even perhaps an element of popular justice, may be obtained through struggles over the enforcement of established rights to welfare. There appear, however, to be inherent limitations to such a strategy. The space in which rights under social legislation may be exercised is administratively closely constrained and even the most litigious of strategies is unlikely in isolation to achieve the substantive enlargement of social justice.

It is the interdependence of rights which is inescapable. The chapter has examined the idea that there is in fact a diversity of rights which must be exercised in order for citizens to achieve autonomy; a diversity which reveals a greater complexity to citizenship than the amelioration of class disadvantage. A failure to develop or enforce such rights of citizenship results in 'nautonomy', a concept which may be articulated with that of poverty. It is possible to debate the idea that, though rights may be complex and interdependent, they reflect none the less a hierarchy of human need in which rights to health and welfare, for example, may be regarded as qualitatively different but in no way subordinate to rights to cultural and political participation.

The subordination of social rights seems to be a problem inherent to welfare state capitalism. Though a full analysis would require at least another volume, this chapter has concluded by introducing for discussion a few of the possible ways in which this tendency to subordination may come in future to be challenged. The chapter has touched on the eco-socialist basic income strategy; the potential in future debate for religious influences from elsewhere in the world; and the idea of an integrative rights-oriented strategy (achievable, conceivably, through some such agency as a reinvigorated trade union movement).

In the meantime, the nature of democratic-welfare-capitalism, as Marshall characterised it, has been changing. This book has sought to demonstrate the ways in which the influences of new managerialism and welfare pluralism, the effects of economic and political globalisation, and shifts towards work-based and private forms of welfare all have implications for the nature of social rights. Bob Jessop (1994) has sought to characterise such changes in terms of a transition from a Keynesian welfare state to a 'hollowed out Schumpeterian workfare state'. Jessop's argument is that the shell of the nation-state which remains following the transfer of powers to supranational forums in one direction and regional and/or non-elected agencies in the other is preoccupied with creating the conditions necessary for flexible patterns of production and diverse patterns of consumption and accumulation. The significance of associating the changing form of democratic-welfare-capitalism with Schumpeter (1942) lies in the latter's rejection, not only of the corporate form of capitalism embodied by the large-scale 'Fordist' enterprise, but also of participative forms of democracy and the notion that democracy necessarily equates to the pursuit of social justice (see, for example, Held 1987: ch. 5). A Schumpeterian workfare state implies a highly heterogeneous and unequal society, populated by a largely passive citizenry, closely ordered by a technocratic elite.

Whether we recognise this scenario, whether we subscribe to a vision such as that embraced by the Commission on Social Justice, or whether we aspire to strategies of resistance to the welfare state, it will be clear to readers that welfare rights and social legislation are critical features within any form of democratic-welfare-capitalist regime. There are at least three senses in which this is so. First, whether they succeed in preventing or merely containing poverty, welfare rights and social legislation are critical to the lives of citizens in such societies; and to some citizens more than others. Second, welfare rights and social legislation are a constitutive component and are critical to maintaining the existence of democratic-welfare-capitalism. Third, the functioning of welfare rights and social legislation throws up critical questions about the capacity of democratic-welfare-capitalism to ensure or to deny social justice.

Recommended additional reading

Commission on Social Justice (1994) *Social Justice: Strategies for national renewal,* Vintage Books, London, Introduction and Chapter 6.
Coote, A. (ed.) (1992) *The Welfare of Citizens: Developing new social rights,* Rivers Oram Press, London, Introduction and Chapters 1–3.
Held, D. (1994) 'Inequalities of power, problems of democracy', in Miliband, D. (ed.), *Reinventing the Left,* Polity Press, Cambridge.
Hunt, A. (1990) 'Rights and social movements: counter-hegemonic strategies', *Journal of Law and Society,* vol. 17, no. 3.

Questions for reflection

Does social justice depend on social equality?

Can social rights guarantee equal autonomy?

REFERENCES

Abbott, E. and Bompas, K. (1943) 'The woman citizen and social security' reproduced in Clarke, J., Cochrane, A. and Smart, C., *Ideologies of Welfare*, 1987 edition, Hutchinson, London.

Abel, R. (ed.) (1982) *The Politics of Informal Justice*, Academic Press, New York.

Abel-Smith, B. and Stevens, R. (1967) *Lawyers and the Courts*, Heinemann, London.

Abel-Smith, B. and Stevens, R. (1968) *In Search of Justice*, Penguin Books, Harmondsworth.

Ainley, P. (1993) 'The legacy of the Manpower Services Commission: training in the 1980s', in Taylor-Gooby, P. and Lawson, R. (eds.) *Markets and Managers*, Open University Press, Buckingham.

Alber, J. (1983) 'Some causes of social security expenditure development in Western Europe 1949–1977', in Loney, M., Boswell, D. and Clarke, J. (eds.) *Social Policy and Social Welfare*, Open University Press, Milton Keynes.

Alcock, P. (1993) *Understanding Poverty*, Macmillan, Basingstoke.

Alinsky, S. (1969) *Reveille for Radicals*, Random House, New York.

Amin, K. and Oppenheim, C. (1992) *Poverty in Black and White: Deprivation and ethnic minorities*, Child Poverty Action Group, London.

Anderson, D. (1991) Paper to 25th Annual Conference of the Social Policy Association, University of Nottingham, 11 July.

Arden, A. and Hunter, C. (1992) *Manual of Housing Law*, 5th edition, Sweet & Maxwell, London.

Audit Commission (1989) *Managing Services Effectively – Performance review*, Audit Commission, London.

Bacon R. and Eltis, W. (1978) *Britain's Economic Problem: Too few producers*, Macmillan, London.

Bagguley, P. (1994) 'Prisoners of the Beveridge dream? The political mobilisation of the poor against contemporary welfare regimes', in Burrows, R. and Loader, B. (eds.) *Towards a Post-Fordist Welfare State*, Routledge, London.

Bailey, S. and Gunn, M. (1991) *Smith and Bailey on the Modern English Legal System*, 2nd edition, Sweet & Maxwell, London.

Baldwin-Edwards, M. and Gough, I. (1991) 'EC social policy and the UK', in Manning, N. (ed.), *Social Policy Review 1990–91*, Longman, Harlow.

Ball, M. (1983) *Housing Policy and Economic Power: The political economy of owner-occupation*, Methuen, London.

Bankowski, Z. and Mungham, G. (1976) *Images of Law*, Routledge & Kegan Paul, London.

Bassett, P. (1989) 'All together now', *Marxism Today*, vol. 33, no. 1 (January).

Bauman, Z. (1987) *Legislators and Interpreters*, Polity Press, Cambridge.

Beedham, B. (1994) 'Islam and the West', *Economist*, 6 August.

Beresford, P. and Croft, S. (1986) *Whose Welfare: Private care or public services?*, Lewis Cohen Urban Studies Centre, Brighton.

Berghman, J. (1991) '1992 and social security', in Room, G. (ed.), *Towards a European Welfare State?*, SAUS, Bristol.

Berlin, I. (1967) 'Two concepts of liberty', in Quinton, A. (ed.), *Political Philosophy*, Oxford University Press, Oxford.

Beveridge, W. (1942) *Social Insurance and Allied Services* ('The Beveridge Report') Cmd. 6404, HMSO, London.

Blackwell, J. (1994) 'Changing work patterns and their implications for social protection', in Baldwin, S. and Falkingham, J. (eds.), *Social Security and Social Change*, Harvester Wheatsheaf, Hemel Hempstead.

Booth, C. (1889) *The Life and Labour of the People in London*, 1902 edition, Macmillan, London.

Bottomore, T. (1992) 'Citizenship and social class: Forty years on', in Marshall, T. H. and Bottomore T. (eds.), *Citizenship and Social Class*, Pluto Press, London.

Boyson, R. (1971) *Down With the Poor*, Churchill, London.

Bradshaw, J. (1972) 'The concept of social need', *New Society*, 30 March.

Bradshaw, J. (1993a) *Household Budgets and Living Standards*, Joseph Rowntree Foundation, York.

Bradshaw, J. (1993b) Foreword to Oldfield, N. and Yu, A., *The Cost of a Child*, Child Poverty Action Group, London.

Bradshaw, J. and Holmes, H. (1989) *Living on the Edge: A study of living standards of families on benefit in Tyne and Wear*, Tyneside Child Poverty Action Group, CPAG, London.

Breugal, I. (1989) 'Sex and race in the labour market', *Feminist Review*, no. 32.

Burghes, L. (1993) *One-parent Families: Policy options for the 1990s*, Family Policy Studies Centre/Joseph Rowntree Foundation, York.

Burns, L. (1994) 'Back of the queue', *Roof*, Sept.–Oct.

Butler, J. (1993) 'A case study in the National Health Service: Working for patients', in Taylor-Gooby, P. and Lawson, R. (eds.), *Markets and Managers: New issues in the delivery of welfare*, Open University Press, Buckingham.

Caiden, G. (1988) 'The challenge of change', in *Proceedings of the Fourth International Ombudsman Conference*, Canberra.

Callinicos, A. (1989) *Against Postmodernism*, Polity Press, Cambridge.

Campbell, T. (1983) *The Left and Rights*, Routledge & Kegan Paul, London.

Castles, F. (1982) *The Impact of Parties*, Sage, London.

Central Statistical Office (CSO) (1992) *Social Trends No. 22*, HMSO, London.

Child Poverty Action Group (CPAG) (1994a) 'The Incapacity for Work Bill: hitting the sick for six', *Welfare Rights Bulletin*, 119, April.

Child Poverty Action Group (CPAG) (1994b) 'Incapacity Benefit', CPAG Factsheet, November, CPAG, London.

Child Poverty Action Group (CPAG) (1994c) 'JSA White Paper: targeting the "workshy" and cutting benefit', *Welfare Rights Bulletin*, 123, December.

Christopher, T. (1992) 'Countering disadvantage now', *Policy Studies* vol. 13, no. 1: 'Training and enterprise councils: the story so far', Policy Studies Institute, London.

Clapham, D., Kemp, P. and Smith, S. (1990) *Housing and Social Policy*, Macmillan, Basingstoke.

Commission for Local Administration (1978) *Complaints Procedures*, CLA, London.

Commission for Local Administration (1992) *Devising a Complaints System*, CLA, London.

Commission of the European Communities (1993) *European Social Policy: Options for the union*, Green Paper, Office for Official Publications of the European Communities, Luxembourg.

Commission on Social Justice (CSJ) (1994) *Social Justice: Strategies for national renewal*, The Report of the Commission on Social Justice, IPPR/Vintage Books, London.

Cook, J. and Watt, S. (1992) 'Racism, women and poverty', in Glendinning, C. and Millar, J. (eds.), *Women and Poverty in Britain: the 1990s*, Harvester Wheatsheaf, Hemel Hempstead.

Cooper, M. (1983) *Public Legal Services*, Sweet & Maxwell, London.

Coote, A. (1992) Introduction, in Coote, A. (ed.), *The Welfare of Citizens: Developing new social rights*, IPPR/Rivers Oram Press, London.

Craig, G. (1992) 'Managing the poorest: the social fund in context', in

Social Work and Social Welfare Yearbook, Open University Press, Buckingham.

Cranston, M. (1973) *What are Human Rights?*, Bodley Head, London.

Cranston, M. (1976) 'Human rights, real and supposed', in Timms, N. and Watson, D. (eds.), *Talking about Welfare*, Routledge & Kegan Paul, London.

Cranston, R. (1985) *Legal Foundations of the Welfare State*, Weidenfeld and Nicolson, London.

Crosland, C. A. R. (1956) *The Future of Socialism*, Jonathan Cape, London.

Cross, M. (1993) 'Generating the "new poverty": a European comparison', in Simpson, R. and Walker, R. (eds.), *Europe: For richer or poorer?*, CPAG, London.

Dale, J. and Foster, P. (1986) *Feminists and State Welfare*, Routledge & Kegan Paul, London.

Deacon, B. (1993) 'Developments in East European social policy', in Jones, C. (ed.), *New Perspectives on the Welfare State in Europe*, Routledge, London.

Deacon, B. *et al.* (1992) *The New Eastern Europe: Social policy past, present and future*, Sage, London.

Dean, H. (1988/9) 'Disciplinary partitioning and the privatisation of social security', *Critical Social Policy*, Issue 24, winter.

Dean, H. (1991) *Social Security and Social Control*, Routledge, London.

Dean, H. (1992) 'Poverty discourse and the disempowerment of the poor', *Critical Social Policy*, Issue 35.

Dean, H. (1993) 'Social Security: the income maintenance business', in Taylor-Gooby, P. and Lawson, R. (eds.), *Markets and Managers: New issues in the delivery of welfare*, Open University Press, Buckingham.

Dean, H. and Hartley, G. (1995) 'Listen to learn', *Community Care*, 30 March.

Dean, H. and Taylor-Gooby, P. (1992) *Dependency Culture: The explosion of a myth*, Harvester Wheatsheaf, Hemel Hempstead.

Dean, M. (1991) *The Constitution of Poverty: Toward a genealogy of liberal governance*, Routledge, London.

Department of Employment/Department of Social Security (DE/DSS) (1994) *Jobseeker's Allowance*, Cm. 2687, HMSO, London.

Department of Health (DH) (1991) *The Right to Complain: Practice guidance on complaints procedures in Social Services Departments*, HMSO, London.

Department of Health and Social Security (DHSS) (1985) *The Reform of Social Security*, vol. 1, Cmnd. 9517, HMSO, London.

Department of Health and Social Security (DHSS) (1989) *Caring for People: Community care in the next decade and beyond*, Cm. 849, HMSO, London.

Department of Social Security (DSS) (1990) *Children Come First*, Cm. 1264, HMSO, London.

Department of Social Security (DSS) (1995) *Improving Child Support*, Cm. 2745, HMSO, London.

Dicey, A. (1885) *Introduction to the Law of the Constitution*, 9th edition 1939, ed. E. Wade, Macmillan, London.

Dicey, A. (1915) 'The development of administrative law in England', *Law Quarterly Review*, vol. 31, pp. 133–48.

Dilnot, A., Kay, J. and Morris, C. (1984) *The Reform of Social Security*, Institute of Fiscal Studies/Clarendon Press, Oxford.

Dominelli, L. (1991) *Woman across Continents*, Harvester Wheatsheaf, Hemel Hempstead.

Donnison, D. (1982) *The Politics of Poverty*, Martin Robertson, Oxford.

Doyal, L. and Gough, I. (1984) 'A theory of human needs', *Critical Social Policy*, Issue 10.

Doyal, L. and Gough, I. (1991) *A Theory of Human Need*, Macmillan, Basingstoke.

Dworkin, R. (1977) *Taking Rights Seriously*, Duckworth, London.

Eardley, T. and Sainsbury, R. (1991) *Housing Benefit Reviews: An evaluation of the effectiveness of the review system in responding to claimants dissatisfied with Housing Benefit decisions*, Department of Social Security Research Report, Series No. 3, HMSO, London.

Economides, K. and Hansen, O. (1992) 'Critical legal practice: Beyond abstract radicalism', in Grigg-Spall, I. and Ireland, P. (eds.), *The Critical Lawyers' Handbook*, Pluto Press, London.

Esam, P., Good, R. and Middleton, R. (1985) *Who's to Benefit? A radical review of the Social Security system*, Verso, London.

Esping-Andersen, G. (1990) *The Three Worlds of Welfare Capitalism*, Polity Press, Cambridge.

Ferge, Z. (1993a) 'Social policy in transition in Eastern Europe', in Simpson, R. and Walker, R. (eds.), *Europe: For richer or poorer?*, CPAG, London.

Ferge, Z. (1993b) 'Winners and losers after the collapse of state socialism', in Page, R. and Baldock, J. (eds.), *Social Policy Review 5*, Social Policy Association, Canterbury.

Ferris, J. (1991) 'Green politics and the future of welfare', in Manning, N. (ed.), *Social Policy Review 1990–91*, Longman, London.

Finch, J. and Mason, J. (1993) *Negotiating Family Responsibilities*, Routledge, London.

Fine, B. (1984) *Democracy and the Rule of Law: Liberal ideals and Marxist critiques*, Pluto Press, London.

Finer, M. (1974) *Report of the Committee on One-Parent Families*, Cmnd. 5629, HMSO, London.

Fitzpatrick, P. (1992) 'Law as resistance', in Grigg-Spall, I. and Ireland, P. (eds.), *The Critical Lawyers' Handbook*, Pluto Press, London.

Foucault, M. (1979) *Discipline and Punish*, Penguin Books, Harmondsworth.

Foucault, M. (1980) *Power/Knowledge*, ed. C. Gordon, Harvester Wheatsheaf, Hemel Hempstead.

Franks, O. (1957) *Report of the Committee on Administrative Tribunals and Enquiries*, Cmnd. 218, HMSO, London.

Friere, P. (1972) *Pedagogy of the Oppressed*, Penguin Books, Harmondsworth.

Galligan, D. (1992) 'Procedural rights in social welfare', in Coote, A. (ed.), *The Welfare of Citizens: Developing new social rights*, IPPR/Rivers Oram Press, London.

Gamble, A. (1988) *The Free Economy and the Strong State*, Macmillan, Basingstoke.

Ganz, G. (1974) *Administrative Procedures*, Sweet & Maxwell, London.

Garnham, A. and Knights, E. (1994a) *Child Support Handbook*, 2nd edition 1994/5, Child Poverty Action Group, London.

Garnham, A. and Knights, E. (1994b) *Putting the Treasury First: The truth about Child Support*, Child Poverty Action Group, London.

Genn, H. and Genn, Y. (1989) *The Effectiveness of Representation at Tribunals*, Lord Chancellor's Department, London.

George, V. (1973) *Social Security and Society*, Routledge, London.

George, V. (1988) *Wealth, Poverty and Starvation: An international perspective*, Harvester Wheatsheaf, Hemel Hempstead.

George, V. (1993) 'Poverty in Russia: from Lenin to Yeltsin', in Page, R. and Baldock, F. (eds.), *Social Policy Review 5*, Social Policy Association, Canterbury.

George V. and Howards, I. (1991) *Poverty amidst Affluence: Britain and the United States*, Edward Elgar, Aldershot.

George V. and Wilding, P. (1985) *Ideology and Social Welfare*, Routledge & Kegan Paul, London.

Giddens, A. (1990) *The Consequences of Modernity*, Polity Press, Cambridge.

Gilbert, B. (1966) *The Evolution of National Insurance in Great Britain*, Michael Joseph, London.

Ginsburg, N. (1992) *Divisions of Welfare: A critical introduction to comparative social policy*, Sage, London.

Glendinning, C. and Millar, J. (eds.) (1992) *Women and Poverty in Britain: the 1990s*, Harvester Wheatsheaf, Hemel Hempstead.

Gold, M. and Mayes, D. (1993) 'Rethinking a social policy for Europe', in Simpson, R. and Walker, R. (eds.), *Europe: For richer or poorer?*, CPAG, London.

Goodman, A. and Webb, S. (1994) *For Richer, for Poorer: The changing distribution of income in the United Kingdom, 1961–91*, Institute of Fiscal Studies, London.

Gordon, P. (1989) *Citizenship for Some? Race and government policy 1979–1989*, Runnymede Trust, London.

Gordon, R. (1993) 'Challenging community care assessments', *Legal Action*, August.

Gough, I. (1979) *The Political Economy of the Welfare State*, Macmillan, London and Basingstoke.

Gould, A. (1993) 'The end of the middle way? The Swedish welfare state in crisis', in Jones, C. (ed.), *New Perspectives on the Welfare State in Europe*, Routledge, London.

Gray, A. and Jenkins, B. (1993) 'Markets, managers and the public service: the changing of a culture', in Taylor-Gooby, P. and Lawson, R. (eds.), *Markets and Managers: New issues in the delivery of welfare*, Open University Press, Buckingham.

Griffiths, J. (1981) *The Politics of the Judiciary*, 2nd edition, Fontana, London.

Griffiths, J. (1991) *The Politics of the Judiciary*, 4th edition, Fontana, London.

Groves, D. (1992) 'Occupational pension provision and women's poverty in old age', in Glendinning, C. and Millar, J. (eds.), *Women and Poverty in Britain: the 1990s*, Harvester Wheatsheaf, Hemel Hempstead.

Gutierrez, G. (1973) *A Theology of Liberation*, Orbis, Maryknoll, N.Y.

Habermas, J. (1976) *The Legitimation Crisis*, Heinemann: London.

Habermas, J. (1985) 'Modernity – an incomplete project', in Foster, H. (ed.), *Postmodern Culture*, Pluto Press, London.

Habermas, J. (1987) *The Philosophical Discourse of Modernity*, Polity Press, Cambridge.

Hadley, R. and Hatch, S. (1981) *Social Welfare and the Failure of the State*, Allen & Unwin, London.

Hall, S. and Held, D. (1989) 'Citizens and citizenship', in Hall, S. and Jacques, M. (eds.), *New Times: The changing face of politics in the 1990s*, Lawrence & Wishart, London.

Hansen, O. (1993) *Legal Aid in Practice*, 3rd edition, Legal Action Group, London.

Harden, I. and Lewis, N. (1986) *The Noble Lie: The British constitution and the rule of law*, Hutchinson, London.

Harlow, C. and Rawlings, R. (1984) *Law and Administration*, Weidenfeld & Nicolson, London.

Hayek, F. (1944) *The Road to Serfdom*, Routledge & Kegan Paul, London.

Hayek, F. (1960) *The Constitution of Liberty*, Routledge & Kegan Paul, London.

Hayek, F. (1976) *Law, Legislation and Liberty*. Vol. 2: *The Mirage of Social Justice*, Routledge & Kegan Paul, London.

Held, D. (1987) *Models of Democracy*, Polity Press, Cambridge.

Held, D. (1994) 'Inequalities of power, problems of democracy', in Miliband, D. (ed.), *Reinventing the Left*, Polity Press, Cambridge.

Henwood, M. and Wicks, M. (1984) *The Forgotten Army: Family care and elderly people*, Family Policy Studies Centre, London.

Hewitt, M. (1993) 'Social movements and social need: Problems with postmodern political theory', *Critical Social Policy*, Issue 37, Summer.

Hewitt, M. (1994) 'Social policy and the question of postmodernism', in Page, R. and Baldock, J. (eds.), *Social Policy Review 6*, Social Policy Association, Canterbury.

Hewitt, P. (1993) *About Time: The revolution in work and family life*, IPPR/Rivers Oram, London.

Hills, J. (ed.) (1990) *The State of Welfare: The welfare state in Britain since 1974*, Clarendon Press, Oxford.

Hindess, D. (1987) *Freedom, Equality and the Market*, Tavistock, London.

Hirst, P. (1980) 'Law, socialism and rights', in Carlen, P. and Collison, M. (eds.), *Radical Issues in Criminology*, Martin Robertson, Oxford.

Holloway, J. and Picciotto, S. (eds.) (1978) *State and Capital: A Marxist debate*, Edward Arnold, London.

Holman, R. (1978) *Poverty: Explanations of social deprivation*, Martin Robertson, Oxford.

Hood, C. (1991) 'A public management for all seasons?', *Public Administration*, vol. 69, no. 1.

Hunt, A. (1978) *The Sociological Movement in Law*, Macmillan, London.

Hunt, A. (1990) 'Rights and social movements: Counter-hegemonic strategies', *Journal of Law and Society*, vol. 17, no. 3.

Hurd, D. (1989) 'Freedom will flourish where citizens accept responsibilities', *Independent*, 13 September.

Ignatieff, M. (1984) *The Needs of Strangers*, Chatto & Windus, London.

Illich, I., McKnight, J., Zola, I., Caplan, J. and Shaiken, H. (1977) *Disabling Professions*, Marion Boyars, London.

Jenkins, S. (1994) *Winners and Losers*, Department of Economics, University of Swansea.

Jennings, W. (1936) 'Courts and administrative law: The experience of English housing legislation', *Harvard Law Review*, vol. 49, p. 426.

Jessop, B. (1994) 'The transition to post-Fordism and the Schumpeterian workfare state', in Burrows, R. and Loader, B. (eds.), *Towards a Post-Fordist Welfare State*, Routledge, London.

Johnson, N. (1987) *The Welfare State in Transition*, Wheatsheaf, Brighton.

Johnson, N. (1990) *Reconstructing the Welfare State*, Harvester Wheatsheaf, Hemel Hempstead.

Jones, C. (1993) 'The Pacific challenge: Confucian welfare states', in Jones, C. (ed.), *New Perspectives on the Welfare State in Europe*, Routledge, London.

Jordan, B. (1973) *Paupers: The making of the claiming class*, Routledge & Kegan Paul, London.

Joseph, K. (1972) 'The cycle of deprivation', speech to Pre-school Playgroups Association, 29 June.

Joseph, K. and Sumption, J. (1979) *Equality*, John Murray, London.

JUSTICE (1961) *The Citizen and the Administration: The redress of grievances*, Stevens, London.

JUSTICE–All Souls (1988) *Administrative Justice: Some necessary reforms*, Oxford University Press, Oxford.

Kamenka, E. and Tay, A. (1975) 'Beyond bourgeois individualism: The contemporary crisis in law and legal ideology', in Kamenka, E. and Neale, R. (eds.), *Feudalism, Capitalism and Beyond*, Edward Arnold, London.

Keane, J. (1988) *Democracy and Civil Society*, Verso, London.

Keithly, J. (1991) 'Social security in a single European market', in Room, G. (ed.), *Towards a European Welfare State?*, SAUS, Bristol.

Kemp, P. (1990) Foreword in Wall, D. (ed.), *Getting There: Steps to a green economy*, Green Print, London.

Kemp, P. and Wall, D. (1990) *A Green Manifesto for the 1990s*, Penguin Books, Harmondsworth.

Kincaid, J. (1975) *Poverty and Equality in Britain: A study of social security and taxation*, Penguin Books, Harmondsworth.

Kingdom, J. (1991) *Government and Politics in Britain*, Polity Press, Cambridge.

Korpi, W. (1983) *The Democratic Class Struggle*, Routledge & Kegan Paul, London.

Laclau, E. and Mouffe, C. (1985) *Hegemony and Socialist Strategy*, Verso, London.

Land, H. (1975) 'The introduction of Family Allowances', in Hall, R., Land, H., Parker, R. and Webb, A. (eds.), *Change, Choice and Conflict in Social Policy*, Heinemann, London.

Land, H. (1992) 'Whatever happened to the social wage?', in Glendinning, C. and Millar, J. (eds.), *Women and Poverty in Britain: The 1990s*, Harvester Wheatsheaf, Hemel Hempstead.

Langan, M. and Ostner, I. (1991) 'Gender and welfare: Towards a comparative framework', in Room, G. (ed.), *Towards a European Welfare State?*, SAUS, Bristol.

Lawson, R. (1993) 'The new technology of management in the personal social services', in Taylor-Gooby, P. and Lawson, R. (eds.), *Markets and Managers: New issues in the delivery of welfare*, Open University Press, Buckingham.

Le Grand, J. (1982) *The Strategy of Equality*, Allen & Unwin, London.

Le Grand, J. (1990a) *Quasi-Markets and Social Policy*, Studies in Decentralisation and Quasi-Markets, No. 1, SAUS, Bristol.

Le Grand, J. (1990b) 'The state of welfare', in Hills, J. (ed.), *The State of Welfare: The Welfare State in Britain since 1974*, Clarendon Press, Oxford.

Leibfried, S. (1993) 'Towards a European welfare state? On integrating poverty regimes into the European Community', in Jones, C. (ed.), *New Perspectives on the Welfare State in Europe*, Routledge, London.

Leung, J. (1994) 'Dismantling the "Iron Rice Bowl": Welfare reforms in the People's Republic of China', *Journal of Social Policy*, vol. 23, no. 3.

Lewis, N. and Birkinshaw, P. (1993) *When Citizens Complain: Reforming justice and administration*, Open University Press, Buckingham.

Lewis, N. and Seneviratne, M. (1992) 'A Social Charter for Britain', in Coote, A. (ed.), *The Welfare of Citizens: Developing new social rights*, IPPR/Rivers Oram Press, London.

Lilley, P. (1993) Speech to Conservative Party Annual Conference, 6 October.

Lipsey, D. (1994) 'Do we really want more public spending?', in Jowell, R. *et al.* (eds.), *British Social Attitudes, the 11th report*, SCPR/Dartmouth, Aldershot.

Lipsky, M. (1976) 'Towards a theory of street-level bureaucracy', in Hawley, W. and Lipsky, M. (eds.), *Theoretical Perspectives on Urban Politics*, Prentice Hall, Englewood Cliffs, N.J.

Lister, R. (1990) *The Exclusive Society: Citizenship and the poor*, Child Poverty Action Group, London.

Lister, R. and Beresford, P. (1991) *Working Together against Poverty*, Open Services Project, London.

Lynes, T. (1975) 'Unemployment Assistance Tribunals in the 1930s', in Adler, M. and Bradley, A. (eds.), *Justice, Discretion and Poverty*, Professional Books, Abingdon.

Lyotard, J. (1984) *The Postmodern Condition: A report on knowledge*, Manchester University Press, Manchester.

Mack, J. and Lansley, S. (1985) *Poor Britain*, Allen & Unwin, London.

Mann, K. (1992) *The Making of an English 'Underclass': The social division of welfare and labour*, Open University Press, Buckingham.

Mann, M. (1987) 'Ruling class strategies and citizenship', *Sociology*, vol. 21, no. 3.

Marsh, A. and McKay, S. (1993) *Families, Work and Benefits*, Policy Studies Institute, London.

Marshall, T. H. (1950) 'Citizenship and social class', reprinted in Marshall, T. H. and Bottomore, T. (1992) *Citizenship and Social Class*, Pluto Press, London.

Marshall, T. H. (1981) *The Rights to Welfare and Other Essays*, Heinemann, London.

Marx, K. (1848) 'The Revolutions of 1848', in *Political Writings*, vol. 2, 1973 edition, Penguin Books, Harmondsworth.

Marx, K. (1859) 'Preface to a contribution to the critique of political economy', in *Marx and Engels Selected Works*, Vol. 1, 1969, edition, Progress, Moscow.

Marx, K. (1887) *Capital*, vol. 1, 1970 edition, Lawrence & Wishart, London.

Mashaw, J. (1983) *Bureaucratic Justice*, Yale University Press, New Haven, Conn.

Maslow, A. (1943) 'A theory of human motivation', *Psychological Review*, vol. 50.

McLaughlin, E. (1991) *Social Security and Community Care: The case of the Invalid Care Allowance*, Department of Social Security Research Report No. 4, HMSO, London.

McLaughlin, E., Millar, J. and Cooke, K. (1989) *Work and Welfare Benefits*, Avebury, Aldershot.

McPherson, S. and Midgley, J. (1987) *Comparative Social Policy and the Third World*, Wheatsheaf, Brighton.

Meadows, D., Meadows, M., Randers, J. and Behrens, W. (1972) *The Limits to Growth*, Pan Books, London.

Miles, R. and Phizacklea, A. (1984) *White Man's Country: Racism in British politics*, Pluto Press, London.

Miliband, R. (1974) 'Politics and poverty', in Wedderburn, D. (ed.), *Poverty, Inequality and Class Structure*, Cambridge University Press, Cambridge.

Miller, S. and Peroni, F. (1992) 'Social politics and the Citizen's Charter', in Manning, N. and Page, R. (eds.), *Social Policy Review 4*, Social Policy Association, Canterbury.

Minister for Disabled People (1995) *Ending Discrimination against Disabled People*, Cm. 2729, HMSO, London.

Mishra, R. (1984) *The Welfare State in Crisis*, Harvester Wheatsheaf, Hemel Hempstead.

Mishra, R. (1990) *The Welfare State in Capitalist Society*, Harvester Wheatsheaf, Hemel Hempstead.

Mishra, R. (1993) 'Social policy in the postmodern world: The welfare state in Europe by comparison with North America', in Jones, C. (ed.), *New Perspectives on the Welfare State in Europe*, Routledge, London.

Modood, T. (1994) *Racial Equality: Colour, culture and justice*, Discussion Paper No. 5, Institute of Public Policy Research, London.

Moore, J. (1989) 'The end of the line for poverty', speech to Greater London Conservative Party constituencies meeting, 11 May.

Moorhouse, P. and Thomas, D. (1994) *Rights Guide for Home Owners*, 10th edition, Child Poverty Action Group, London.

Murray, C. (1984) *Losing Ground: American social policy 1950–1980*, Basic Books, New York.

National Association of Citizen's Advice Bureaux (1991) *Barriers to Benefit*, NACAB, London.

National Consumer Council (1977) *The Fourth Right of Citizenship: A review of local advice services*, NCC, London.

Newman, B. and Thompson, R. (1989) 'Economic growth and social development: a longitudinal analysis of causal priority', *World Development*, vol. 17, no. 4.

Niner, P. (1989) *Homelessness in Nine Local Authority Areas: Case studies of policy and practice*, Department of Employment, HMSO, London.

Nissel, M. (1987) *People Count*, Office of Population Censuses and Surveys, HMSO, London.

Novak, T. (1988) *Poverty and the State*, Open University Press, Milton Keynes.

Nozick, R. (1974) *Anarchy, State and Utopia*, Basil Blackwell, Oxford.

O'Connor, J. (1973) *Fiscal Crisis of the State*, St Martin's Press, New York.

Offe, C. (1984) *Contradictions of the Welfare State*, MIT Press, Cambridge, Mass.

Offe, C. (1992) 'A non-productivist design for social policies', in von de Parijs, P. (ed.), *Arguing for Basic Income*, Verso, London.

Offe, C. and Heinze, R. (1992) *Beyond Employment: Time, work and the informal economy*, Polity Press, Cambridge.

Ogus, A. and Barendt, A. (1988) *The Law of Social Security*, 3rd edition, Butterworths, London.

Oldfield, N. and Yu, A. (1993) *The Cost of a Child*, Child Poverty Action Group, London.

Oliver, M. (1990) *The Politics of Disablement: A sociological approach*, Macmillan, Basingstoke.

Oppenheim, C. (1993) *Poverty: The facts*, Child Poverty Action Group, London.

Orshansky, M. (1969) 'How poverty is measured', *Monthly Labour Review*, vol. 92.

Pahl, J. (1989) *Money and Marriage*, Macmillan, Basingstoke.

Papadakis, E. and Taylor-Gooby, P. (1987) *The Private Provision of Public Welfare: State, market and community*, Wheatsheaf, Brighton.

Parker, H. (1989) *Instead of the Dole*, Routledge, London.

Partington, M. (1975) 'Supplementary Benefits and the Parliamentary Commissioner', in Adler, M. and Bradley, A. (eds.), *Justice, Discretion and Poverty*, Professional Books, Abingdon.

Partington, M. (1993) 'The future of tribunals', *Legal Action*, May.

Pascall, G. (1986) *Social Policy: A feminist analysis*, Tavistock, London.

Pashukanis, E. (1978) *General Theory of Law and Marxism*, Ink Links, London.

Peden, G. (1991) *British Economic and Social Policy*, 2nd edition, Philip Allan, Hemel Hempstead.

Pepinsky, H. (1975) 'Reliance on formal written law, and freedom and social control in the United States and The People's Republic of China', *The British Journal of Sociology*, vol. 26, pp. 330–42.

Piachaud, D. (1981) 'Peter Townsend and the Holy Grail', *New Society*, 10 September; reprinted in Townsend, P. (1993) *The International Analysis of Poverty*, Harvester Wheatsheaf, Hemel Hempstead.

Pirie, M. (1991) *The Citizen's Charter*, Adam Smith Institute, London.

Piven, F. and Cloward, R. (1974) *Regulating the Poor: The functions of public welfare*, Tavistock, London.

Piven, F. and Cloward, R. (1977) *Poor People's Movements*, Pantheon Books, New York.

Plant, R. (1992) 'Citizenship, rights and welfare', in Coote, A. (ed.), *The Welfare of Citizens: Developing new social rights*, IPPR/Rivers Oram Press, London.

Plant, R., Lesser, H. and Taylor-Gooby, P. (1980) *Political Philosophy and Social Welfare*, Routledge & Kegan Paul, London.

Polanyi, K. (1944) *The Great Transformation*, Rinehart, New York.

Portillo, M. (1993) Interview on *Westminster Live*, BBC television, 7 December.

Powell, E. (1972) *Still to Decide*, Elliot Right Way Books, London.

Poynter, R. and Martin, C. (1994) *Rights Guide to Non-Means Tested Benefits*, 17th edition, Child Poverty Action Group, London.

Prime Minister's Office (1991) *The Citizen's Charter: Raising the Standard*, Cm. 1599, HMSO, London.

Prosser, T. (1983) *Test Cases for the Poor*, Child Poverty Action Group, London.

Raz, J. (1984) 'On the nature of rights', *Mind*, vol. XCIII, 194.

Reich, C. (1964) 'The new property', *Yale Law Journal*, vol. 73, no. 5.

Reidy, A. (1980) 'Legal rights and housing policy', *Social Policy and Administration*, vol. 14, no. 1.

Reifner, U. (1982) 'The theory and practice of legal advice for workers in pre-facist Germany', in Abel, R. (ed.), *The Politics of Informal Justice*, vol. II, Academic Press, New York.

Roche, M. (1993) *Rethinking Citizenship: Welfare, ideology and change in modern society*, Polity Press, Cambridge.

Rodes, R. E. Jr (1986) 'Law, history and the option for the poor', in Lucas, G. R. Jr (ed.), *Poverty, Justice and the Law*, University Press of America, Lanham, MD.

Room, G. (1991) 'A time for change', in Becker, S. (ed.), *Windows of Opportunity: Public policy and the poor*, CPAG, London.

Room, G., Lawson, R. and Laczko, F. (1989) 'New poverty in the European Community', *Policy and Politics*, vol. 17, no. 2.

Rose, H. (1981) 'Rereading Titmuss: The sexual division of welfare', *Journal of Social Policy*, vol. 10, no. 4.

Rose, H. (1982) 'Who can de-label the claimant?' in Adler, M. and

Bradley, A. (eds.), *Justice, Discretion and Poverty*, Professional Books, Abingdon.

Rose, R. (1988) *Ordinary People in Public Policy*, Sage, London.

Rose, R. (1993) 'Bringing freedom back in: Rethinking priorities of the welfare state', in Jones, C. (ed.), *New Perspectives on the Welfare State in Europe*, Routledge, London.

Rowlingson, K. and Berthoud, R. (1994) *Evaluating the Disability Working Allowance*, Policy Studies Institute, London.

Rowntree, B. S. (1901) *Poverty: A study of town life*, Macmillan, London.

Rowntree, B. S. (1937) *The Human Needs of Labour*, Longman, London.

Royal Commission on Legal Services (1979) *Report of the Royal Commission on Legal Services*, Cmnd. 7648, HMSO, London.

Sarre, P. (1989) 'Recomposition of the class structure', in Hamnett, C., McDowell, L. and Sarre, P. (eds.), *The Changing Social Structure*, Sage, London.

Saville, J. (1958) 'The welfare state: an historical approach' *New Reasoner*, vol. 1, no. 3.

Schiengold, S. (1974) *The Politics of Rights*, Yale University Press, New Haven, Conn.

Schumpeter, J. (1942) *Capitalism, Socialism and Democracy*, 1976 edition, Allen & Unwin, London.

deSchweinitz, K. (1961) *England's Road to Social Security*, Perpetua, University of Pennsylvania.

Scott, A. (1990) *Ideology and New Social Movements*, Unwin-Hyman, London.

Scott, J. (1993) 'Wealth and privilege', in Sinfield, A. (ed.), *Poverty, Inequality and Justice*, New Waverley Papers, Social Policy Series No. 6, University of Edinburgh.

Scruton, R. (ed.) (1991) *Conservative Texts: An anthology*, Macmillan, Basingstoke.

Seabrook, J. (1985) *Landscapes of Poverty*, Basil Blackwell, Oxford.

Select Committee on the Parliamentary Commissioner for Administration (1987/88) *First Report*, HC 706, HMSO, London.

Sen, A. (1984) *Resources, Values and Development*, Basil Blackwell, Oxford.

Sen, A. (1985) *Commodities and Capabilities*, Elsevier, Amsterdam.

Short, J. (1982) *Housing in Britain: The post-war experience*, Methuen, London.

Simpson, R. (1993) 'Fortress Europe?', in Simpson, R. and Walker, R. (eds.), *Europe: For richer or poorer?*, CPAG, London.

Simpson, R. and Walker, R. (eds.) (1993) *Europe: For richer or poorer?*, CPAG, London.

Smart, C. (1989) *Feminism and the Power of Law*, Routledge, London.

Smith, A. (1776) *An Inquiry into the Nature and Causes of the Wealth of Nations*, 1900 edition, George Routledge, London.

Social Security Advisory Committee (1994) *In Work – Out of Work: The role of incentives in the benefit system*, The Review of Social Security, Paper 1, BA Publishing, Leeds.

Social Security Committee (SSC) (1992a) *Low Income Statistics: Low Income Families 1979–89*, second report, HMSO, London.

Social Security Committee (SSC) (1992b) *The Operation of Pension Funds*, HCP 61–II, 1991–92, HMSO, London.

Solomos, J. (1989) *Race and Racism in Contemporary Britain*, Macmillan, Basingstoke.

de Sousa Santos, B. (1979) 'Popular justice, dual power and socialist strategy', in Fine, B., Kinsey, R., Lea, J., Picciotto, S. and Young, J. (eds.), *Capitalism and the Rule of Law*, Hutchinson, London.

Spicker, P. (1993) 'Needs as claims', *Social Policy and Administration*, vol. 27, no. 1.

Squires, P. (1990) *Anti-Social Policy: Welfare ideology and the disciplinary state*, Harvester Wheatsheaf, Hemel Hempstead.

Stacey, F. (1978) *Ombudsmen Compared*, Oxford University Press, Oxford.

Street, H. (1975) *Justice in the Welfare State*, Stevens & Sons, London.

Taylor-Gooby, P. (1991) *Social Change, Social Welfare and Social Science*, Harvester Wheatsheaf, Hemel Hempstead.

Taylor-Gooby, P. (1993) 'The new educational settlement: National Curriculum and local management', in Taylor-Gooby, P. and Lawson, R. (eds.), *Markets and Managers: New issues in the delivery of welfare*, Open University Press, Buckingham.

Taylor-Gooby, P. (1994) 'Postmodernism and social policy: A great leap backwards?', *Journal of Social Policy*, vol. 23, no. 3.

Therborn, G. (1989) 'The two-thirds, one-third society', in Hall, S. and Jacques, M. (eds.), *New Times: The changing face of politics in the 1990s*, Lawrence & Wishart, London.

Thompson, E. P. (1968) *The Making of the English Working Class*, Penguin Books, Harmondsworth.

Thompson, E. P. (1975) *Whigs and Hunters*, Parthenon, New York.

Titmuss, R. (1958) *Essays on the Welfare State*, Allen & Unwin, London.

Titmuss, R. (1968) *Commitment to Welfare*, Allen & Unwin, London.

Titmuss, R. (1971) 'Welfare rights, law and discretion', *Political Quarterly*, vol. 42, no. 2.

Townsend, P. (1979) *Poverty in the United Kingdom*, Penguin Books, Harmondsworth.

Townsend, P. (1987) 'Deprivation', *Journal of Social Policy*, vol. 16, no. 2.

Townsend, P. (1991) 'The structured dependency of the elderly: a creation of social policy in the twentieth century', *Ageing and Society*, vol. 1, no. 1.

Townsend, P. (1992) *Hard times: The prospects for European social policy*, Eleanor Rathbone Memorial Lecture, Liverpool University Press, Liverpool.

Townsend, P. (1993) *The International Analysis of Poverty*, Harvester Wheatsheaf, Hemel Hempstead.

Travers, M. (1994) 'The phenomenon of the radical lawyer', *Sociology*, vol. 28, no. 1.

Turner, B. (1990) 'Outline of a theory of citizenship', *Sociology*, vol. 24, no. 2.

Turner, B. (1991) 'Prolegomena to General Theory of Social Order', position paper for ESRC workshop, *Citizenship, Civil Society and Social Cohesion*, London, 23 February.

Turpin, C. (1990) *British Government and the Constitution*, 2nd edition, Weidenfeld & Nicolson, London.

Tweedie, J. (1986) 'Rights in social programmes: the case of parental choice of school', *Public Law*, p. 407.

Unemployment Unit (1994) *Turning up the Heat: Will Jobseeker's Allowance get the jobless back to work?*, Unemployment Unit, London.

Ungerson, C. (1994) 'Housing: need, equity, ownership and the economy', in George, V. and Miller, S. (eds.), *Social Policy Towards 2000: Squaring the welfare circle*, Routledge, London.

United Nations (UN) (1948) 'Universal Declaration of Human Rights', reprinted in Centre for Human Rights, Geneva (1988), *Human Rights: A compilation of international instruments*, UN, New York.

Van Praag, B., Hagenaars, A. and Van Weeren, H. (1982) 'Poverty in Europe', *Review of Income and Wealth*, vol. 28.

Veit-Wilson, J. (1994) *Dignity not Poverty: A minimum income standard for the UK*, The Commission on Social Justice, IPPR, London.

Wade, E. (1939) 'Introduction', to Dicey, A., *Introduction to the Law of the Constitution*, 9th edition, Macmillan, London.

Walker, A. (1984) *Social Planning*, Basil Blackwell, Oxford.

Walker, A. (1987) 'The social construction of dependency', in Loney, M. *et al.*, *The State or the Market?*, Sage, London.

Walker, A. (1990) 'Community care', in McCarthy, M. (ed.), *The New Politics of Welfare: An agenda for the 1990s*, Macmillan, Basingstoke.

Walker, C. (1993) *Managing Poverty: The limits of social assistance*, Routledge, London.

Walker, R., Middleton, S. and Thomas, M. (1994) 'Mothers' attachment to Child Benefit', *Benefits*, Issue 11.

Waltzer, M. (1983) *Spheres of Justice*, Basil Blackwell, Oxford.

Ward, M. (1994) *Council Tax Handbook*, 2nd edition, Child Poverty Action Group, London.

Ward, S. (1990) *The Essential Guide to Pensions: A worker's handbook*, 3rd edition, Pluto Press, London.

Watson, D. (1980) *Caring for Strangers*, Routledge & Kegan Paul, London.

Weale, A. (1983) *Political Theory and Social Policy*, St Martin's Press, New York.

Webb, B. and Webb, S. (1935) *Soviet Communism: A new civilisation?*, 2 vols, Longmans, London.

Webster, L. *et al.* (1994) *National Welfare Benefits Handbook*, 24th edition, Child Poverty Action Group, London.

West Midlands Low Pay Unit (WMLPU) (1993) *Employment Law: An advisor's guide to the rights of employees*, WMLPU, Birmingham.

Whiteley, P. and Winyard, S. (1983) 'Influencing social policy: the effectiveness of the poverty lobby in Britain', *Journal of Social Policy*, vol. 12, no. 1.

Wilensky, H. (1975) *The Welfare State and Equality*, University of California Press, Berkeley.

Wilkinson, M. (1986) 'Tax expenditure and public expenditure in the UK', *Journal of Social Policy*, vol. 15, no. 1.

Williams, F. (1989) *Social Policy: A critical introduction*, Polity Press, Cambridge.

Williams, F. (1992) 'Somewhere over the rainbow: universality and diversity in social policy', in Manning, N. and Page, R. (eds.), *Social Policy Review 4*, Social Policy Association, Canterbury.

Wood, E. M. (1986) *The Retreat from Class*, Verso, London.

Wraith, R. and Hutchinson, P. (1973) *Administrative Tribunals*, Allen & Unwin, London.

Zander, M. (1978) *Legal Services for the Community*, Temple-Smith, London.

INDEX